W9-AZG-605

Hoyle

UP-TO-DATE

EDITED BY

ALBERT H. MOREHEAD

AND

GEOFFREY MOTT-SMITH

Grosset & Dunlap

PUBLISHERS   NEW YORK

1972 Printing

CONTENTS

iii

Hoyle Up-To-Date

BRIDGE *is consistently the most popular card game of the English-speaking world and is almost as popular in other countries. It is of English origin and developed from the game* WHIST, *which is still played in parts of the United States. From Whist came* BRIDGE *or* BRIDGE-WHIST, *about 1896—a game in which the dealer could name the trump suit; his partner's hand (called the dummy) was exposed and played by the dealer; and the hand could be played either with a trump suit or at no-trump. Next came* AUCTION BRIDGE, *about 1904, a game in which all four players could bid for the right to name the trump suit. The latest version,* CONTRACT BRIDGE, *dating from 1926 and the most popular form since 1930, has ridden serenely through such fads as Gin Rummy and Canasta and in the end has always survived as the most popular game. It is the same game as Auction Bridge except in the scoring.*

CONTRACT BRIDGE

PLAYERS. Four, two against two as partners, facing each other.

CARDS. The regular 52-card pack. In each suit the cards rank: A (high), K, Q, J, 10, 9, 8, 7, 6, 5, 4, 3, 2. The suits

1

rank: spades (high), hearts, diamonds, clubs; in bidding the rank is the same except that no-trump ranks highest, above spades. Properly two packs are used so that while one player is dealing the other pack is being shuffled for the next deal by dealer's partner.

PRELIMINARIES. A pack is spread face down on the table and each player draws a card, not one of the four at either end. The two highest are partners against the two next-lower, and if there are more than four who want to play they have right of entry into the game in order after the fourth-highest, the first four players going out in order of precedence, the player who drew the highest card going out last. Highest card has choice of seats and cards with which to deal, and deals first; or there may be a new draw for seats, cards, and first deal. The pack is shuffled by the player at the dealer's left (the dealer may shuffle last if he wishes, but seldom does) and must be cut by the player at dealer's right.

THE DEAL. The deal gives each player thirteen cards, one at a time in order to his left (clockwise), thus dealing the full pack.

THE AUCTION. Beginning with the dealer, each player in turn may *call* (pass, bid, or double or redouble if appropriate) until any call has been followed by three passes. A player may pass and then on a later turn bid, double, or redouble.

A *pass* simply signifies disinclination at that time to make any other call.

A *bid* is an undertaking to win more than six tricks with a named suit as trump (or at no-trump); the bid must name the suit or no-trump plus the number of *odd tricks*, which are tricks *over six*, that the bidder undertakes to win. For example, "one spade," a bid to win seven tricks with spades trumps. Each bid must be higher than any preceding bid, either by naming a greater number of tricks or by naming the same number of tricks in a higher-ranking denomination. For example, "two hearts" may be overcalled by two spades, two no-trump, or three or more of any denomination, but not by two diamonds, which would be an *insufficient bid*.

A player in turn may *double* an opponent's bid, meaning that he does not contest the opponent's bid but wishes its scoring values to be doubled if it is played; or he may *redouble* a bid that he or his partner made and an opponent doubled. Doubling and redoubling do not affect the ranking of bids; a bid of two clubs doubled or redoubled may still be overcalled by a bid of two diamonds or higher, and the new bid is not doubled, though it may be later.

An example of legal bidding: South, "One no-trump"; West, "Double"; North, "Redouble"; East, "Two hearts." This is usually written as follows:

SOUTH	WEST	NORTH	EAST
1 N T	Double	Redouble	2 ♡

West can double because the last bid was made by an opponent. North can redouble because an opponent has doubled. East can overcall with two hearts, because that is higher than one no-trump, regardless of whether the no-trump bid is undoubled, doubled or redoubled. The heart bid cancels the double and redouble.

If the auction commences with four successive passes, the cards are thrown in and the next dealer deals the other pack. In any other case the auction is *open* and calling continues until three players in succession pass. The last pass *closes* the auction.

The highest bid of the auction becomes the *contract* (its status as undoubled, doubled, or redoubled affects only the scoring, not the play). The member of the contracting side who first bid the declaration named in the contract becomes the *declarer*. Examples:

SOUTH	WEST	NORTH	EAST
1 N T	Pass	3 N T	Pass
Pass	Pass		

North-South are the contracting side, and South is declarer because he was first to bid no-trump.

SOUTH	WEST	NORTH	EAST
1 ♧	Double	1 ♤	2 ♡
2 ♤	3 ♧	Double	Pass
4 ♧	4 ♡	Pass	Pass
4 ♤	Pass	Pass	Pass

The contract is "Four spades"; North-South are the contracting side, and North is the declarer.

THE PLAY. The object in play is to win tricks, to fulfill or defeat the contract. Each trick consists of a card led by one player plus a card played by each other player in turn, four cards in all. The player at declarer's left makes the first or opening lead and thereafter the winner of each trick leads to the next. A player may lead any card. A player must follow suit to the card led if able, and if not able to follow suit may play any card. A trick is won by the highest card played of the suit led, or, if it contains a trump, by the highest trump it contains.

As soon as the opening lead is made, declarer's partner spreads his hand (called the *dummy*) face up on the table; his cards should be grouped in suits and his trumps, if any, should be the group he places at his right. The declarer plays dummy's cards as well as his own, but from each hand in proper turn.

Declarer gathers in all tricks won by his side. One opponent—the one who did not win his side's first trick—gathers in all tricks won by his side. Tricks are kept bunched and piled on but distinctly separated from other tricks won by the same side.

Declarer's partner, also called the *dummy*, may not help or advise declarer but may warn declarer or any other player who seems about to violate a law of the game. Declarer's opponents, called *defenders*, may not expose cards or by any means except legal plays convey information to each other.

SCORING. The two members of a partnership score as a unit. Scores are recorded on paper. There are two columns, one for each side. A horizontal line is ruled somewhat below the center of the scoresheet. *Below the line* go trick scores, which can result only when declarer makes his contract; *above the line* go all other scores, including those variously called honors, premiums, bonuses, overtricks, and undertrick penalties.

When all thirteen tricks have been played, the result is scored. If declarer has won at least as many tricks as his contract required, he has made his bid and the value of all the tricks he won is scored in the column of his side. If declarer has won too few tricks, his side receives no credit for the tricks it has won and the defenders score the value of undertricks, the tricks by which declarer fell short of his contract. The value of undertricks depends on whether the contract was doubled or redoubled and on whether declarer's side was vulnerable (as explained later).

TRICK SCORES may be earned only by declarer's side. If the contract is fulfilled, the amount of the bid is scored below the line as follows:

	CONTRACT IS		
DECLARATION	UNDOUBLED	DOUBLED	REDOUBLED
No-trumps, 1st odd trick	40	80	160
each subsequent odd trick	30	60	120
Spades or hearts, each odd trick	30	60	120
Diamonds or clubs, each odd trick	20	40	80

Whenever a side accumulates 100 or more points in trick scores, it wins a game. A horizontal line is then drawn under the trick scores of both sides. Each side starts on the new game from zero score. The side that first wins two of three games wins a *rubber*. After each rubber, there is a new draw for partnerships, and also a shift in the active players if there are more than four candidates. For winning a rubber, a side scores above the line:

Winning rubber in two games	700
Winning rubber in three games	500

Settlement for the rubber is made on the difference of grand totals, the column for each side being added up, all scores above and below the line together. (It has been legally ruled that the question of who will "win the rubber" means who will make the higher grand total, not who will first win two games. A side may earn the *rubber bonus* and still "lose the rubber.")

VULNERABILITY. A side that has won a game toward the rubber is *vulnerable;* a side having no game is *not vulnerable.*

The vulnerability of the contracting side affects certain scoring quantities. (Vulnerability of the defending side never makes any difference.)

OVERTRICKS. Tricks won by declarer in excess of the contract are known as *overtricks*. Each is scored above the line (not counting toward game) as follows:

| DECLARATION | DECLARER NOT VULNERABLE | | | DECLARER VULNERABLE | | |
	Un-doubled	Doubled	Re-doubled	Un-doubled	Doubled	Re-doubled
No-trumps	30	100	200	30	200	400
Spades or hearts	30	100	200	30	200	400
Diamonds or clubs	20	100	200	20	200	400

BONUS FOR MAKING CONTRACT. If a contract is doubled or redoubled, and is made, declarer's side scores a bonus of 50 above the line. (No variation for vulnerability.)

SLAMS. A bid of six odd tricks is *little slam* (or *small slam*); a bid of all seven odd tricks is *grand slam*. For making a slam contract, declarer's side scores above the line:

	DECLARER NOT VULNERABLE	DECLARER VULNERABLE
Small slam	500	750
Grand slam	1000	1500

UNDERTRICKS are tricks by which declarer falls short of making the contract. For example, if the contract is three no trump and declarer wins seven tricks, there are two undertricks. When the contract is defeated, declarer's side scores nothing (except for honors, as explained below), and the defending side scores above the line for each undertrick as follows:

CONTRACT IS	DECLARER NOT VULNERABLE	DECLARER VULNERABLE
Undoubled	50	100
Doubled		
first trick	100	200
each subsequent trick	200	300
Redoubled		
first trick	200	400
each subsequent trick	400	600

HONORS at a trump declaration are the A, K, Q, J, 10 of the trump suit. At no-trump, the honors are the four aces. If one player is dealt all the honors, his side scores 150 above the line. If one player is dealt four of the five trump honors, his side scores 100 above the line. This honor premium is scored regardless of which side assumes the contract.

BACK SCORE. It is customary to reduce the final net score for a rubber to a multiple of 100, 50 becoming 100 and any smaller fraction of 100 becoming 0. If the partnerships change each rubber, a separate *back score* or *ledger score* is kept for each player, in which is entered the amount he has won or lost in a rubber, as either a plus or minus quantity. The net score of the rubber goes in full to each member of the winning pair and is debited in full against each of the losing pair. The separate items in a player's ledger score are added algebraically, and the total of all net ledger scores must add algebraically to zero. Whenever settlement is made, those who are minus pay out and those who are plus collect.

NAME	+	−	+	−
Smith		13		6
Jones		13		20
Brown	13		20	
Green	13		6	

Four-Deal Bridge

In a cut-in game, a player who is "cut out" often has a long wait till the rubber ends and he can get back in. Playing Four-Deal Bridge, no player ever has to wait more than 15 or 20 minutes. The game is often called "Chicago" because it originated in the Standard Club of Chicago, Illinois.

A round consists of four deals, one by each player in turn. Vulnerability is automatic, as follows:

First deal: Neither side vulnerable.

Second and third deals: Dealer's side vulnerable, opponents not vulnerable (even if they previously made game).

Fourth deal: Both sides vulnerable.

A passed-out deal is redealt by the same dealer. There is a bonus of 300 for making game when not vulnerable and 500 when vulnerable. A part-score carries over as in rubber Bridge and can help to make game in the next deal or deals, but is canceled by any game. There is a bonus of 100 for making a part-score on the fourth deal. After four deals have been played, the scores are totaled and entered on the back score, as in rubber Bridge, and there is a new cut for partners, deal, and seats. Some play that the first dealer must always sit in the same seat at the table.

BRIDGE LAWS

The provisions of the laws of Contract Bridge governing irregularities are as follows. The same laws apply to Auction Bridge.

MISDEAL. There must be a new deal by the same dealer if the deal is not correct in all respects, if a card is exposed in dealing or found faced in the pack, if a player sees and can name correctly two cards dealt to another hand, or if at any time one hand is found to have too few cards and another too many. Before the last card is dealt, any player may require a new deal if the wrong player deals or if the pack was not cut.

INCORRECT HAND. If one hand is found short, the others being correct, and the missing cards are found elsewhere than in quitted tricks, they are restored to the short hand. If the partner of the short hand sees them, and is a defender, the cards are deemed exposed. The short hand is deemed to have held the cards continuously, and so is liable to penalty for revoke by failure to play them. If the missing cards are found in the quitted tricks, they are left there, the short hand plays on with too few cards and does not play to the last trick or tricks. If it wins a trick with its last card, the right to lead passes to the opponent at the left.

If a player has a card too many, by reason of failure to play to a trick, he must discard one card from his hand, if possible one that could have been played to the defective trick. This card cannot change the ownership of the defective trick unless the correction was made before a member of each side has played to the next trick.

IRREGULARITY IN THE AUCTION. Any player may call attention to an irregularity during the auction. Left-hand opponent (called L. H. O.) of the offender *condones* the error if he calls before a penalty has been enforced. Either opponent individually may select and enforce a penalty, but may not consult except to have the applicable law stated. Consultation constitutes waiver of penalty.

CHANGING A CALL. If a player makes a call and "changes it in any way practically in the same breath" this correction stands without penalty. The attempt to change a call, other than a "misnomer," may be penalized. If his first call was proper, the offender may let it stand and his partner must pass on the next round; or may change it and his partner must pass throughout the auction. If the first call was improper, it is dealt with under the appropriate section below.

INSUFFICIENT BID. A bid not sufficient to overcall the previous bid, and also any attempted correction thereof, is void if L. H. O. does not condone. The offender must then make any sufficient bid, or pass. If he chooses the lowest sufficient bid in the same declaration of his insufficient bid, there is no penalty. If he chooses any other bid, his partner must pass during the rest of the auction. If he passes, his partner must pass thereafter and declarer, if an opponent, may require or forbid the opening lead of a specified suit.

CALL OUT OF TURN. If a call out of turn is penalized, the call is void and the turn reverts to the rightful player. The penalty depends on the erroneous call.

(a) If it was a pass, made before the opening bid, or later in the turn of the offender's right-hand opponent, the offender must pass at his next turn only.

(b) In any other case, the offender's partner must pass during the rest of the auction, but the offender himself may call as he pleases in turn.

OTHER IMPROPER CALLS. A player should say simply "Double," not "I double four spades." If he does name the bid to be doubled or redoubled, and misstates the bid as to declaration or odd tricks, he is deemed to have doubled or redoubled the actual preceding bid. If a player doubles or redoubles a bid which his partner has already doubled or redoubled, his call is void, either opponent may cancel all previous doubles and redoubles, and the offender's partner must pass during the rest of the auction. If a player doubles his partner's bid, doubles when there has been no bid, or redoubles when there has been no double, he must substitute any proper call and his partner must pass during the rest of the auction. If a player bids more than seven, or makes a positive call when bound by penalty to pass, he is deemed to have passed, both partners of the offending side must pass during the rest of the auction, and if they become the defenders, declarer may require or forbid the opening lead of a specified suit.

INFORMATION. Until the opening lead is made, any player is entitled to have all the calls restated for his information. Thereafter, a player (not dummy) is entitled to be informed only what the contract is, including whether it is doubled or redoubled.

IRREGULARITY DURING THE PLAY. Any player or dummy may call attention to an irregularity during the play (but dummy is limited as below). Either defender for his side, or declarer, has the right to condone an adverse error, or to penalize it. Dummy may participate in discussions of fact and law, but may not advise declarer what course to pursue.

EXPOSED CARDS. A card is deemed exposed during the auction if the partner of the owner sees its face. There is no penalty for exposing one card lower than a jack if it is not a premature lead. In any other case, each card so exposed becomes a *penalty card* and must be placed face up on the table. The partner of the owner must pass during the rest of the auction. If the owner becomes declarer or dummy, there is no further penalty. If the owner becomes a defender, declarer may treat the card as a penalty card during the play (see below).

During the play, declarer may expose his own cards without penalty. But a defender's card becomes a penalty card if it is dropped face up on the table, played with another intended to be played, played when another should have been played in response to a legal requirement, or is seen by partner of the owner.

A penalty card must be played at the first legal opportunity, whether in leading, following suit, ruffing or discarding. If a defender has two or more playable penalty cards, declarer chooses which is to be played. If a penalty card is higher than a jack, declarer has the option if it is still on the table when the owner's partner first gets in the lead: He may forbid a lead in the suit of the penalty card. If he exercises this option, the penalty card may be picked up and ceases to be subject to penalty. In any other case, the obligation to play a penalty card continues until it is played.

CARDS AND TRICKS. A card is deemed to be played if it is detached from the hand and its back touches the table, or if detached from a defender's hand and seen by his partner.

or if it is named as an intended play. If a defender exposes a card in the attempt to change a legal play, this card becomes a penalty card.

Tricks must be gathered and placed face down by one player for each side, and arranged so that the identity of each trick can be determined and the number ascertained at a glance. Until he or his partner has played to the next trick, a player is entitled to look at all the cards of a trick and be informed which hand played each, even if the trick has been gathered and turned. No earlier tricks may be examined except to settle the facts in a claim of irregularity.

DUMMY may call attention to an irregularity, discuss questions of fact and law after they arise, answer a proper request for information, and warn a player that he is about to commit an irregularity, as by inquiring whether a play is a revoke, or warning declarer not to lead from the wrong hand. Dummy loses these rights if he looks at a card in another player's hand.

No penalty may be enforced against the dummy hand for revoke, wrong number of cards, or any other irregularity (but it may be rectified to allow play to continue).

PLAY OUT OF TURN. If declarer leads out of turn, either opponent may let it stand or require correction. In the latter case, if the lead must be made by the opposite hand, declarer must if possible lead a card of the same suit as his incorrect lead. If he plays (not leads) out of turn, there is no penalty, but his play may not be changed unless it is a revoke.

If a defender leads out of turn, when it was his partner's turn, declarer may either treat the incorrect lead as a penalty card, or forbid the other defender to lead the suit of the out-of-turn lead. If a defender leads when it was the turn of declarer or dummy, declarer may treat the incorrect lead as a penalty card.

PREMATURE PLAY. If a defender leads before his partner has played to the current trick, or plays fourth hand to a trick before his partner (or third hand) has played, declarer may require his partner to follow suit with his highest or lowest card, or to play a specified suit; but he may not specify a suit after calling for the highest or lowest card of the suit led and discovering that the defender has none of that suit.

REVOKE. A revoke is failure to follow suit, when able to do

so. A revoke must be corrected if noted before it becomes established, and a revoke in the twelfth trick must be corrected without penalty at any time before the cards are mixed together. A defender's card withdrawn to correct a revoke becomes a penalty card; a member of the non-offending side may change a play made after the revoke.

A revoke becomes established when a member of the revoking side leads or plays to the next trick, and the revoke trick may no longer be changed. After play ends, two tricks (if available) are transferred to the opponents of the revoking side and are scored as though won in play; a trick won before the revoke trick may not be transferred. A revoke due to failure to play any faced card (including dummy's cards) is not subject to penalty, nor is a second revoke in the same suit by the same player.

CLAIMS. A defender may show all or part of his hand to declarer for the purpose of establishing a claim to some or all of the remaining tricks, but no such claim or concession is binding unless the other defender accedes. If declarer claims any or all of the remaining tricks "or suggests that play may be curtailed," he must put his hand face up on the table and "forthwith make any adequate statement of his intended line of play." Either defender may dispute the claim and require declarer to play on with his hand exposed, and (in effect) the defenders may direct his play in any situation not specifically covered by his prior statement. Cards exposed by a defender in consequence of a claim by declarer are not subject to penalty, and a defender may suggest a play to his partner.

CONTRACT BRIDGE BIDDING

There are numerous systems for bidding skillfully in Contract Bridge. The most popular by far is the one devised by Charles H. Goren. In this system a player first values his hand by a *point-count system,* to determine how strong it is; then he bids in accordance with general rules of guidance provided by Mr. Goren, each bid in each situation requiring a given number of points. In many cases, a bid requires that the bidder have a certain minimum of points but not have more than a certain maximum. An authorized outline of the Goren System, approved by Mr. Goren, follows.

GOREN POINT-COUNT TABLE

HIGH-CARD POINTS			QUICK TRICKS		
Ace	=	4 pts.	A-K	=	2
King	=	3 pts.	A-Q	=	1 1/2
Queen	=	2 pts.	A or K-Q	=	1
Jack	=	1 pt.	K-x	=	1/2

High-card points (usually called simply *points*) are counted for nearly every bid. To them are often added distributional points, described below. Quick tricks are counted only for opening bids on borderline hands and, often, when considering a double of an opponent's bid.

GAME AND SLAM REQUIREMENTS. 26 points will normally produce a game. 33 points will normally produce a small slam. 37 points will normally produce a grand slam.

DISTRIBUTIONAL POINTS
(In Addition to High-Card Points)

Opening Bidder Counts For Original Bids

Void Suit = 3 pts.
Singleton = 2 pts.
Doubleton = 1 pt.

Add 1 pt. for all 4 aces.

Deduct 1 pt. for an aceless hand.

Deduct 1 pt. for each unguarded honor (examples: Q-x, J-x, singleton K, Q, or J).

Responder Counts When Raising Partner's Suit

Void Suit = 5 pts.
Singleton = 3 pts.
Doubleton = 1 pt.

Promote honors in partner's bid suit by 1 pt. (unless these honors already total 4 pts.).

Deduct 1 pt. from total distributional points if hand contains only three trumps or if hand has 4-3-3-3 distribution.

For Rebids: After Partner has raised opening bidder's suit:
Add 1 additional pt. for the fifth card in the trump suit.
Add 2 additional pts. for the sixth and each subsequent trump.

MINIMUM BIDDABLE SUITS

For an Opening Bid

4-Card Suits: Must contain 4 high-card points (example—K-J-x-x, A-x-x-x)

5-Card Suits: Any 5-card suit (x-x-x-x-x)

For a Response or Rebid

Q-10-x-x or better (example —Q-10-x-x, K-x-x-x, A-x-x-x)

Any 5-card-suit (x-x-x-x-x)

REBIDDABLE SUITS

4-Card Suits   No 4-card suit is rebiddable
5-Card Suits   Must be Q-J-9-x-x or better
6-Card Suits   Any 6-card suit is rebiddable (x-x-x-x-x-x)

OPENING BID REQUIREMENTS

One of a suit

(a)   14-pt. hands must be opened.
(b)   13-pt. hands may be opened if a good rebid is available (a rebiddable suit or a second rebiddable suit).
(c)   All openings must contain two quick tricks.
(d)   A third-position opening is permitted with 11 pts. if hand contains a good suit.

Two of a suit
(forcing to game)

(a)   25 pts. with a good 5-card suit (1 pt. less with a second good 5-card suit).
(b)   23 pts. with a good 6-card suit.
(c)   21 pts. with a good 7-card suit.

Three, four, or five of a suit
(preëmptive bids)

Preëmptive bids show less than 10 pts. in high cards and the ability to win within two tricks of the contract vulnerable and within three tricks not vulnerable. They should usually be based on a good 7-card or longer suit.

One no-trump   16 to 18 pts. (in no-trump bidding only high-card points are counted) and 4-3-3-3, 4-4-3-2 or 5-3-3-2 distribution with Q-x or better in any doubleton.

Two no-trump   22 to 24 pts. and all suits stopped (J-x-x-x; Q-x-x; K-x; or better).

Three no-trump   25 to 27 pts. and all suits stopped.

CHOICE OF SUITS. Generally speaking, bid your longest suit first. With two 5-card suits bid the higher-ranking first. With two or more 4-card suits, bid the suit immediately lower in rank to your short suit (doubleton, singleton, or void).

EXAMPLES:

♠ J 10 x x x   ♡ A x   ◇ A K J 10   ♣ x x
Bid one spade, your longest suit.

♠ A J 10 5   ♡ 9   ◇ A 10 x x   ♣ K J x x
Bid one diamond, the suit immediately below the singleton.

♠ x x x   ♡ A Q 10 x   ◇ A K J x   ♣ x x
Bid one heart, the first biddable suit below the doubleton. (The spades are not biddable.)

♠ J x x x   ♡ Q x x x   ◇ K x   ♣ A K x
Bid one club. This hand is a mandatory opening (14 pts.) and neither major suit is biddable. With no biddable 4-card suit or only one 4-card suit, an exception is sometimes made in favor of a 3-card suit. This bid is employed as a matter of convenience.

RESPONSES

GENERAL PRINCIPLES. Usually the combined hands must have 26 points to make a game contract. Partner's opening bid promises at least 13 of these, but he may have much more. Therefore every effort should be made to keep the bidding open to give him a second chance to speak. A response should be made with as little as 6 points, because partner may have made a simple one-bid with as much as 20 points.

Often the responder holds a good hand, sometimes even better than that of the opening bidder; but to keep the bidding low, any bid of a new suit by the responding hand is forcing on the opening bidder for one round. Thus, each time the responder bids a new suit the opener must bid again. If responder should jump, his bid is forcing to game.

Game in a major suit is easiest to make (the required 26 points can include distribution as well as high cards). The next-easiest game is three no-trump. The most difficult is game in a minor (requiring 28 or 29 points).

With a mediocre hand (less than 10 points), responder should prefer to raise partner if partner has opened in a major suit, and to bid a new suit himself at the one level in preference to raising a minor-suit opening bid.

With 11 or 12 points, responder can make two bids but should not force to game. With 13 points or more he should see that the bidding is not dropped before a game contract is reached. With 19 points he should make a strong effort to reach a slam.

RESPONSES TO SUIT BIDS OF ONE. *Raise.* To raise partner's suit responder must have adequate trump support. This consists of J-x-x, Q-x-x, x-x-x-x, or better for a non-rebid suit; and Q-x, K-x, or x-x-x for a rebid suit.

Raise partner's suit to two with 7 to 10 points and adequate trump support.

Raise to three with 13 to 16 points and at least four trumps.

Raise to four with no more than 9 high-card points plus at least five trumps and a short suit (singleton or void).

Bid of a New Suit. At the one level a bid of a new suit requires 6 points or more. This response may be made on anything ranging from a weak hand, where responder is just trying to keep the bidding open, to a very powerful one when he is not sure where the hand should be played.

At the two level it requires 10 points or more.

A jump in a new suit requires 19 points or more. (The jump shift is reserved for hands where a slam is very likely. Responder should hold either an independent suit or strong support for opener's suit.)

No-Trump Responses. These responses are usually made on balanced hands. One no-trump requires 6 to 9 points in high cards (this bid is often made on an unbalanced hand if responder's suit is lower in rank than the opening bidder's and responder lacks the 10 points required to take the bidding into the two level).

Two no-trump requires 13 to 15 points in high cards, all unbid suits stopped, and a balanced hand.

Three no-trump requires 16 to 18 points in high cards, all unbid suits stopped, and 4-3-3-3 distribution.

RESPONSES TO SUIT BIDS OF TWO. An opening bid of two in a suit is unconditionally forcing to game and responder may not pass until game is reached. With 6 points or less he bids two no-trump regardless of his distribution. With **7** points and one quick trick, he may show a new suit or raise the opener's suit. With 8 or 9 high-card points and a balanced hand, responder bids three no-trump.

RESPONSES TO PREËMPTIVE BIDS. Since the opener has overbid his hand by two or three tricks, aces, kings, and potential ruffing values are the key factors to be considered when responder is contemplating a raise. One or two trumps constitute sufficient support.

RESPONSES TO A ONE NO-TRUMP BID. *Balanced Hands.* Raise to 2 N T with 8 or 9 points, or with 7 points and a good 5-card suit. Raise to 3 N T with 10 to 14 points. Raise to 4 N T with 15 or 16 points. Raise to 6 N T with 17 or 18 points. Raise to 7 N T with 21 points.

Unbalanced Hands. With less than 8 points plus a 5-card suit, bid two diamonds, two hearts, or two spades. (Do not bid two clubs on a 5-card club suit.) With 8 points or more and a 4-card major suit, bid two clubs. (This is an artificial bid asking opener to show a 4-card major if he has one. See section on rebids by opening one no-trump bidder.) With 10 points and a good suit, bid three of that suit. With a 6-card major suit and less than 10 points in high cards, jump to game in the suit.

RESPONSES TO A TWO NO-TRUMP OPENING. *Balanced Hands.* Raise to 3 N T with 4 to 8 points. Raise to 4 N T with 9 to 10 points. Raise to 6 N T with 11 or 12 points. Raise to 7 N T with 15 points.

Unbalanced Hands. With a 5-card major suit headed by an honor, plus 4 points, bid the suit at the three level. Show any 6-card major suit.

RESPONSES TO A THREE NO-TRUMP OPENING. Show any 5-card suit if the hand contains 5 points in high cards. Raise to 4 N T with 7 points. Raise to 6 N T with 8 or 9 points. Raise to 7 N T with 12 points.

REBIDS

REBIDS BY OPENING BIDDER. The opener's rebid is frequently the most important call of the auction, as he now has the opportunity to reveal the exact strength of his opening bid and therefore whether game or slam is in contemplation. His opening is valued according to the following table:

13 to 16 pts.	Minimum hand
16 to 19 pts.	Good hand
19 to 21 pts.	Very good hand

Minimum Hand (13 to 16 points). If partner has made a limit response (one no-trump or a single raise), opener should pass, as game is impossible. If partner bids a new suit at the one level, opener may make a single raise with good trump support, rebid one no-trump with a balanced hand, or, with an unbalanced hand, rebid his own suit or a new suit (if he does not go past the level of two in the suit of his original bid).

Good Hand (16 to 19 points). If partner has made a limit response (one no-trump or a single raise) opener should bid again, as game is possible if responder has maximum values. If responder has bid a new suit, opener may make a jump raise with four trumps, or jump in his own suit if he has a 6-card suit, or bid a new suit.

Very Good Hand (19 to 21 points). If partner has made a limit response (one no-trump or a single raise), opener may jump to game in either denomination, according to his distribution. If responder has bid a new suit, opener may make a jump raise to game with four trumps, or jump to game in his own suit if it is solid. With a balanced hand and 19 or 20 points, opener should jump to two no-trump. With 21 points he should jump to three no-trump. With 22 points and up he should jump in a new suit (forcing to game and suggesting a slam).

REBIDS BY OPENING NO-TRUMP BIDDER. *Two-Club Convention.* This is usually called the Stayman Convention.* When the responder bids two clubs, the opening bidder must show a 4-card biddable major suit if he has one:

---

* Introduced by Samuel M. Stayman of New York. The name "two-club convention" is also, more often, applied to the use of an opening two-club bid as an artificial game-forcing bid; see page 22.

With four spades, he bids two spades.

With four hearts, he bids two hearts.

With four cards in each major, he bids two spades.

With no 4-card major suit, he bids two diamonds.

Opening No-Trump Bidder Must Pass: When responder raises to two no-trump and opener has a minimum (16 points); when responder bids two diamonds, two hearts, or two spades, and opener has only 16 or 17 points and no good fit for responder's suit; when responder bids three no-trump, four spades, or four hearts.

DEFENSIVE BIDDING

OVERCALLS. An overcall is a defensive bid (made after the other side has opened the bidding). Prospects for game are not as good as they are for the opening bidder, in view of the announced adverse strength, and safety becomes a prime consideration. Overcalls are therefore based not on a specified number of points but rather on a good suit. Generally speaking, the overcaller should employ the same standards as a preëmptor; he should be able to win in his own hand within two tricks of his bid if vulnerable and within three tricks not vulnerable.

ONE NO-TRUMP OVERCALL. An overcall of one no-trump is similar to a one no-trump opening bid and shows 16 to 18 points with a balanced hand and the opening bidder's suit well stopped.

JUMP OVERCALL. Any jump overcall, whether it is a single, double or triple jump, is pre-emptive in nature and shows a hand weak in high cards but with a good suit that will produce within three tricks of the bid if not vulnerable and within two tricks vulnerable.

TAKEOUT DOUBLES (also called *negative* or *informatory doubles*). If a defender doubles when all the following conditions are present: (a) his partner has made no bid; (b) the double was made at the doubler's first opportunity; (c) the double is of one, two or three of a suit—it is intended for a takeout and asks partner to bid his best (longest) suit. This defensive call is employed on either of two types of hand: (1) a hand of opening-bid strength where the doubler has no good or long suit of his own but has good support for any of the unbid suits; and (2) where the doubler has a good suit and so much high-card strength that he fears a mere overcall might be passed out and a possible game missed.

OVERCALL IN OPPONENT'S SUIT (CUE-BID). The immediate cue-bid (example: opponent opens one heart; defender bids two hearts) is the strongest of all defensive bids. It is unconditionally forcing to game and shows the equivalent of an opening forcing bid. It normally announces first-round control of the opening-bid suit and is usually based on a void with very fine support in all unbid suits.

ACTION BY PARTNER OF OVERCALLER. The overcaller's bid is based on a good suit; therefore less than normal trump support is required to raise (Q-x or x-x-x). A raise should be preferred by the partner to bidding a suit of his own, particularly if the overcaller has bid a major. The partner of the overcaller should not bid for the sole purpose of keeping the bidding open. A single raise of a one no-trump response should be made only in an effort to reach game. If appropriate values are held, a leap to game is in order, since a jump raise is not forcing.

ACTION BY PARTNER OF TAKEOUT DOUBLER. In this situation, the weaker the hand the more important it is to bid. The only holding that would justify a pass would be one that contained four defensive tricks, three in the trump suit. The response should be made in the longest suit, though preference is normally given to a major over a minor.

Since the partner of a doubler may be responding on nothing, it is a good policy for the doubler to subsequently underbid, while doubler's partner should overbid. If doubler's partner has better than an average hand, game is very probable (and doubler's partner should so indicate by jumping in his best suit, even if it is only four cards in length).

ACTION BY PARTNER OF THE OPENING BIDDER (when the opening bid has been overcalled or doubled). When the opener's bid has been overcalled, the responder is no longer under obligation to keep the bidding open; so a bid of one no-trump or a raise should be based on a hand of at least average strength. Over a takeout double, the responder has only one way to show a good hand—a redouble. This bid does not promise support for opener's suit but merely announces a better-than-average holding. Any other bid, while not indicative of weakness, shows only mediocre high-card strength.

SLAM BIDDING

When the two partners have been able to determine that they have the assets for a slam (33 points between the combined hands plus an adequate trump suit) the only thing that remains is to make certain that the opponents are unable to cash two quick tricks. Various control, asking and control-showing bids have been employed through the years, but only three have stood the test of time—Blackwood, Gerber, and cue-bids (individual ace-showing).

BLACKWOOD CONVENTION.* After a trump suit has been agreed upon, a bid of four no-trump asks partner to show his total number of aces. A response of five clubs shows either no aces or all four aces; five diamonds shows one ace; five hearts shows two aces; five spades shows three aces. After aces have been shown, the four no-trump bidder may ask for kings by now bidding five no-trump. The responder to the five no-trump bid now shows kings as he showed the number of aces in response to the four no-trump bid: by bidding six clubs if he has no king, six diamonds if he has one king, etc., but six no-trump if he has all four kings.

GERBER CONVENTION.† This convention is similar to Blackwood in that it asks for the number of aces. Its advantage lies in the fact that it initiates the response at a lower level. A sudden bid of four clubs where it could not possibly have a natural meaning (example: opener, one notrump; responder, four clubs) is Gerber and asks partner to show the number of his aces. If he bids four diamonds, he shows no aces; four hearts, one ace, etc. If the asking hand desires information about kings, he bids the next-higher suit over his partner's ace-showing response. Thus, if the responding hand has bid four hearts over four clubs to show one ace, a bid of four spades would now ask him for kings and he would now reply four no-trump to show no king, five clubs to show one king, etc.

CUE-BIDDING (*individual ace-showing*). The Blackwood and Gerber conventions are designed to cover only a small

---

* Devised 1934 by Easley Blackwood of Indianapolis, Ind.
† Devised 1937 by John Gerber of Houston, Tex.

number of potential slam hands. Many slams depend on possession of a specific ace, rather than a wholesale number of aces. Cue-bids are employed in such cases. For example: Opener bids two spades, responder bids three spades, opener now bids four clubs; the four-club bid shows the ace of clubs and invites responder to show an ace if he has one. Frequently, in this method of slam bidding, controls will be shown in all side suits but one. Then if one partner "signs off" (by bidding the agreed trump suit), the other partner may bid the slam if he can guarantee no more than one loser in the unmentioned suit (as by having second-round control, the king or a singleton, in that suit).

OTHER CONTRACT BRIDGE CONVENTIONS

CLUB CONVENTION. This method of bidding was devised by Harold S. Vanderbilt, who invented the modern game of Contract Bridge, and for that reason it is often called "the Vanderbilt Club." It is very popular in Europe. An opening bid of one club is artificial; it does not necessarily show a club suit but it shows a strong hand with 3 1/2 or more quick tricks. The opener's partner must respond one diamond if he has less than 2 quick tricks. Any other response shows at least 2 quick tricks. After the opening bid and response the partners show their suits naturally.

TWO-CLUB CONVENTION. This convention, used by many expert players, is usually combined with "weak two-bids." An opening bid of two clubs is artificial, not necessarily showing a club suit but showing a very powerful hand. It is forcing to game. The opener's partner must respond two diamonds if he has a weak hand. Any other response shows strength, usually at least 1 1/2 quick tricks. An opening bid of two diamonds, two hearts, or two spades is a pre-emptive bid, made on a fairly weak hand that includes a good 5- or 6-card suit but does not have the 13 or more points needed for an opening one-bid.

Any hand that would justify an opening bid of two in a suit (page 14) is suitable for an artificial two-club bid. For example:

♠ A K Q J 6 3   ♡ A K 8   ◇ K 7   ♣ A 5

The following hands are typical for the "weak two-bid":

♠ 6   ♡ K Q 10 7 5 3   ◇ K 6 2   ♣ 7 5 2
(Bid two hearts)

♠ 7 5　　♡ A 4　　◇ K 10 9 7 6 3　　♣ J 10 4
(Bid two diamonds)

The opening bidder's partner passes a weak two-bid unless he has a strong hand, usually 15 or more points. Some players treat any response in a new suit to a weak two-bid as forcing; some treat a two no-trump response as forcing.

CONVENTIONAL LEADS
(Contract or Auction Bridge)

HOLDING IN SUIT	LEAD AT SUIT BIDS	LEAD AT NO-TRUMP
A-K-Q alone or with others	K, then Q	K, then Q
A-K-J-x-x-x-x	K, then A	*A, then K
A-K-J-x-x or A-K-x-x(-x)	K, then A	Fourth best
A-Q-J-x-x	A**	Q
A-Q-10-9	A**	10***
A-Q-x-x(-x)	A	Fourth best
A-J-10-x	A**	J
A-10-9-x	A	10
A-x-x-x(-x)	A	Fourth best
A-K-x	K	K
A-K alone	A	K**
K-Q-J alone or with others	K, then J	K, then Q
K-Q-10 alone or with others	K	K
K-Q-x-x(-x-x)	K	Fourth best
K-Q alone	K	K
K-J-10 alone or with others	J	J
K-10-9-x	10	10
Q-J-10 or Q-J-9 alone or with others	Q	Q
Q-J-x or Q-J	Q	Q
Q-J-8-x (four or more)	Q	Fourth best
Q-10-9 alone or with others	10	10
J-10-9 or J-10-8 alone or with others	J	J
J-10-x or J-10	J	J
J-10-x-x or more	J	Fourth best
10-9-8 or 10-9-7 alone or with others	10	10
10-9-x-x(-x)	10	Fourth best
K-J-x-x(-x-x)	Fourth best	Fourth best
Any other four-card or longer suit not listed above	Fourth best	Fourth best

* The lead of the ace of an unbid suit at a no-trump contract requests partner to play his highest card of the suit led, even the king or queen, unless dummy reveals that such a play might risk losing a trick.
** Usually not a good lead at this contract.
*** When dummy seems likely to have the king, the queen is a better lead.

23

LEADS IN PARTNER'S BID SUIT

HOLDING IN SUIT	LEAD AT SUIT BIDS	LEAD AT NO-TRUMP
A-x, K-x, Q-x, J-x, 10-x, or any other doubleton	High card	High card
J-10-x or x-x-x	Highest	Highest
A-J-x or A-x-x	A	Lowest
K-J-x, K-x-x, Q-10-x, Q-x-x, J-x-x	Lowest	Lowest
Q-J-x(-x)	Q	Q
A-x-x-x or better	A	Fourth best
K-Q-x(-x)	K	K
Any other 4 or more cards	Fourth best	Fourth best

Progressive Bridge

When a Bridge party is given for sixteen or more guests—especially when it is a mixed group who wish to play in a social atmosphere—the best game is Progressive Bridge.

The hostess divides her expected guests into two groups, preferably one of gentlemen and one of ladies. She prepares "tally cards" (combination seating assignments and score slips) of two colors, one color for each group.

One card table is set up for each four players; if possible, all the tables should be in the same room. On each table are placed two packs of cards, a Bridge score pad, and a marker designating the table number; table 1 is the "head" table.

When the guests arrive, each draws a tally card of the color assigned to his or her group, and goes to the table designated by the card; each two players having cards identically marked (though of different colors) are partners for the first round. The players draw for first deal and play exactly four deals, each player in rotation dealing first. When a deal is passed out it is not redealt.

The scoring is the same as in Contract Bridge except that there are no rubber bonuses; when declarer makes his contract, he adds to the trick score

50 points for less than game;
300 points for game in one hand, not vulnerable;
500 points for game in one hand, vulnerable.

Vulnerability does not depend on winning a game. On the first deal of each four, neither side is vulnerable; on the second and third deals, dealer's side only is vulnerable; on the fourth deal both sides are vulnerable.

In PROGRESSIVE AUCTION BRIDGE, no rubber bonus is awarded and a pair that scores game in one hand receives a bonus of 125 points.

PROGRESSION. When the fourth deal is completed, the scores for all four deals are added up and each player writes on his tally card the number of points he scored on that round. When all tables have completed play, the hostess announces the change: The pair with the higher score at each table moves to the next-lower-numbered table, exchanges partners with the pair who remained there, and another round is begun.

The only exception is at the head table, where the winning pair remains (without changing partners) and the losing pair moves to the highest-numbered table (the "booby" table).

Play may continue for any convenient number of rounds. After the game, each player totals the scores on his tally card. There is usually a prize for the highest score, and a consolation prize for the lowest score, together with such other prizes as the hostess wishes to give.

PROGRESSIVE RUBBER BRIDGE. This differs only in that six deals are played to each round, with regular Rubber Bridge scoring, as explained on pages 5 to 7. After the sixth deal, the play ceases even if a rubber is not completed. (There is a bonus of 300 for having the only game in an unfinished rubber, and a bonus of 50 for having the only part-score(s) in an unfinished game of an unfinished rubber.)

PLUS-OR-MINUS SCORING. The Laws of Progressive Bridge require that at the end of each round the lower total be deducted from the higher; the winners enter the difference as a "plus" score and the losers enter it as a "minus" score. This is popular only with very serious players.

SCORING LIMITS. Neither side may score more than 1,000 points on a single deal, except by *bidding and making* a slam.

It is not proper to prohibit doubles or redoubles, or to alter the Contract Bridge laws except as explained above.

AUCTION BRIDGE *follows exactly the same rules as*
CONTRACT BRIDGE, *with the exception of the scoring.*
The one essential difference—which, however, makes
considerable difference in the strategy of the game—is
that in Contract Bridge only the amount of the bid is
scored "below the line," whereas in Auction all the
tricks won in play, not merely those bid, contribute to
winning the game. Auction Bridge scoring is as follows.

AUCTION BRIDGE

TRICKS. If declarer's side makes its contract, it scores all
the odd tricks won, below the line:

DECLARATION	UNDOUBLED	DOUBLED	REDOUBLED
No-trump, for each odd-trick	10	20	40
Spades	9	18	36
Hearts	8	16	32
Diamonds	7	14	28
Clubs	6	12	24

The side that first accumulates 30 points below the line
wins a game. A horizontal line is then drawn below the trick
scores of both sides. Each side starts on the new game from
zero score.

The side that first wins two out of three games wins a
rubber and adds 250 points to its score.

BONUSES. If a doubled contract is made, declarer's side
scores above the line: 50 for making the contract, plus 50

26

for each trick won in excess of the contract. If a redoubled contract is made, these bonuses are raised to 100 each.

UNDERTRICKS. If declarer fails to make his contract, his side scores nothing for tricks and the other side scores above the line, for each undertrick: at an undoubled contract, 50; doubled contract, 100; redoubled contract, 200.

SLAMS. If either side wins twelve tricks (*little slam*) it scores 50 above the line. If either side wins all the tricks (*grand slam*) it scores 100 above the line. These premiums are independent of the contract and whether it is fulfilled.

HONORS. At a trump declaration, the honors are the A, K, Q, J, and 10 of the trump suit. At no-trump, the honors are the four aces. The side to whom three or more honors are dealt scores for them above the line:

3 honors	30
4 trump honors, divided	40
5 trump honors, divided	50
4 trump honors in one hand	80
All trump honors, divided 4-1	90
4 aces in one hand	100
5 trump honors in one hand	100

Honors are scored regardless of which side assumes the contract.

WHIST

Whist follows the rules of play stated on page 1, but there is no bidding and no dummy. Each player holds and plays his own hand, closed from the view of the others.

The pack is dealt out one card at a time, thirteen cards to each player. Dealer places the last card, belonging to him, face up on the table, and it fixes the trump suit for the deal. Eldest hand makes the opening lead, and before playing to the first trick dealer restores the trump card to his hand. The object of play is solely to win as many tricks as possible.

The side that wins the majority scores 1 point for each trick in excess of six. The side first to accumulate 7 points wins the game, the value of which is 7 minus the loser's score. Thus, beginning the last deal of a game, one side has 6 points, the other side 4. The former side wins three odd-tricks, but it wins $7 - 4 = 3$, not $9 - 4 = 5$.

BRIDGE FOR THREE

Cutthroat Bridge

The three players take any three seats at the table and draw for deal, but not for partners. The dealer deals the usual four hands; the one opposite him is the dummy and is not touched. The three players bid in regular order, beginning with the dealer, and when any call is followed by two consecutive passes the auction is closed. The player at declarer's left makes the opening lead. Declarer then sorts the dummy and lays it out opposite him, between the two defenders. Play proceeds precisely as in Contract or Auction Bridge.

There are three columns on the score sheet, one for each player. If declarer fulfills the contract, he scores its value in his column. If declarer falls short, each defender scores the undertrick penalties in his column. Honors held by one defender are scored by both defenders.

The rubber ends when any player has won two games. Each player's column is added up and he settles separately with each of the other players, depending on the difference in their scores. If Contract Bridge scoring is being used, the winner of the rubber scores only 500 points bonus if either defender was vulnerable.

An irregular bid stands if both opponents call before attention is called to it, but is void if attention is called to it earlier. An irregular double may be canceled by the player who is doubled; and no player may double him thereafter at any contract. If a defender bids after the auction is closed, declarer may require or forbid an opening lead in a specified suit.

Bridge for Three

This form of three-hand Bridge has been published under the names TRIO and TRIANGLE CONTRACT. It was devised by George S. Coffin of Waltham, Massachusetts, and is the best form of Bridge for three.

The players sit in the compass positions South, North, and East. South and North are partners against East and the dummy. After the deal the full dummy is immediately spread in the West position. All players see it throughout the bidding and play.

South always bids first. The bidding proceeds as in Contract Bridge. East bids dummy and his own hand, each in proper turn. Any player (including dummy) may become declarer, and the hand at declarer's left makes the opening lead, but the original dummy hand is the only one that is exposed. The play and scoring are the same as in regular Contract Bridge (pages 4-7), with East winning or losing doubly. At the end of the rubber the previous South becomes the new East and has the dummy for the next rubber; the previous North becomes the new South, and East the new North.

Towie

Only three may play at a time, but others may participate in the same game. The deal is as in Cutthroat Bridge, but after dealing the dealer turns up six cards of the extra hand. The auction proceeds, then the play (with dummy's remaining cards exposed), and any additional player who is sitting out scores the same as the defenders.

No contract of less than game (that is, worth less than 100 points trick score, at its undoubled, doubled or redoubled value as the case may be) is played; nor does the dealer change if the hands are passed out. Instead there is a *goulash*. Each player sorts his hand into suits, the hands are stacked and cut but not shuffled, and dealer gives each player thirteen cards, 5, 5 and 3 at a time. Six of dummy's cards are turned up as usual, and the auction proceeds.

When more than three are playing, the declarer retires from the table after each hand and his place is taken by the inactive player who is highest in order of precedence except that no vulnerable player may re-enter the game while a non-vulnerable player sits out.

A player who makes his first game receives a bonus of 500 points; for winning the rubber there is an additional bonus of 1000.

Any call out of turn is void and the offender must pass thereafter unless both opponents condone the offense and let the irregular call stand. An insufficient bid must be made sufficient, and the offender must pass thereafter unless he made the correction before attention was called to the irregularity.

BRIDGE FOR TWO

Draw Bridge or Domino Bridge

The two players face each other across the table, as in other two-hand games. They draw for deal, using a regular 52-card pack; the dealer shuffles, his opponent cuts, and he deals thirteen cards to each player, one at a time. The remainder of the pack is the stock.

Non-dealer leads, and the rules of play are as in Bridge; but after each trick the winner and then his opponent draw from the stock, so that each has a thirteen-card hand until the stock is exhausted, at which time the auction is held.

Dealer bids first; the auction ends when any call is passed, and non-dealer leads. The last thirteen tricks are played and scored as though it were a four-hand bridge game.

Honeymoon Bridge

Instead of facing each other, the two players sit beside each other. Four complete hands are dealt, as in Bridge. Each player looks at both his own hand and the hand opposite him (his dummy). Only the two players bid, dealer first; the high bidder becomes declarer, and the hand at his left (whether it is his opponent or his opponent's dummy) leads first. Play proceeds as in Bridge, all four hands playing to each trick, each in proper turn. The result is scored as in Bridge (Auction or Contract).

For convenience in playing, it is almost necessary for each player to have a device (such as a wooden rack) in which he can stick the cards of his dummy in such a way that he can see them but his opponent cannot.

OH HELL

OH HELL *(called* OH PSHAW *or* BLACKOUT *in family journals) made its appearance in New York card clubs in the late 1930s. It was said to have come from England, but nothing more is known of its origin. It is one of the best round games for sheer relaxation, yet it is comparable to Hearts in its opportunity for skillful play.*

PLAYERS. From three to seven; best is four-hand, each playing for himself.

CARDS. A regular pack of 52. In each suit the cards rank: A (high), K, Q, J, 10, 9, 8, 7, 6, 5, 4, 3, 2.

THE GAME. A game comprises a fixed number of deals. In the first deal, each player receives one card; in the second deal, two; and so on. In three-hand, there are fifteen deals; in four-hand, thirteen; in five-hand, ten; in six-hand, eight; in seven-hand, seven. The number of deals can be reduced, by agreement, to make the game shorter.

THE DEAL. The turn to deal rotates to the left (clockwise). The dealer distributes cards one at a time clockwise, up to the number per hand due in that deal. He turns the next card of the pack face up on the table; this *turn-up* fixes the trump suit for that deal. The rest of the pack is laid aside and is not used during that deal. In the last deal of a game the trump card is not turned, the hands being played out at no-trump.

THE BIDDING. The player at left of the dealer bids first. Each player in turn must make a bid (he cannot pass); he bids the number of tricks that he will undertake to win. He may bid zero if he pleases, and this bid is sometimes indicated by saying "Pass." The size of the bid is of course limited by the number of cards per hand. In the first deal, the only possible bids are one and zero. In the last deal of a four-hand game, the bids may range from zero to thirteen.

THE SCOREKEEPER. One player should be appointed to keep score. The scoresheet should be divided into columns (or double columns), one for each player. The scorekeeper must record each bid, and must furnish information about the bids on request. During the bidding, any player in his turn may ask how many tricks (total) have been bid before him. During the play, any player in his turn may ask what were the bids made by various players. When the bidding is ended, the scorekeeper should announce whether the deal is overbid, underbid, or even (that is, if the total of the bids of all players makes more, less, or the same as the number of cards in each hand).

THE PLAY. The player at left of the dealer makes the opening lead. The hands are played out in tricks. A hand must follow suit to a lead, if able; if unable to follow suit, the hand may play any card. A trick is won by the highest trump in it, or, if it contains no trump, by the highest card played of the suit led. The winner of a trick leads to the next. Each player must keep his tricks segregated so that any other may readily ascertain their number.

SCORING. In Oh Hell (as contrasted with Bridge, Pinochle, etc.) a player does not fulfill his bid by winning *more* tricks than he bid. To score, he must win the exact number he bid. He *busts* if he takes either more or less.

After the end of play, the scorekeeper records all due scores in running totals on the scoresheet. Each player who busts scores nothing. Each player who makes his bid scores the amount of the bid plus 10. (Some players prefer a different scoring for zero bids; the bidder receives 5 plus the number of tricks in the deal. The theory is that a zero bid is easy to make in the early deals, but becomes progressively harder as the hands grow in size.)

At the end of a game, the player with highest cumulative score wins.

IRREGULARITIES IN OH HELL

IRREGULAR BID. If a player bids out of turn, his bid stands but the turn reverts to the rightful player. If a player bids in proper turn, then attempts to change his bid, the change is allowed only if the next player in turn has not bid.

EXPOSED CARD. If a player exposes a card from his hand, or leads or plays out of turn, he must leave the card face up on the table and play it at his first legal opportunity thereafter.

REVOKE. Failure to follow suit when able is a revoke. A revoke may be corrected before the lead to the next trick, and any cards played to the trick after the revoke may be retracted without penalty. The card retracted by the revoker becomes exposed. If a revoke is not corrected in time, the deal is void; there must be a redeal of the same number of cards by the same dealer, and 10 points are deducted from the score of the offender.

STRATEGY OF OH HELL

Generally speaking, it is easier to lose than to win tricks. Especially when there are four or more cards in each hand, a player is safer to underbid his hand by one trick than to bid for the full number of tricks he estimates he can win. The dealer has an advantage because he bids last. He should try to make it even if he is doubtful about how many tricks he can win, for then he may get co-operation from other players trying to make the exact number they have bid. When his hand is clear-cut, he should bid its exact value and tend if possible to make the total uneven.

The ideal suit has both high and low cards; the worst suit has several intermediate cards. For example:

Diamonds are trumps. Bid one. If forced to win a club trick, you will not have to take your ace of hearts.

The normal policy in leading is to open one's dangerous suits, forcing clarification thereof, so as to know how to play one's "two-way" suits. In an example previously given, a hand holds ♡ A 6 4 2 ♣ J 10 9, with diamonds trumps, and bids one. Having the lead, this hand should open a club. If a club trick is taken, the heart ace must be withheld, while if there is no club trick, the ace must be taken. If the opening lead is won by another hand, this hand should seek to discard both remaining clubs, thereby eliminating the danger and relying on the ace alone.

If the deal is underbid, the natural policy of each player is to hold back in the early tricks, avoiding taking any unnecessarily. But the necessity for clarifying danger suits often overrides this principle. Above all, a player must be sure to take his tricks before his last small exit card is bailed out. As an extreme example, with ♢ A 2 there is scarcely conceivable any reason for holding up the ace on the first round to win the second diamond lead.

EXAMPLE DEAL

```
                    NORTH
                    ♠ 7
                    ♡ A K 8
                    ♣ A K 9 8 4
                    ♢ 6 3
  WEST                                    EAST
  ♠ 10 4                                  ♠ A J 9 2
  ♡ 2                                     ♡ J 10 4 3
  ♣ 3                                     ♣ 7
  ♢ K J 10 9 8 4 2                        ♢ Q 7
                    SOUTH (Dealer)
                    ♠ Q 6
                    ♡ Q 9 7 6 5
                    ♣ Q 10 5
                    ♢ A
```

♠ 8 turned.

The bids are: West, 1; North, 3; East, 3; South, 3. West bids one because if the hand is underbid he will probably be forced to win the ♠ 10, while if it is overbid he still has a good chance to make it by ruffing, especially as he has the opening lead. North counts that he can probably win three top tricks by force, and probably can be forced to win three hearts. East counts two trump tricks anyhow, with either a forced trick in diamonds or a voluntary third trick in trumps. South counts a trump and a diamond, with everything else problematical. To bid only two, leaving the deal two underbid, is dangerous. South makes a guess and tries three.

In the play below, West leads first; the card that is starred wins the trick, and the card below it is the lead to the next.

TRICK	WEST	NORTH	EAST	SOUTH
1	♣ 3	♣ A*	♣ 7	♣ 10

North steps right up to clarify the heart situation.

2	♡ 2	♡ A*	♡ J	♡ 9
3	♠ 10*	♡ K	♡ 3	♡ 7

This is just what West wanted.

4	♠ 4	♠ 7	♠ J	♠ Q*

South wants to get in to cash the ◇ A, so as to be able to discard, if need be, on later diamond leads. On the following lead he seeks to clarify the club situation.

5	◇ J	◇ 6	◇ 7	◇ A*
6	◇ 10	♣ 9	♠ 9*	♣ Q

East ruffs in order to find out at once whether the ◇ Q is a trick.

7	◇ 9	◇ 3	◇ Q	♠ 6*

South's ruff looks like the best play. East surely has some more trumps for his bid, and North still wants another trick. If South doesn't step in now, he may find himself swamped by trumps and high cards in the end.

8	◇ K	♡ 8*	♡ 4	♡ 5

Here and on the next trick East plays very astutely. It would seem natural to take the ♡ 8 with the ♡ 10 and exit with the ♠ 2. But maybe both remaining trumps are long, placing the ♠ K 5 3 in the stock. At all events, the bidding and play show that there cannot possibly be more than one more trump in play. Even if there is one, it is best to let the ♡ 8 win. Then if North leads a heart which East has to win, the ♠ 2 will be an exit. In any other contingency, East can surely win the last two tricks with his trumps.

9	◇ 8	♣ 4	♡ 10	♣ 5*
10			♠ 2*	
11			♠ A*	

All make their contracts except South.

FAN TAN

There is *a Chinese gambling game called Fan Tan, based on guessing the number of beans in a pot. The card game Fan Tan may have been named for it but is in no way similar to it. The card game is a member of the* Stops *family of games; it is sometimes called* Stops *or* Sevens.

Players. Three to eight; best for four or five.

Cards. A regular pack of 52. In each suit the cards rank: K (high), Q, J, 10, 9, 8, 7, 6, 5, 4, 3, 2, A.

The Deal. All the cards are dealt out, one at a time in rotation to the left. It does not matter if some players hold one more card than others.

The Pool. All players receive equal numbers of poker chips at the outset. Before the deal, a pool is formed by antes: one chip from each player with a greater number of cards, two chips from each with a lesser number.

The Play. The player at left of the dealer has first turn. He must play a seven or pass. Each hand in turn must play if able; if unable, the hand passes and must pay a forfeit of one chip to the pool.

Sevens are always playable. The four sevens are placed in a row in the center of the table, forming foundations that open the way for other cards. Once a seven is played, the eight and six of the same suit are playable. The eights are placed in a row on one side of the sevens, the sixes in a row on the other side. On these cards additional cards may be played in suit and sequence—upward on the eights to the kings, downward on the sixes to the aces.

THE OBJECT OF PLAY is to get rid of all the cards in the hand. The player first to do so wins the game. Each other player must pay to the pool one chip for each card remaining in his hand, then the winner takes the entire pool.

IRREGULARITIES. If a player passes, and later is found to hold a seven, he must pay 3 chips to the pool and 5 chips each to the holders of the eight and six of that suit. If a player passes, and later is found to have had a playable card but not a seven, he must pay 3 chips to the pool.

STRATEGY OF FAN TAN

Given a choice of play, the player should (a) prefer first of all a card from a sequence, to prepare additional plays for himself; (b) build toward other cards of the same suit in his hand, rather than play a card which is his last in that direction of sequence; (c) choose the card nearest the king or ace, so as to minimize the plays opened to his opponents.

EIGHTS

This game is also called CRAZY EIGHTS or SWEDISH RUMMY. It is identical with a game called CRAZY JACKS except that in the latter jacks are the wild cards. Whereas most of the Stops games are best for five or more players Eights is best for two.

PLAYERS. From two to seven.

CARDS. A regular pack of 52, with five or fewer players. With more, use two packs shuffled together.

THE DEAL. With two players, each receives seven cards, dealt one at a time. With more than two, each receives five cards. The rest of the pack is placed face down in the center of the table to form the *stock*. Its top card is turned face up beside it as the *starter*.

THE PLAY. The turn to play rotates to the left (clockwise), beginning with the opponent at left of the dealer. A play consists of placing one card face up on the pile begun by the starter. Each card played must match the previous play in either suit or rank: on the ♡ 6 any heart or any six may be played. If unable to play in turn, a player must draw cards from the top of the stock and add them to his hand until able to play. After the stock is exhausted, a player unable to play must pass. A player may draw from the stock even when he has a playable card.

EIGHTS. The eights are wild. An eight may be played upon any preceding card, regardless of its suit or rank. The owner of the eight must specify a suit (not necessarily its own) which the eight calls for, and the next player must follow with that suit or with another eight.

SCORING. Play ends when any player gets rid of the last card in his hand. He scores the total of the cards remaining in all other hands: 50 for each eight, 1 for each ace, 10 for each face card, the index value for each other card. Score is kept on paper. Each deal may be settled as a separate game, but when two play, it is usual to award the game to the one who first reaches 100 points or more.

STRATEGY OF EIGHTS

An eight should be saved for a special purpose. It should not be played merely to avoid drawing. Often it is advantageous to draw a few additional cards, especially in two-hand play.

One's long suit is most often the best to play, as is any suit that the opponent was previously unable to match without drawing.

MICHIGAN

MICHIGAN *is the best-known member of the* STOPS *family of card games, which includes also* EIGHTS *and* FAN TAN, *as well as many other games of great antiquity. Each of these games is likely to be known by several different names; for example, Michigan with slight variations is known as* NEWMARKET *or* BOODLE. *All these are mild gambling games, often played "for buttons" at social parties.*

PLAYERS. From three to about eight.

CARDS. A regular pack of 52. In each suit the cards rank: A (high), K, Q, J, 10, 9, 8, 7, 6, 5, 4, 3, 2 (low).

LAYOUT. From a second pack are taken the ♡ A, ♣ K, ♢ Q, and ♠ J. These four cards, placed in a square in the center of the table, form the *layout;* they and the corresponding cards of the pack used for play are called *boodle cards.*

CHIPS. All participants are provided at the beginning of a game with equal numbers of poker chips, matchsticks, or other tokens. Before each deal, the dealer must place two chips on each boodle card, and every other player must place one chip on each. (An alternate rule is that each player may distribute his chips as he pleases on the boodle cards in the layout.)

THE DEAL. The right to deal first should be decided by chance. The usual way is for any player to deal cards one at a time until the first jack shows; that player deals first.

The turn to deal passes in rotation to the left (clockwise), and a game is completed when each player has dealt once.

The dealer distributes cards one at a time to his left until the pack is exhausted. Thus, some hands may have one more card than others, but this does not matter. One more hand is dealt than the number of players; this extra hand, the *widow,* is placed at dealer's immediate left.

THE AUCTION. After looking at his hand, dealer may elect to discard it and take the widow instead. If he decides to keep his original hand, he must offer the widow for sale. The others, after looking at their hands, may bid for it in chips, and it goes to the highest bidder, the chips in payment going to the dealer. If no bid is made, the widow is set aside. It may not be seen except by the player who buys it or the dealer if he takes it.

THE PLAY. A play consists of showing a card face up. Cards as played may be thrown into a common pile, or may be kept face up in front of their owners.

The opponent at left of the dealer plays first. He may play any suit, but must play the lowest card he holds in that suit. The player having the next-higher card of the same suit must then play it, and so following—the turn to play does not rotate, but passes to whoever can continue the upward sequence in the same suit.

In order to facilitate the play, the leader customarily names the suit and sequence of his card, and the following players call out the ranks they add to it, as, "Five of hearts," "Six of hearts."

The sequence of plays is eventually stopped, either because it reaches the ace or because the next card in sequence is not available (being in the discarded hand or in the previous plays). The last player is then entitled to start a new sequence. He must play his lowest card in the suit he selects and he must choose a new suit; if he has only cards of the old suit, he must pass, and the turn goes to his left.

The play ends as soon as one player gets rid of the last card in his hand. The winner collects from each other player one chip for each card remaining in his hand.

BOODLE CARDS. When a player is able to play a card matching one of those in the layout, he collects all the chips on that card. It frequently happens that not all four boodle cards are played during a deal. Uncollected chips remain on the boodle cards, swelled by further antes, until finally won.

IRREGULARITIES. A player who violates a rule of play may not win the deal or collect by playing a boodle card, and must pay each other player one chip; if he goes out first, the others continue play. If the offender fails to play a card next-lower than a boodle card of the same suit, and that boodle card is not played during the deal, the offender must pay the holder of the card the number of chips on it.

The error of leading the same suit is not subject to penalty: it must be corrected, or must stand as regular if the next hand plays before attention is called to the irregularity.

STRATEGY OF MICHIGAN

Having a boodle card or average high-card strength, keep your hand—don't speculate on the widow. The only time to exchange or bid is when you hold an extraordinary hand of low cards. Even then, there is little percentage in paying more than about five chips for the widow. As dealer, however, you may gain an advantage by discarding an indifferent hand, for then you will know in advance all the natural stops.

In the play, keep track of the first plays in each suit. Each is a stop card; e.g., if the ♡ 7 is a first play, a later lead of lower hearts will surely be stopped at the ♡ 6. When you gain the lead, first play those cards that are stopped or begin new sequences you can stop, so that you may hold or quickly regain the lead.

SEVEN UP

THERE IS *a large family of games in which the object is to win "high, low, jack and game." Almost surely this principle originated in England in the ancient game* ALL FOURS. *Brought to America in Colonial times, this game developed into* SEVEN UP, *also called* OLD SLEDGE *or* HIGH-LOW-JACK. *Many other forms of All Fours grew popular in the United States. One of them—*PITCH, *described on a later page—still flourishes.*

PLAYERS. Two to four. Four may play in two partnerships.

CARDS. A regular pack of 52. In each suit the cards rank: A (high), K, Q, J, 10, 9, 8, 7, 6, 5, 4, 3, 2.

THE DEAL. Each player receives six cards, dealt three at a time. Dealer turns the next card of the pack face up; this turn-up proposes the trump suit. If it is a jack, dealer scores 1 point.

THE TRUMP. The opponent at left of the dealer, after looking at his hand, must say "I stand" or "I beg." To stand is to accept the suit of the turn-up as trump, whereupon play begins. To beg is to pass the decision to the dealer. The latter may then say "Take it" or "Refuse." The first declaration means that dealer accepts the turn-up, whereupon left opponent scores 1 point for *gift*. The second (called *refusal of gift*) rejects the turn-up. Thereupon the turn-up is discarded, and dealer *runs the cards*, i.e., deals a batch of three more cards to each hand, and makes a new turn-up. If this new turn-up is of the same suit, it must be discarded and the cards must be run again, and so on until a new suit is turned. This suit becomes trumps. (If a jack is turned for the new suit, dealer scores 1. If the pack is exhausted before a new suit is turned for trump, all the cards are gathered, shuffled, and redealt by the same dealer.)

THE PLAY. Once the trump is decided, each player reduces his hand (if necessary) to six cards, by discarding the excess face down.

Opponent at left of the dealer makes the opening lead. The hands are played out in tricks. A hand if able to follow suit to a lead must either do so or (on a nontrump lead) play a trump; that is, he may trump even if able to follow suit. A trick is won by the highest trump in it, or, if it contains no trump, by the highest card played of the suit led. The winner of a trick leads to the next.

SCORING. The object of play is to win points in tricks. There are at most 4 points:

High, the highest trump in play.

Low, the lowest trump in play. This is scored by the player to whom it was dealt, regardless of who wins it in play.

Jack, the jack of trumps, scored by the player winning it in a trick.

Game, a plurality of points for high cards taken in tricks, counting.

Each ten	10
Each ace	4
Each king	3
Each queen	2
Each jack	1

If there is only one trump in play, it scores 2 as both high and low (or 3 if it is the jack). The 1 for game is not scored if there is a tie for the highest count.

GAME. The player or side first to reach a total of 7 points wins a game. If more than one might reach 7 as a result of the same deal, the points are counted in order: high, low, jack, game; and the first to reach 7 wins. Dealer is bound to refuse gift when left-hand opponent, having 6, begs.

IRREGULARITIES IN SEVEN UP

NEW DEAL. There must be a new deal by the same dealer if a card is exposed in the original deal, or if the pack was not shuffled or was not offered for cut.

EXPOSED CARD. If a player's card is exposed through no fault of his own (as when the pack is run), he may have it replaced from the top of the pack after all others have received their cards.

In partnership play only, a card exposed except in legal play must be left face up on the table and must be played on demand of either opponent (provided that its play is legal).

REVOKE. Failure to follow suit (or trump) when able is a revoke. A player may correct his revoke before the lead to the next trick, and cards played to the trick after his revoke may be withdrawn. If not corrected in time, a revoke stands; from the offender's score is deducted 2 (if the jack is in play) or 1 (if it is not). In two-hand Seven Up, the opponent of the offender may instead add the penalty points to his own score.

AUCTION PITCH, or SETBACK

Seven Up grew into Pitch, in which the maker of the trump had the first lead and had to "pitch" (lead) a trump; and this game became Auction Pitch when bidding was added. Now the earlier game has vanished and Auction Pitch is called simply Pitch.

PLAYERS. Two to seven; best for four. There are no partnerships.

CARDS. A regular pack of 52. In each suit the cards rank: A (high), K, Q, J, 10, 9, 8, 7, 6, 5, 4, 3, 2.

THE DEAL. Each player receives six cards, dealt three at a time.

THE BIDDING. Each player in turn to left of the dealer has one chance to bid or pass. The only possible bids are one, two, three, and four. No suit is mentioned. A player may indicate that he bids four by pitching (making an opening lead).

THE PLAY. The high bidder (pitcher) makes the first lead, and its suit becomes trump for that deal. (If he names one suit but leads another, the lead governs.) A hand able to follow suit to a lead must either do so or (to a nontrump lead) trump; that is, he may trump even when able to follow suit. A trick is won by the highest trump in it, or, if it contains no trump, by the highest card played of the suit led. The winner of a trick leads to the next.

SCORING. The object of play is to win points in tricks. There are four points at stake:

High, the highest trump in play.

Low, the lowest trump in play.

Jack, the jack of trumps.

Game, a plurality of points for high cards, counting:

Each ten	10
Each ace	4
Each king	3
Each queen	2
Each jack	1

If two or more players tie for the game point, it is not scored. Low and jack are scored by the players winning them in tricks. The jack does not score if it was not dealt. If there is only one trump in play, it scores 2 as both high and low, and 3 if it is the jack.

If the pitcher (high bidder) wins at least as many points as he bid, he scores all he makes; if he wins less, he is "set back"—the bid is deducted from his score. It is thus possible for a player to have a minus score, when he is said to be "in the hole" (from the custom of drawing a circle around his score). Each opponent of the pitcher scores what he himself wins.

Score may be kept on paper or with poker chips. The player first to reach a total of 7 points wins a game. The pitcher scores first, and other players score their points in this order: high, low, jack, game.

SMUDGE, played in many games: See page 46.

IRREGULARITIES IN AUCTION PITCH

MISDEAL. If the dealer exposes a card or misdeals in any way, he loses the deal; there must be a new deal by the next dealer.

EXPOSED CARD. A card exposed during the bidding is not penalized. A card exposed during the play must be put face up on the table and played at the first legal opportunity.

PITCH OUT OF TURN. If a player pitches out of turn, the correct pitcher may let it stand and immediately name the trump suit, and must lead a trump at his first opportunity; or he may require the incorrect pitch to be retracted and may require the offender, at his first turn to play, to trump or not to trump or to follow suit with his highest or lowest card.

REVOKE. A player revokes if he fails to follow suit (or trump) when able. A revoke may not be corrected; play continues, and the offender is set back by the amount of the bid, while each other player scores what he wins.

STRATEGY OF AUCTION PITCH

The dealer, bidding last, has a great advantage and should press it by taking risks to win the bid. The first two hands to the left of the dealer should be conservative.

A holding of three trumps is worth a bid of one, for it will usually capture the game point, if nothing else. The jack once guarded is worth a bid of one, and the two spot even once guarded has a good chance of being saved. It is reasonable to bid in the hope that a king in hand will prove to be high, or a threespot low. Side aces and tens strengthen the hand but cannot be relied upon to capture the game point.

Smudge, or Pitch

The rules given for Auction Pitch in the preceding pages are followed, with certain differences:

Provided a player is not "in the hole" (that is, provided he does not have a minus score at the time) he can make game in one hand by bidding four and making his bid. The bid of four is called _smudge_. If he was in the hole, a bid of four, if made, counts only the same four points for him.

Low is scored by the player who wins it, no matter to whom it was dealt.

CALIFORNIA JACK

CALIFORNIA JACK is All Fours adapted for two-hand play. The full pack of 52 cards is used. The ranking is normal, with ace high. The dealer gives six cards to each player, one at a time. The thirteenth card is turned up to fix the trump suit for the deal, then buried in the middle of the stock. The stock is placed face up in the middle of the table.

The non-dealer makes the first lead. The second player must follow suit to the lead when able; if unable, he may play any card. A trick containing a trump is won by the higher trump; any other trick, by the higher card of the suit led. The winner of a trick leads to the next.

Prior to leading, the winner of the previous trick takes the top card of the stock, and his opponent takes the next card. The hands are thus kept filled to six cards, until the stock is exhausted, when the hards are played out without drawing. Since the top card of the stock is exposed, the card that will go to the winner of a trick is always known. The play is a continual battle to capture the valuable cards that show, while losing the trick when a worthless card appears. There is also a battle to capture tenspots. Each player scores what he takes in tricks, of the 4 points at issue:

High, the ace of trumps.

Low, the two of trumps.

Jack, the jack of trumps.

Game, majority of the high-card points.

For determination of *game,* each ace counts 4, king 3, queen 2, jack 1, ten 10.

The player who first reaches 7 points wins a game. The points are scored in the given order, so that, for example, at score of 6-6 the player who gets *high* wins the game, even though his opponent should capture the other three points.

A player may at any time claim that he has reached 7 points. Play stops at once, and the game is won or lost at once, according as the claim is proved to be true or false.

CINCH

CINCH, a partnership game for four players, is the aristocrat of the high-low-jack games, for it gives the greatest opportunity for skillful play. Indeed, Cinch was rapidly becoming the most popular partnership game in this country, when Bridge muscled in and took over.

Partners sit opposite each other across the table. The regular pack is used, ranking normally with ace high. The dealer gives nine cards to each hand, three at a time.

The game commences with one round of bidding for the right to name the trump. Eldest hand has first say. Each player in turn may pass or bid. Each bid must of course be higher than any preceding bid. The bids are made by number alone, without mention of what suit the bidder intends to name. The bids may range from "One" to "Fourteen," as there are 14 points to be won in play. *The object of the game is to win these 14 points.*

The 14 points are cards of the trump suit, as follows:

High. The highest trump in play. Barring accidents, this is sure to be the ace. Counts 1.

Low. The lowest trump in play. Almost sure to be the deuce. Counts 1.

Jack. The jack of trumps. Counts 1.

Game. The ten of trumps. Counts 1.

Right pedro. The five of trumps. Counts 5.

Left pedro. The other fivespot of same color as right pedro. For example, the ♣ 5 when spades are trumps. Left pedro is a trump, ranking between right pedro and the four of trumps. Counts 5.

The highest bidder names the trump suit. Every player then discards all cards but trumps from his hand. As the hands must be reduced to six cards, a player who happens to be dealt more than six trumps has to discard some. He must show these discards to the other players, for all players are entitled to know what trumps if any are not in play.

The dealer serves cards to each hand in turn, beginning with eldest, so as to fill each to six cards. When it comes to his own draw, dealer *robs the pack*. Instead of taking his draw blind from the top of the stock, he searches all the rest of the cards and takes out all the trumps, together with enough plain cards to fill his hand. The object in allowing the dealer to rob is to be sure that all trumps get into play— or at least, that if any are left out, they shall be disclosed. For if dealer finds more than six trumps in his hand and the stock together, he must show the trumps that he is compelled to discard.

The opening lead is made by the player who named trump. He may lead any card (he does not have to pitch a trump). When able to follow suit to a lead, another hand may either do so or trump. A trump lead always calls for trumps, but without restriction as to playing high or low. If unable to follow suit to the lead, a hand may play any card. The highest card of the suit led wins the trick, except that trumps always win over other suits. The winner of a trick leads to the next.

The object in play is to capture the six counting cards, which score as they fall in tricks, not as they are dealt. Partners cooperate in the play, and score as a unit.

If the bidder's side wins at least as much as they bid, the difference of what is won by the two sides goes to the higher. For example, if West bids 9 and just makes it, East-West score 9 — 5 = 4. Opponents of the bidder may score even though he makes his contract. For example, if West bids 6 and just makes it, North-South score 8 — 6 = 2.

If the bidder's side fails to make its contract, the opponents score what they take, plus the amount of the bid (or, what is the same thing, 14 plus the amount by which the bidder falls short of contract).

The side that first accumulates 51 points wins a game, and settlement is made on the difference of the final totals.

PENALTIES

There is a misdeal, which loses the deal, if an incorrect hand is dealt. The opponents may demand a new deal if a card is faced in dealing. But the deal stands after the first bid is made, and an incorrect hand is corrected in the draw.

A bid out of turn is void and bars the offender's side from bidding thereafter.

A lead or play out of turn stands unless an opponent demands correction before he or his partner plays. When correction is demanded, the card illegally led may be called by either opponent; or, if the offender led in his partner's turn, the partner may be required to lead or not to lead a trump. If a player revokes, his side may not score, but play continues. The bidding side cannot be set when opponent revokes.

STRATEGY

The play is not to win the most tricks, but to win specific cards; above all, the pedros. Therefore it is not the number but the quality of tricks won that determines the result.

The bidding is based primarily on the prospect of saving pedros held or catching pedros not held.

The average number of trumps dealt originally is nine to ten (there are fourteen trumps). An average share per player is between two and three. A bid is scarcely feasible on less than three trumps, preferably four. To bid "Five," which for practical purposes is the minimum bid (some players do not even allow lower bids), requires either a pedro that can probably be saved, or top strength to catch a pedro. The normal minimums are respectively K-5-3, A-Q-3.

Many players, however, bid five when holding any pedro, with as few as two trumps. Tactically such a bid has the effect of shutting out an adverse minimum bid. Occasionally it operates to let partner infer the intended trump suit, and so bid higher when he happens to have strong support.

Bids of six and seven usually require a pedro, plus one or two of the other counting cards: a holding say as good as A-Q-5 or J-9-8-5. Any higher bid requires a practically "ironclad" hand, especially as to top trumps. Thus A-K-J-9-8 is fairly sure to win 8 points, but J-9-8-7-5 has to find the right tops in partner's hand to score more than 6.

In the play, the chief point to remember is not to let the fourth hand to a trick win with a pedro, if he may have one. If no higher trump has been played, third hand must usually *cinch* a trick by playing some trump higher than the five. Most hands are properly played by cross-ruffing, the third hand cinching so long as he can.

NAPOLEON

In one *of the most ancient and universal families of card games, originally called the "Triumph" family, each player holds five cards and the primary object is to win three out of five tricks. Such games include* Écarté *(France),* Spoil Five *(Ireland),* Euchre *(United States), and* "Nap" *or* Napoleon, *the English version, described below.*

Players. From two to six.

Cards. A regular pack of 52. In each suit the cards rank: A (high), K, Q, J, 10, 9, 8, 7, 6, 5, 4, 3, 2.

The Deal. Each player receives five cards, dealt in batches of 3-2 or 2-3. (Dealer must adhere to whichever plan he commences.)

The Bidding. Each player in turn to left of the dealer has one chance to bid or pass. A bid is a number of tricks, from one to five; no suit is mentioned. Each bid must be higher than any previous bid.

The Play. The high bidder makes the opening lead, and the suit of his lead becomes trump. (In other words, the high bidder names his intended trump suit by leading it.) The hands are played out in tricks with rotation to the left (clockwise). A player must follow suit to the lead if able; if unable to follow suit he may play any card. A trick is won by the highest trump in it, or, if it contains no trump, by the highest card played of the suit led. The winner of a trick leads to the next.

SCORING. Settlement is made after each deal in chips or other tokens. If the bidder fails to make his bid, he pays each other player; if he succeeds, he collects from all. Nothing is gained by winning extra tricks beyond what is necessary to make or defeat the bid.

The rate of settlement is usually one unit for each trick bid. But if *nap* (all five tricks) is bid, the bidder collects 10 if he wins but pays only 5 if he loses.

ADDED BIDS. Features often added are the bids of Wellington and Blucher. Like nap, these are bids to win all five tricks and collect 10 if they succeed. But Wellington pays 10 if it loses, and so overcalls nap, while Blucher pays 20, and so overcalls Wellington.

IRREGULARITIES IN NAPOLEON

MISDEAL. If the deal is irregular in any way, the same dealer redeals.

WRONG NUMBER OF CARDS. A player dealt the wrong number of cards may demand correction before declaring; otherwise he must play on with the incorrect hand. If he is the high bidder (all other hands being correct) he cannot collect if he wins but must pay if he loses. If the bidder's hand is correct and an opponent's incorrect, the bidder does not pay if he loses but collects if he wins.

PLAY OUT OF TURN. There is no penalty against the bidder for a lead or play out of turn, but the error must be corrected if noticed before the trick is gathered. If an opponent leads or plays out of turn, he must pay 3 units to the bidder and he collects nothing if the bid is defeated.

REVOKE. Failure to follow suit when able is a revoke. If a revoke is detected and claimed before settlement for the deal has been made, the cards are thrown in. A revoking bidder then pays as though he had lost. A revoking opponent pays the bidder the full amount he would have won for making the bid, the others paying nothing.

Nap Variants

MISERY is a bid to win no tricks. It overcalls a bid of 3 and may be overcalled by a bid of 4. It is settled at the value of 3. When "misery" prevails, there is no trump suit.

PURCHASE NAP. Before the bidding begins, each player discards as many cards as he wishes from his original hand, and the dealer then serves each in turn with replacements from the stock. For each card "purchased," the player pays the value of one trick into a pool. The usual practice is to let the pool accumulate from deal to deal and award it to the first player to bid and make nap.

SEVEN-CARD NAP. In this recent innovation, each player receives seven cards. Bids up to 4 are settled at single stake, a bid of 5 (still called nap) at double stakes, a bid of 6 at triple, and a bid of 7 at quadruple. The bid of misery ranks just below nap and is likewise settled at double stakes.

Loo

Loo is almost as fast a gambling game as cutting the pack for highest card. It dominated English gaming tables in the 18th and 19th centuries, and though now overshadowed by Poker, Bridge, etc., is still played. Many variants of Loo developed; the principal survivor is described here.

FIVE TO SEVEN players make the best game, though it can be played by more or less. A regular pack is used, ranking as usual with ace high. Each player receives three cards, dealt one at a time. The next card of the stock is exposed; it fixes the trump suit for that deal.

The dealer antes three chips into a pool. When that is the entire content of the pool, the game is a *single;* when the pool contains additional chips, the game is a *double.*

SINGLE POOL. Eldest hand makes the opening lead. He and all subsequent leaders must if possible lead a trump—the highest, if he has more than one. After a lead, each other hand must follow suit if able, must *head* the trick if able by playing a card better than any previously played. Hence it is compulsory to trump, if able, a plain-suit lead when one is void. A trick is won by the highest trump, or, if it contains no trump, by the highest card of the suit led. The winner of a trick leads to the next.

At the end of the play, the pool is distributed: one chip for each trick won. Each player who won no trick at all is *looed* and must pay a forfeit into the next pool (usually three chips), thereby making it a *double*.

DOUBLE POOL. An extra hand of three cards, called the *miss*, is dealt face down at the dealer's left. Beginning with eldest hand, each player in turn must declare whether he will play or *pass;* to pass is to drop out of that deal. Any player who stays may take the miss in exchange for his hand, if none has already taken it. The dealer has the duty of requiring every player to declare himself, and must not look at his own hand until his turn comes to declare.

The active player nearest the left of the dealer makes the opening lead, and the rules of play are as in single pool. After the play, one-third of the pool is paid out for each trick won, and then each player who was looed pays a forfeit into the next pool. (The game can revert to a single only when three or fewer players stay and none is looed.)

If one player takes the miss and all the rest pass, he takes the entire pool. If all pass ahead of the dealer, he takes the pool. The dealer may not pass if only one other player stays, without taking the miss. In this event, dealer may either stay and play for himself, or take the miss and *defend the pool*. When he defends, he collects and pays nothing, only the opponent settling with the pool.

Loo Variants

The foregoing game is "three-card limited Loo," limited because the forfeit for loo is a fixed amount. In "unlimited" Loo the forfeit is equal to the entire previous pool.

FIVE-CARD LOO differs from three-card only in that each player receives five cards, payments to the pool are in multiples of five, and one-fifth of the pool is paid out for each trick won. This game gave rise to Napoleon.

PAM-LOO makes *pam*, the jack of clubs, always the highest trump whatever the trump suit. Pam also may be used as a wild card to complete a *flush* (five cards of one suit) or a *blaze* (five face cards). Such a hand wins the entire pool.

AUCTION FORTY-FIVES

This game developed from the Irish game Spoil Five and its variant FORTY-FIVE, so called because 45 points win the game. Although in Auction Forty-Fives the number 45 ceased to have any special scoring significance, the name persisted. This game is popular in Canada and especially in Nova Scotia.

PLAYERS. Four or six, in two partnerships with partners sitting alternately.

CARDS. A regular pack of 52. The highest trump is the fivespot; second is the jack; third is the ♡ A, whatever the trump suit. In the black suits, the cards from two to ten rank in reverse of the normal order; the traditional saying is "highest in red; lowest in black."

The full rank in the trump suit is:

Hearts: ♡ 5 (high), J, A, K, Q, 10, 9, 8, 7, 6, 4, 3, 2.

Diamonds: ♢ 5 (high), ♢ J, ♡ A, ♢ A, K, Q, 10, 9, 8, 7, 6, 4, 3, 2.

Clubs or Spades: ♣ 5 or ♠ 5 (high), ♣ J or ♠ J, ♡ A, ♣ A or ♠ A, K, Q, 2, 3, 4, 6, 7, 8, 9, 10.

In nontrump suits the rank is:

Hearts or Diamonds: K (high), Q, J, 10, 9, 8, 7, 6, 5, 4, 3, 2, (♢ A).

Clubs or Spades: K (high), Q, J, A, 2, 3, 4, 5, 6, 7, 8, 9, 10.

THE DEAL. Each player receives five cards, dealt in batches of 3-2 or 2-3. (Dealer must adhere to whichever plan he commences.)

THE BIDDING. Beginning at the left of the dealer, each player in turn to the left may bid or pass. Bids are made in multiples of 5, up to 30, no suit being mentioned. Each bid must be higher than the preceding bid, except that the dealer may in his turn say "I hold," meaning that he bids the same as the last preceding bid; he has the vested right to name the trump if no one bids *higher* than he. After dealer holds, each player in turn who has not previously passed may bid again, and so on until all players but one have passed. The winning bidder then names the trump suit.

DRAWING. Each player discards face down from his hand as many cards as he pleases. The dealer then serves each, in turn to the left, with enough cards to restore his hand to five. (Local custom sometimes permits the dealer to "rob the pack," that is look through the remainder and pick out what replacements he pleases for his own discards.)

THE PLAY. The opponent at the left of the winning bidder makes the opening lead. The hands are played out in tricks. If unable to follow suit to a lead, a hand may play any card. A trick is won by the highest trump in it, or, if it contains no trump, by the highest card played of the suit led.

A hand must follow suit to a lead, if able, with these exceptions:

(a) Even though able to follow to a nontrump lead, a player may trump if he pleases.

(b) The three highest trumps (5, J, ♡ A) have the privilege of *reneging* when a lower trump is led. For example, if the trump seven is led, a player holding any of these three top trumps without lower trumps may discard instead of following suit (having lower trumps also, he must play a trump). But there is no reneging against a higher trump. For example, if the trump jack is led, the holder of the five may renege but not the holder of the ♡ A.

SCORING. Each trick counts 5, and the highest trump in play counts 5. After the play, each side counts what it has taken. If the bidder's side has taken at least the amount of the bid, it scores all that it has won. If this side fails, the amount of the bid is deducted from its score. The other side in either case scores what it has won in tricks. But a side that bids and makes 30 (all the points) scores 60 instead of 30.

GAME. The side that first reaches a total of 120 points wins a game. A side having 100 or more points is not allowed to bid less than 20.

IRREGULARITIES IN AUCTION FORTY-FIVES

NEW DEAL. There must be a new deal by the same dealer: (a) if he deals any hand a wrong number of cards and attention is drawn to this before there has been a bid; (b) if he fails to adhere to his chosen plan of dealing; or (c) if a card is exposed during the deal.

WRONG NUMBER OF CARDS. If, after the first bid but before the opening lead, any hand is found to be incorrect, it must be rectified. A short hand must draw additional cards from the stock; a long hand has the excess drawn out and discarded face down by its right-hand opponent.

If any hand is found incorrect after the opening lead, it must be discarded and play continues without this hand. The side of the player with the incorrect hand may not score for the deal, and if it made the trump its bid is scored as lost.

EXPOSED CARD. If, after the opening lead, a player illegally exposes any of the three highest trumps, he must discard his hand, and the paragraph above applies. If a lower card is exposed, it must be left face up on the table and must be played at the first legal opportunity.

Forty-Five

Two, four or six may play. Four or six play in two partnerships, with each player seated between two opponents.

The rank of cards and the deal of five cards to each player are the same as in Auction Forty-Fives (page 55). The next card of the pack is turned for trump. If it is an ace, dealer may take it in exchange for any card he chooses to discard from his hand. If any player holds the ace of trumps, he may if he wishes exchange it for the turn-up.

The player at left of the dealer leads first. If able to follow suit to a lead, each other hand must either do so or trump; if unable to follow suit, a player may discard or trump as he pleases. A trick is won by the highest trump, or by the highest card of the suit led if it contains no trump. The winner of a trick leads to the next.

The three highest trumps, the 5, J, and ♡ A, have the privilege of *reneging:* None of these cards need be played, even on a trump lead, except when a higher trump is led. Thus the five can never be forced, the jack can be forced only when the five is led and the jack is alone in a player's hand, etc.

The side that wins three of four tricks scores 5 points; a side taking all five tricks scores 10. The side that first reaches 45 points wins a game.

| One | Two | Three | Four |

EUCHRE SCORING WITH SMALL CARDS

EUCHRE

EUCHRE *originated among the Pennsylvania Dutch prior to 1864. The term* bower *is the German* Bauer *(farmer), one of the names for the jack. The game is now played chiefly in the northeastern states. It gave rise to Five Hundred.*

PLAYERS. From three to seven. The four-hand partnership game is first described below. Partners face each other across the table.

CARDS. A pack of 32 cards: from a regular pack of 52 discard all twos to sixes inclusive.

The highest trump is the jack, called *right bower*. The second-highest is the other jack of same color, called *left bower*. For example, if spades are trumps, the ♠ J is right bower and the ♣ J is left bower. The rest of the trump suit ranks: A (third-best), K, Q, 10, 9, 8, 7. In each nontrump suit the rank is: A (high), K, Q, J (if not left bower), 10, 9, 8, 7.

THE DEAL. Each player receives five cards, dealt in batches of 3-2 or 2-3. (The dealer must adhere to whichever plan he commences.) The last card of the pack (belonging to the dealer) is turned face up on the table; this is the *turn-up*.

MAKING. The turn-up proposes the trump suit for that

deal, but it becomes trump only if some player accepts it. Beginning with the player at the left of the dealer, each player in turn may pass or may accept the suit of the turn-up (if it has not been accepted before him). An opponent of the dealer accepts by saying "I order it up." The dealer's partner says "I assist." Dealer says "I take it up."

If all four players pass (dealer passes by saying "I turn it down"), the turn-up is turned face down. Then each in turn to left of the dealer has a second chance to pass or to name a trump suit (if none has been named ahead of him). The named trump suit must be different from the turn-up.

Whoever decides the trump suit, by accepting the turn-up or naming a trump in the second round, becomes the *maker*. The maker has the right to say "I play alone," whereupon his partner must discard his hand and stay out of the play. Either opponent of a lone maker may say "I defend alone," whereupon *his* partner must stay out.

THE PLAY. If the turn-up is accepted, dealer has the right to use it as part of his hand, discarding any other card face down. (The turn-up is customarily left on the table until played.)

Against a lone maker, the opening lead is made by the opponent at his left. Otherwise, the opening lead is made by the player at left of the dealer, regardless of who is the maker.

The hands are played out in five tricks. A player must follow suit to a lead if able; if unable to follow suit, he may play any card. A trick is won by the highest trump in it, or, if it contains no trump, by the highest card played of the suit led. The winner of a trick leads to the next.

SCORING. Only the side that wins three or more tricks scores. Winning all five tricks is called *march*. When the making side fails to win the majority it is said to be *euchred*.

The making side, when both are playing, score 1 point for winning three or four tricks, or 2 for march. A maker playing alone scores 1 for three or four tricks, or 4 for march.

Opponents of the maker, when both are playing, score 2 for euchre. When there is a lone defender the score is 2 for winning three or four tricks, or 4 for march.

GAME. The side first to reach a total of 5 points wins a game. (By agreement this is sometimes fixed at 7 or 10 points.)

IRREGULARITIES IN EUCHRE

NEW DEAL. There must be a new deal by the same dealer if a card is exposed or found faced in the pack during the deal, or if the pack is found to be incorrect.

FALSE DECLARATION. If a player uses the wrong term in accepting the turn-up (as "I order it up" by dealer's partner), there is no penalty; he is deemed to have accepted the turn-up. If in a second round of declaring a player names the suit of the rejected turn-up, his call is void and his side may not make the trump.

DECLARATION OUT OF TURN. If a player declares out of turn, except in saying "Pass," his call is void and his side may not make the trump.

WRONG NUMBER OF CARDS. If, before the first trick is quitted, any hand is found to have the wrong number of cards, there must be a new deal by the same dealer; if the error is discovered at a later time, play continues and the offending side may not score for that deal.

LEAD OUT OF TURN. If a player leads out of turn and the trick is gathered before the error is noticed, it stands as regular. Otherwise, the erroneous lead becomes an exposed card (see below) and any other cards played to the trick may be retracted without penalty. At the next proper turn of the offending side to lead, the opponent at the right of the leader may name the suit to be led. This penalty does not apply to a lone player, but he may be required to retract a lead out of turn.

EXPOSED CARD. If a player (not playing alone) exposes a card from his hand except in proper play, he must leave it face up on the table and must play it at the first legal opportunity.

ILLEGAL INFORMATION. If a player looks at a quitted trick or gives illegal information to his partner, the opponent at the right of the leader may name the suit to be led at the next opportunity of the offending side to lead.

REVOKE. Failure to follow suit when able to do so is a revoke. A player may correct his revoke before the trick is gathered; otherwise it stands as established. For established revoke, the opponents of the offender may score 2 points or may deduct 2 from the revoking side (both playing) or 4 from a lone player.

STRATEGY OF EUCHRE

Two fairly probable tricks in the hand usually justify "taking action." It is correct to expect partner to furnish one trick. Any three trumps are a "take," and A-x or K-x is a fair try. At 0-0 score, however, neither opponent of dealer should accept the turn-up without three very probable tricks, for his side will have first chance to make if the turn-up is rejected. For the same reason, dealer should take it up if he can, even at some risk.

Advanced scores often compel special tactics. With the score 4-2 or 4-1, the side "at the bridge" (having 4 points) will often accept the turn-up regardless of the cards. The idea is to be the maker; opponents can then score at most 2 points for euchre. But if an opponent becomes the maker, he might play alone, make march, and thus win the game.

If the opening leader has two or more trumps, he should usually lead one. Otherwise, he should usually open a plain suit in which he has no high card, rather than one in which he has. In following to a lead, try to win the trick (or let your partner win) at all costs. Holding up a high card for a possible later trick in a suit once led is a losing policy.

Three-Hand Euchre

This game is commonly called Cutthroat. Each plays for himself. The trump maker plays alone against the other two, who temporarily become partners. The maker scores 1 point for winning three or four tricks, or 3 for march. If he is euchred, each opponent scores 2. The rules on irregularities are applied with due allowance for the difference between the maker, as a lone hand, and the opponents, as a partnership.

Railroad Euchre

Various special rules are adopted by groups of players, especially commuters, to speed up the game. All such variants go under the name of Railroad Euchre. Some of the special rules are as follows.

JOKER. The joker is added to the pack, ranking as the

highest trump. If the turn-up is the joker, it proposes hearts for trumps.

CALLING FOR BEST. A lone player is entitled to discard one card face down and call for his partner's best card as a replacement. The partner must make his own choice of his best card, without consultation. When a player "assists" and plays alone, dealer is entitled to give him the turn-up.

LAPS. If a player (or side) reaches a total of more than 5 points, he may carry forward the excess toward the next game.

SLAMS. A game counts double if the losing side has scored no point.

Call-Ace Euchre

This is a "cutthroat" form of Euchre (each plays for himself). Four, five or six may play.

Trump is made by ordering up, taking up, or naming a new suit, as explained on pages 58-59. The maker then calls any suit (which may or may not be trumps) and the holder of the best card dealt in that suit becomes his partner. At the start of the play, the maker does not know who his partner is; nor can another player often be sure he is the maker's partner, unless he holds the ace of the suit called. Even if he does hold this ace, he must say nothing to reveal the fact that he is the maker's partner. The identity of the maker's partner is not revealed until the fall of the cards in play makes it apparent.

The maker may instead call *alone*. He may unexpectedly turn out to be a lone player if he himself holds the highest card of the suit he called.

When the maker proves to have a partner, scoring is as in regular Euchre. When the maker plays alone, he wins from or loses to each of the other players. The only difference from four-hand scoring is that when there are five or six players a march made by a partnership counts 3. Each member of each side receives the full amount for making or for euchre.

FIVE HUNDRED

FIVE HUNDRED *is one of the few "invented" games that have achieved a popularity comparable with that of the "developed" games. It sprang into being full-blown in 1904, when the United States Playing Card Company published its first set of rules, which have remained unchanged with a few additions. The idea was to provide Euchre enthusiasts with a game having greater opportunity for skill, by dealing out the full pack. Five Hundred became popular immediately, and for twenty years it shared with Auction Bridge the lead among trick-winning games.*

PLAYERS. From two to five. The game for three is first described.

CARDS. For three players, a pack of 33: from a regular pack of 52 discard all twos to sixes inclusive, and add the joker. For two, four, or five players, see the rules on the following pages; for six players, a special 62-card pack is available.

The joker is always the highest trump. At a suit bid, the jack of that suit, called *right bower*, is the second-best trump. Third-best is the jack of the other suit of same color as the trump; this jack is *left bower*. Thus, if hearts are trumps, the three highest trumps are: joker, ♡ J, ◇ J. The

63

rest of the trump suit ranks: A (fourth-best), K, Q, 10, 9, 8, 7.

In each nontrump suit the rank is: A (high), K, Q, J (if it is not left bower), 10, 9, 8, 7.

THE DEAL. Each player receives ten cards, dealt in batches of 3-4-3. After the first round of the deal, three cards are dealt face down in the center of the table, forming the *widow*.

THE BIDDING. The player at the left of the dealer declares first. Each in turn has one chance to declare, either passing or making a bid higher than any preceding bid. Each bid must name a denomination and a number of tricks, e.g., "six spades," "seven no-trump." A bid is sufficient to overcall a preceding bid if it has a higher scoring value, according to the table below:

| | NUMBER OF TRICKS | | | | |
DENOMINATION	6	7	8	9	10
Spades	40	140	240	340	440
Clubs	60	160	260	360	460
Diamonds	80	180	280	380	480
Hearts	100	200	300	400	500
No-trump	120	220	320	420	520

If all players pass, the deal is abandoned without score and the next dealer deals. Otherwise the highest bid becomes the contract and the two other players combine in temporary partnership against the contractor.

THE PLAY. The contractor takes the widow into his hand, then discards any three cards face down. Next he makes the opening lead.

The hands are played out in tricks. A player must follow suit to the lead, if able; if unable to follow suit he may play any card. A trick is won by the highest trump in it, or, if it contains no trump, by the highest card played of the suit led. The winner of a trick leads to the next.

At no-trump, the joker is in effect the sole trump. It wins any trick to which it is played, but it may not be played to a trick by a nonleader unless he is void of the suit led. When the joker is led, its owner specifies a suit that all other hands must play to the trick, if able.

Each opponent of the contractor gathers separately the tricks that he himself wins. But the two opponents should co-operate in trying to defeat the contract.

SCORING. The score is kept on paper, with a separate column for each player.

If the contractor wins at least the number of tricks he bid, he scores the value of his bid according to the table above; but if he wins all the tricks, he scores either his bid or 250, whichever is greater. If the contractor is *set* (fails to make contract), the value of his bid is deducted from his score. (Hence a player can have a minus score; he is then said to be "in the hole," since the usual way of marking a minus score is to draw a circle around it.)

Whether the contract is made or defeated, each opponent scores 10 for each trick he himself has won.

GAME. The player first to reach a total score of plus 500 wins a game. If two or more reach 500 in the same deal, the contractor wins against an opponent; as between opponents, the first to reach 500 in the course of play wins, and the deal is nòt played out unless the contractor also could reach 500 in that deal.

NULLO. By agreement the players may adopt an additional bidding denomination: nullo. This is an offer to lose every trick at no-trump. The value of this bid is 250; it is thus higher than "eight spades" and lower than "eight clubs." If the nullo contractor fails, he is set back 250, and each opponent scores 10 for each trick taken by the contractor.

IRREGULARITIES IN FIVE HUNDRED

NEW DEAL. There must be a new deal by the same dealer if a card is found exposed in the pack; or if the dealer gives the wrong number of cards to any hand; or if, before the last card is dealt, a player demands a new deal because the cut was omitted or because the dealer departed in any way from the prescribed method of dealing.

BID OUT OF TURN. There is no penalty (in three-hand play) for a pass or bid out of turn; the declaration is void, and the offender may make any legal declaration in his turn.

WRONG NUMBER OF CARDS. If, during the bidding, two hands (excluding the widow) are found to have the wrong number of cards, there must be a new deal by the same dealer. If the widow and one hand are found to be incorrect, they must be rectified; another player draws out the excess cards and gives them to the short hand; and a player whose hand was incorrect is barred from bidding.

If, during the play, the contractor and an opponent are found to have the wrong number of cards, or if there is an incorrect hand due to an incorrect pack, there must be a new deal by the same dealer. If two opponents are found to have incorrect hands, the contractor's being correct, the bid is deemed to have been made and the opponents may not score. The contractor may continue play in an effort to win all the tricks, and he is deemed to win all final tricks to which the short hand cannot play.

If the contractor's hand and discard are found incorrect, the opponents' hands being correct, the bid is lost, but the deal is played out to determine how many tricks are to be credited to each opponent.

EXPOSED CARD. There is no penalty against a player for exposing any card to an opponent. But if he exposes a card to his partner, such card must be placed face up on the table and must be played at the first legal opportunity. (Dropping a card face up on the table, or naming a card as being in one's hand, is deemed "exposure to partner"— when one has a partner.)

LEAD OR PLAY OUT OF TURN. A lead out of turn must be retracted on demand of the other side. An opponent's card led out of turn is treated as exposed (see above); in addition, the contractor may require the offender's partner to lead a named suit, or not to lead the suit of the exposed card.

If an opponent plays out of turn, not in leading, his card is treated as exposed (see above).

If an error in leading or playing is not noticed until the trick is gathered, it stands as regular.

REVOKE. Failure to follow suit to a lead when able is a revoke. A revoke may be corrected at any time before the next lead; otherwise it stands as established. When a revoke is corrected, the incorrect card is deemed exposed, even if it belongs to the contractor. An established revoke may be claimed at any time before the cut for the next deal; if it is proved, and the offender was an opponent, the bid is scored as made and neither opponent may score; if the offender was the contractor, his bid is defeated.

ILLEGAL INFORMATION. If an opponent gives illegal information to his partner, or looks at a trick after it is gathered and quitted (except to settle a claim of an irregularity), or if the contractor's discards are looked at by him after the opening lead or by an opponent at any time: The player at the right of the leader may name the suit to be led on the next occasion when the offender or his partner gains the lead.

ERROR IN SCORE. A proved error in recording scores must be corrected on demand made before the first bid (not pass) of the next deal after that to which the error pertains. In any other case, recorded scores may not be changed.

STRATEGY OF FIVE HUNDRED

A suit bid is rarely advisable with less than five trumps. A no-trump bid normally requires stoppers in all four suits. To bid no-trump without the joker is speculative; with the joker, a stopperless suit is admissible if the rest of the hand is fairly solid in top cards.

Count primarily the tricks you can probably win by force: e.g., a nontrump ace or king-queen is one trick, a king without the ace is only a "possible trick." Count each card beyond a length of four in trumps (or in a long side suit if the hand as a whole is strong enough to establish it) as a "long card" trick.

Do not bid in the hope of finding a specific card (e.g., the joker) in the widow. However, you are entitled to expect *some* help from the widow: this expectation is one or two tricks when you have six in hand, or one when you have seven. With a stronger hand don't reckon the widow as a "bidding value."

Since you have only one chance to bid, you must make the highest safe bid you can. You must often "stretch" the normal bidding requirements to reach six or seven; but be conservative in higher bids.

At a suit contract, after taking the widow, usually discard from your short suits (three cards or less), saving all long suits intact. At no-trump, save your longest suit intact and discard what you can afford from the others, keeping all your stoppers guarded. (Minimum stoppers are A, K-x, Q-x-x.)

At a normal suit bid, the contractor begins by leading trumps, to pull two adverse trumps to his one. At no-trump, the contractor should usually open his longest suit (regardless of its top strength) and continue it at every opportunity. With no real long suit (five cards or more) he should try to force out the adverse aces and kings that stand in the way of his lower-card tricks.

As an opponent of the contractor, try to avoid helping him by opening new suits. Usually try to develop your own longest or strongest suit. When you find the contractor void of a plain suit, force him with it at every opportunity. It is especially important for the left-hand opponent, who leads "up to" the contractor, to exit safely. The right-hand opponent, who leads "through" him, can often afford to open a new suit when he himself has neither ace nor king.

Four-Hand Five Hundred

When four play, each two players sitting opposite each other are partners. All tricks and scores made by partners are pooled in a common score. If either side reaches minus 500 it loses the game. The pack is 43 cards: from a pack of 52 discard the twos, threes, and black fours, then add the joker. Each player receives ten cards in the deal, and three cards form the widow. If a player bids out of turn, the bid is void and the offender's partner is barred from bidding. All other rules are as in the three-hand game, above.

Two-Hand Five Hundred

When two play, the 33-card pack may be used and a dead hand dealt to left of the dealer, this hand not being used in the play (and it must not be looked at by either player); bidding is highly speculative, as compared with three-hand, for the contractor will have only one opponent and a weak hand may be greatly strengthened if the right ten cards are out of play. Or a 25-card pack may be used, ace to nine in each suit, plus the joker.

Five-Hand Five Hundred

Use the full 52-card pack plus joker. Each player receives ten cards and the widow three. After the bidding, the contractor may name any other player to be his partner, or, if he bid for eight or more tricks, he may name two partners. The others combine in temporary partnership against the contracting side.

HASENPFEFFER

This is a bidding form of Euchre. The name is a German word for a hare or rabbit stew. Four play, in two partnerships. The pack has 25 cards—A, K, Q, J, 10, 9 in each suit—plus the joker, which is always the highest trump. Each player is dealt six cards, three at a time. The last card is left face down on the table as the *widow.*

Eldest hand bids first, and each player has one bid. Each bid is a number, from one to six. The high bidder picks up the widow, names the trump suit, discards one card face down, and leads any card to the first trick. The rules of play are as in Euchre. If the bidding side wins at least as many tricks as it bid, it scores one for each trick it wins. If it falls short of its bid it is *set back*—the amount of the bid is deducted from its score. A side may have a minus score (be *in the hole*). Game is 10 points plus.

If all four players pass, the player holding the joker must show it and play a bid of three.

Double Hasenpfeffer

Four or six play, in two partnerships. A 48-card Pinochle pack is used, ranking as in Euchre, with no joker. All the cards are dealt. Each player has one bid, as in Hasenpfeffer, but the lowest bid is for half the tricks and if the first three players pass, dealer must bid at least this minimum. The high bidder may elect to play alone. If he does, he discards two cards face down and his partner selects and gives him two cards, then discards his hand. They still score as partners.

Game is 62 points. A dealer who bid the minimum can be set back only half his bid. A lone player scores or loses double.

ÉCARTÉ

ÉCARTÉ is a French gambling game, which has been reduced almost to an exact science. It is played by two, but casino rules permit and encourage the "gallery" to participate in the stakes as well as place side bets on the outcome.

The pack comprises 32 cards, made from a regular pack by stripping out the sixes and all lower cards. The rank in each suit is K (high), Q, J, A, 10, 9, 8, 7. Each player receives five cards dealt in batches of three and two or two and three. The eleventh card is turned face up and its suit is trumps for the deal. If the turned card is a king, the dealer scores 1 point for it immediately.

The non-dealer, after looking at his hand, either *stands* or *proposes*. If he stands, the original hands are played out. The proposal is to draw cards from the stock in the hope of bettering the original hand; dealer may refuse it (in which case play begins) or accept it. If it is accepted, non-dealer discards as many cards as he wishes; he must discard at least one. Dealer gives him enough cards from the top of the stock to restore his hand to five cards. Then dealer discards and draws, though he may keep his original hand intact if he wishes.

Non-dealer may repeatedly propose, and dealer may repeatedly accept, until either one player elects to stand or the pack is exhausted. In the latter case, the deal is abandoned without score. When either player stands, the hands are played out.

Non-dealer makes the first lead. He may lead any card. In responding to a lead, the other hand must follow suit if able, must win the trick if able, must play a trump if able when void of a plain suit led. A trick is won by the higher trump, or if it contains no trump, by the higher card of the suit led. The winner of a trick leads to the next.

The cards are not thrown together in tricks, but kept segregated, for if a revoke or other irregularity is committed the hands are reassembled and replayed according to rule. Furthermore, the French custom is to announce the suit of each card led, as a safeguard against revoke, but American players usually omit this formality.

The object of play is to win tricks. Either player taking three or four tricks scores 1 point; for *vole,* all five tricks, 2 points. There is one exception to this uniform rule. If a player stands on his original hand and fails to win a majority, the opponent scores 2 for three, four, or five tricks. The king of trumps counts 1 point to the player that holds it (or to the dealer if it is turned for trump), provided that he shows it before playing to the first trick.

A game is won by the player who first accumulates 5 points. If a player has 4 points and is dealt the king of trumps, he may show it and claim the game at once.

The strategy of the game consists almost entirely in knowing when to stand and when to propose or accept. This is a matter of knowing the *jeux de règle*—the minimum hands that will in the abstract win three or more tricks in a majority of the cases, considering all possible hands that may be held by the opponent. The *jeux de règle* may be summarized as follows:

(a) Any hand with three or more trumps.

(b) A hand with two trumps, plus one plain king or two queens or three jacks. (Certain weaker holdings are also admissible: ace-ten in one plain suit and ace in another; jack-ten in one suit and ten in another.)

(c) A hand with one trump, plus two plain suits headed by king or queen-jack. (Certain weaker holdings are also admissible: three jacks and a queen; a three-card plain suit headed by king-queen.)

(d) A hand with no trumps, but a king or queen-jack at the top of each plain suit. (Or, with one suit headed by queen without the jack, two kings and a queen or two kings and two jacks in the other suits.)

Discarding after a proposal is largely mechanical—trumps and kings are saved, all else discarded. The correct opening lead is usually the top card of the strongest plain suit. After the first lead, significant choices of play are rare.

HEARTS

HEARTS *is so called because every card of the heart suit counts "minus" when won in tricks. The object of play is usually the reverse of that in Bridge and other games, where the object is to win certain cards or tricks. Indeed, the 18th-century ancestor of Hearts was called* REVERSE. *The traditional game of Hearts is described first, but other forms such as* BLACK LADY *and* OMNI-BUS HEARTS *(described later) have become more popular.*

PLAYERS. Three to six; the best game is four-hand. In every case, each plays for himself.

CARDS. A regular pack of 52. With more or less than four players, discard enough low cards (♣2, ♦2, ♣3, ♠2) so that all players have the same number of cards. In each suit the cards rank: A (high), K, Q, J, 10, 9, 8, 7, 6, 5, 4, 3, 2.

THE DEAL. The whole pack is dealt, one at a time in rotation to the left.

THE PLAY. The player at left of the dealer leads first. A player must follow suit to a lead if able; if unable to follow suit, he may play any card. A trick is won by the highest card played of the suit led. The winner of a trick leads to the next.

SCORING. All players are provided at the outset with equal numbers of chips. Before each deal, equal antes are put into a pool. After the play, if one player alone is *clear* (has taken no heart), he wins the whole pool. If two are clear, they divide the pool. If all four are *painted* (win hearts), or if all the hearts are taken by one player, the pool is a *jack*, that is, it remains on the table to be won later, increased by the subsequent antes.

IRREGULARITIES IN HEARTS

MISDEAL. It is a misdeal if dealer exposes a card, or gives any hand an incorrect number of cards, or otherwise departs from prescribed procedure. A misdeal may be called at any time before the first trick is completed; otherwise the deal stands as regular. On a proper call of misdeal, the cards are thrown in and redealt by the next dealer (the offender thus losing his turn to deal).

INCORRECT HAND. If at any time after the first trick any hand is found to have an incorrect number of cards, this hand must take all the cards remaining in the hands after the last complete trick is played. If two or more hands are incorrect, these excess cards go to all alike, and each faulty hand is charged with the full number of hearts in the excess cards.

PLAY OUT OF TURN. There is no penalty for a lead or play out of turn, but any player who has not yet played to the trick may demand that it be retracted (in which case any other cards subsequently played must also be retracted). If no player (entitled to do so) demands retraction, the out-of-turn play stands as regular. The owner of an out-of-turn card may not retract it except on proper demand of another player.

REVOKE. If a player fails to follow suit when able, he may correct his error without penalty before the trick is turned down and quitted. If a revoke is not corrected in time, and is discovered before the deal has been scored, the offender is charged for all the hearts in that deal.

STRATEGY OF HEARTS

When the play begins, each hand is intent on avoiding hearts. But once a player has taken a heart he does not care how many more he may have to take. His only chance at the pool will be to paint every other player, or to win all the hearts himself. If two or three are painted, they naturally conspire to paint the others also.

The basis of the play is straight "nullo"—the effort to win no trick, or only harmless tricks. High cards that can be forced to take tricks in three leads of a suit should be played early rather than late. Aces and high cards accompanied by some low cards are not dangerous, but middle cards without low cards are very dangerous. A holding such as Q-9-8 should be led each and every time the opportunity offers, in the effort to dispose of it before cards of this suit are discarded from other hands. A holding such as J-10-9-8-6 is desperately bad and should be discarded whenever opportunity offers, so long as any lower cards of the suit remain unplayed.

Adequately guarded high cards should, however, be saved so long as there is no danger in doing so. Nullo play alone will not suffice, if another player has a chance to win all the hearts. A high-card entry sometimes is invaluable in letting a clear hand interrupt a "take-all" to make a killing lead that paints another hand.

Black Lady

See Hearts, page 72, for rules as to Players, Cards, The Deal, The Play, and Irregularities. Black Lady differs only in the following features.

THE BLACK LADY. The ♠ Q is a "minus" card additional to the hearts, counting 13. The focus of play is thus to avoid winning the Black Lady (also called Black Maria or Calamity Jane), the hearts being relatively minor.

In club play this rule is usually adopted: The player holding the ♠ Q must get rid of it on the first trick he can, either by discard or by playing it under the ♠ A or ♠ K already in the trick. The purpose of this rule is to forestall quarrels that may arise from the feeling that favoritism is shown in the disposal of the ♠ Q. But often "favoritism" (in self-interest) is the soul of the strategy.

THE PASS. After the deal is completed, each player must pass any three cards from his hand to his left neighbor. He must select his pass before looking at the cards received from his right neighbor. (*Alternative:* In some circles the rule is to pass alternately to the left and right in successive deals.)

TAKE-ALL. If a player takes all thirteen hearts and the ♠ Q: (a) there is no score or settlement for the deal; or (b) this player scores + 26.

SCORING. When there is no take-all, the points taken by each player are charged against him in a running total on the scoresheet. A session ends at a prefixed time or when one player reaches 100, as agreed. Then each player settles with every other according to the differences of their scores. The simplest way to settle is to total all the scores and divide by the number of players, thus determining the average score. Each player is charged with his difference from the average: those who are above pay the difference, and those who are below collect.

STRATEGY OF BLACK LADY

The most important consideration in selecting cards to pass is to mitigate spade danger. Any high spades (A, K, or Q) in a holding of less than four spades are very dangerous. Usually pass them; except that the ♠ Q is often safer in the hand than out, so that if you are dealt the ♠ Q adequately guarded (three or more others) keep it.

Unguarded high hearts are also unpleasant, since they may capture many minus cards. Pass them if you can afford to do so. High cards in general are not dangerous if accompanied by two or more low cards. A suit as a whole is dangerous if it is long (four or more cards) and contains no low cards, e.g., ♣ Q J 9 8. If you can afford it, pass two or three cards from such a holding.

Every player who does not have "spade trouble" after the pass has an interest in leading spades and should do so. To force out the ♠ Q by spade leads is the best insurance against taking it later by discard.

With two to four diamonds or clubs, having both high cards and low cards, usually play your high cards early, saving your low cards to escape the more dangerous later rounds. The same advice applies to hearts in some degree. If hearts are led through you and you hold ♡ A 7 2, you might risk playing low, but if you hold ♡ A 2 the low play would be folly: put up your ace and take your licking. The outcome to be avoided at all costs is to give up all your exit cards early, whereupon you may be stuck in the lead and forced to win the last five or six tricks.

Cancellation Hearts

This is a variant for six or more players. Shuffle together two regular 52-card packs and deal them out as far as they will go evenly. Leave the extra cards face down on the table; these go to the winner of the first trick. The rules are as in Black Lady, plus one added rule: When identical cards (as two jacks of clubs) fall on the same trick, they cancel each other: neither can win the trick. It may happen under this rule that no card in a trick can win it; in such case, the trick is held aside and goes to the winner of the next trick. The same leader leads again when a trick must be so held aside. If the last trick of the deal is canceled out, the cards are dead and are not scored.

The most convenient way of scoring is to provide a common pool of poker chips or matchsticks. Each player must take from the pool one chip for each point taken (each heart 1, the ♠ Q 13). When a session ends, each player settles with every other as in Black Lady. If the pool nears exhaustion, all players return an equal number of chips to it.

Omnibus Hearts

This latest and best variant of Hearts is Black Lady plus two rules:

The ♦ 10 (in many circles, the ♦ J) counts "plus 10" to the winner.

If a player wins all thirteen hearts, the ♠ Q and the ♦ 10, he scores plus 26 (in some circles, 36) instead of minus 16.

STRATEGY. The strategy of Black Lady largely applies here. If you could go through a session of Omnibus Hearts taking no more than an average of one or two hearts per deal, you would very probably win. But you must expect to be "painted" with 13 or more on some occasions. Winning policy is therefore to try to capture the ♦ 10 or make take-all, whenever chances are good, in order to offset the bad hands.

The ♦ 10 is rarely won by the hand that holds it after the pass. Lacking an exceptional hand, the player to whom the ♦ 10 is dealt therefore passes it if he has any good prospect of catching it. The ◇ 10 usually falls by forced discard in the last tricks. After the ♤ Q has been forced out, high cards and long suits are desirable; the object is now to win tricks rather than to lose tricks. It should be noted that if you can catch the ◇ 10 you should usually go for it regardless of the number of hearts you take in the process, for you *may* emerge with a net plus, and in any event it is worth while to keep the ◇ 10 from falling to someone else.

The take-all obviously depends on exceptional top strength. But this alone is not sufficient. Most fatal to take-all intentions are low diamonds and low hearts (except as end cards of long near-solid suits), and the ◇ 10. If you cannot pass all such danger cards, don't aim for take-all. On the other hand, aces are not an absolute necessity (except in hearts if you have more than one or two hearts).

Defensive strategy is greatly influenced by the take-all. A successful take-all campaign costs each opponent about 9 points at least. If necessary to prevent a take-all a player will profit considerably by taking a heart trick (4 points) that he could have lost. He should seldom take or risk taking 7 or 8 points to prevent a take-all unless he is sure it could not be prevented otherwise.

CRIBBAGE

CRIBBAGE *is believed to have been invented and christened by the English poet Sir John Suckling, who lived 1609-1642. Some of its features were taken from an older game,* NODDY, *of which little is known. Early colonists brought Cribbage to America, where it flourishes. In New England there are clubs devoted to Cribbage, conducting intra- and intercity tournaments.*

PLAYERS. Two. Adaptation can be made for three or four.

CARDS. A regular pack of 52. The cards rank: K (high), Q, J, 10, 9, 8, 7, 6, 5, 4, 3, 2, A. The suits play little part; the cards are used chiefly as numbers. Each face card represents 10, each ace 1, each other card its index value. Face cards and tens are called "tenth cards."

THE DEAL. Each player receives six cards, dealt one at a time.

THE CRIB. From his hand each player selects two cards, and the four cards are placed face down near the dealer. They form the *crib*, an extra hand that belongs to the dealer.

THE STARTER. After the crib is laid away, the nondealer cuts the rest of the pack, and the dealer turns up the top card of the lower portion. This card is the *starter*. If it is a jack, the dealer pegs (scores) 2 points.

THE CRIBBAGE BOARD. Scores accrue so rapidly that a special scoring device is used, a *Cribbage board*. As shown in the illustration, the board is an oblong panel having four rows of 30 holes each, plus some extra *game holes* at one end. Each player uses two pegs, which at the outset are placed in the game holes. Each item of score is marked by jumping the rearward peg ahead of the other by a corresponding number of holes. The pegs are marched away from the head of the board (the end with the game holes) along an outer row of holes, then back along an inner row. The game may be played "once around," for a total of 61 points, but far more common is "twice around" for a total of 121.

THE PLAY. In playing his cards, each player retains possession of them, merely exposing them face up in a pile in front of himself.

The nondealer begins by playing any card, announcing its point value, as "Ten" if he leads a face card or ten. Dealer then plays a card, announcing the total of the two cards, as "Seventeen" if he plays a seven. Play continues alternately, the new total being announced each time, until the player in turn is unable to play without carrying the total over thirty-one. He must then say "Go." The other pegs for the *go* (as explained below); then the player who called the go must lead again for a new series of plays. The count begins again at zero, and again the total must not be carried beyond thirty-one.

After go is called, the other must play additional cards if he can do so without exceeding thirty-one. Thus the same player may play two or three times in succession. For making exactly thirty-one the player pegs 2; for a go at less than thirty-one he pegs 1. Playing the last card of all (of the eight in play) counts 1 for last, or 2 if it makes thirty-one.

SCORING IN PLAY. Other points may be scored in play besides the go's. These are as follows.

Fifteen. For making the count fifteen, peg 2.

Pairs. For playing a card of same rank as that just played by an opponent, peg 2. (Pairing goes by rank, e.g., a king with a king, not with a queen, though both have the point value of 10.) For playing the third card of a rank peg 6, and for playing the fourth peg 12.

Runs. For playing a card that is in sequence of rank with two or more played just previously, peg the number of cards in the *run* (sequence.) For example, if the cards played are 4, 6, 5, the last player pegs 3 for run plus 2 for fifteen. The cards need not be played in sequential order to score for run, so long as no foreign cards intervene. For example, if the cards played are 4, K, 6, 5 there is no run.

SHOWING. By *showing* is meant counting and scoring a hand. The hands are shown in strict order: nondealer, dealer's hand, crib.

The starter is treated as a fifth card belonging to each of these three hands. The combinations that score are as follows.

Fifteen. For each combination of cards that total fifteen, score 2. "Combination" here is meant in the strict sense. Thus, a hand (with starter) of 9, 8, 7, 7, 6 has three combinations of fifteen: 9 and 6, 8 with one 7, 8 with the other 7. A hand of J, 5, 5, 5, 5 has no less than eight combinations of fifteen: four of J and 5, four of three 5's. (This hand, when the J also scores as *his nobs*, makes 29, the largest possible score.)

Pairs. For a pair, score 2; for three of a kind (called *pair royal* or "proil"), 6; for four of a kind (*double pair royal*), 12.

Runs. For each combination that makes a run of three or more, peg the number of cards in the run. In the hand 9, 8, 7, 7, 6 there are 8 points for two runs of four, using the 7's in turn.

Flush. For four cards in hand (not crib, and excluding the starter) of the same suit, score 4, or 5 if the starter is also of the same suit. For crib and starter all of the same suit, score 5. (There is no score for a four-flush in the crib.)

His Nobs. For a jack in hand, of same suit as the starter, score 1. The jack scored as starter by dealer is called *his heels.*

Proper etiquette is to count aloud, taking the categories in the order given above, and indicating the source of the scores briefly. For example, in scoring K, K, 10, 5, 4, the player would say "Fifteen two, fifteen four, fifteen six, and a pair makes eight." The opponent must be given time to verify the score. It is proper to announce the scores for certain combinations *in toto*, as pair royal and double pair royal (call "Six" or "Twelve"; do not count the separate pairs). Other standard combinations count as follows for runs and pairs alone (exclusive of fifteens and other items):

Double run, as K, Q, Q, J, scores 8.

Double run of four, as K, Q, Q, J, 10, scores 10.

Triple run, as K, Q, Q, Q, J, scores 15.

Quadruple run, as K, Q, Q, J, J, scores 16.

MUGGINS. If a player overlooks a score to which he is entitled, either in playing or in showing, the opponent may call "Muggins!" and take the score himself. This rule should be waived when a beginner plays against an experienced player.

GAME. When a player pegs into the game hole that gives him 121 (or 61) points, he wins the game forthwith—nothing more is scored. If the loser has not passed the halfway mark—has not reached 61 in "twice around" or 31 in "once around"—he is *lurched* and loses a double game.

IRREGULARITIES IN CRIBBAGE

NEW DEAL. There must be a new deal by the same dealer if, before nondealer lays away to the crib, it is found that a wrong number of cards was dealt, or a card is exposed in dealing.

WRONG NUMBER OF CARDS. If a player is found (too late for a new deal) to have an incorrect number of cards in his hand, the opponent may either have the hand corrected or may let it stand and peg 2. A short hand is corrected by drawing cards from the stock; a long hand is corrected by discarding cards drawn from it by the opponent. If the crib has the wrong number of cards it must be corrected and nondealer pegs 2.

FAILURE TO PLAY. If a player calls go when able to play,

or fails to play when able after opponent calls go, the card or cards he could have played are dead and opponent pegs 2. Dead cards are unplayable; the owner must complete his play with a short hand; but the cards are counted in showing.

ERROR IN SCORING. A player may correct his own error in announcing his score before he has pegged it, but a score once pegged may not be changed except on demand of opponent.

A player may demand correction of an incorrect amount pegged by his opponent, provided that he does so before making his next play, or showing his own hand, or gathering the cards, etc.

STRATEGY OF CRIBBAGE

The choice of cards to give the crib is often easy. Count all the points in the six cards, then lay away the two picked to leave the maximum possible score in the remaining four. But sometimes this course would put points or valuable cards in the crib, so that if the crib is not yours you may do better to deplete your hand somewhat in order to *balk* the crib. Dangerous cards to put in the adverse crib are fives, sevens, and eights, and *near* cards—two in sequence or in sequence-but-one. The best balking cards are very high, very low, and *wide* cards generally—separated in rank by two or more.

Sometimes you are forced to split combinations, even when the crib is yours. As a rule, keep a run of three or more, splitting a pair instead, if necessary. Holding a run gives you maximum chance of increasing your count by help of the starter.

In the play, the main principle is to try to prevent your opponent from making fifteen, or a run, unless you can riposte with a score. Obviously the safest opening lead is a four, because opponent can then neither make fifteen nor pass fifteen and so deprive you of a chance to make it. (He might pair your four—but against pairs there is no defense.)

A tenth card is supposed to be a bad lead, but actually is no more dangerous than a seven, eight, or any other middle card. In fact, a tenth card is a good lead if you have a five: if your opponent makes fifteen, you make a pair. Similarly, a lead from two cards that total fifteen (9 and 6, 7 and 8) is good.

After a lead, the question sometimes arises whether to *play on* or *play off*, that is, play a near card making sequences possible, or play a wide card. Naturally you should play on only if you can extend any sequence that your opponent might make.

When no other considerations supervene, play your high cards first, saving low cards to eke out a go.

EXAMPLE DEAL

NONDEALER   DEALER

Nondealer lays away 10-3. He cannot keep his entire score, so saves one sequence combination (8-7) and the valuable fivespot, with the jack to make a fifteen. He gives the ten rather than the jack so as to avoid giving *his nobs*.

Dealer has an easy discard, the K-A, saving the double run. After the starter is turned, the situation is:

NONDEALER   STARTER   DEALER

The play card by card is as follows:

1. Nondealer leads his eight. "Eight." Either the eight or seven should be led, but which one is a guess.
2. Dealer plays the seven. "Fifteen, and two." He pegs 2. He might have made a pair of eights for the same score, but prefers to "play on" by building toward a run.
3. Nondealer plays the seven. "Twenty-two and a pair." Pegs 2.
4. Dealer plays ◇ 9. "Thirty-one." Pegs 2.
5. Nondealer leads the jack. "Ten." On general principle, the lower card is saved as giving a better chance for go.

6. Dealer plays the other nine. "Nineteen." He does not play the eight because Nondealer's last card might be an eight. It surely is not a nine, else Nondealer on the third play would have made a run of three rather than a pair.

7. Nondealer plays the five. "Twenty-four." Dealer calls "Go," and Nondealer pegs 1.

8. Dealer plays the eight. "One for last." Pegs 1.

Nondealer shows as follows: "Fifteen two (J-5), fifteen four (8-7), and a run (8-7-6-5) makes eight." Pegs 8.

Dealer shows his hand: "Fifteen two (8-7), fifteen four (9-6), fifteen six (9-6 using the other nine), and double run of four (counting 10) makes sixteen." Pegs 16. He then turns up the crib. "I have nineteen!" (i.e., no score; for there is no possible hand that counts 19).

Three-Hand Cribbage

Three-Hand Cribbage follows the rules of two-hand except in the following respects. Five cards are dealt to each player, and one card is dealt to the crib. Each player lays away one card to the crib. Eldest hand cuts for the starter and leads first. On a call of go, the other hands must continue to play if able and the last to play scores for the go. The new lead is made by the first to call go. In showing, the order is: eldest hand first, then player at his left, then dealer's hand, finally the crib. Triangular Cribbage boards are made for scoring this game.

Four-Hand Cribbage

Four-Hand Cribbage is played in two partnerships, which may be determined by drawing cards, the two lowest playing against the two highest. Lowest card deals first. Five cards are dealt to each player, of which one is laid away to the crib. Eldest hand cuts for the starter and makes the first lead. On a call of go, the other hands continue to play if able, and the last side to play scores for the go. The new lead is made by the first player to call go. Only one score is kept for each side. In showing, the order is: non-dealing side first, then dealer's side, finally the crib, which belongs to dealer's side.

POKER

POKER *is a popular game throughout the world. It combines principles of card games known hundreds of years ago in Europe and probably long before that in the Orient, but in its present form it is distinctly of American origin. There are hundreds of forms of Poker, but they differ only in details and all follow the same basic principles, so a person who has learned these principles can play without difficulty in any game. The main divisions of Poker are:* CLOSED POKER, *in which all of a player's cards are unknown to his opponents; and* OPEN POKER, *or* STUD POKER, *in which some of a player's cards are face up and others face down. Closed Poker is now usually encountered in the form of* DRAW POKER. *Subdivisions of these basic forms are:* LOW POKER, *or* LOWBALL, *in which the worst hand wins;* HIGH-LOW POKER, *in which the best and worst hands split; and Freak or "Dealer's Choice" Games. These forms are described separately on the following pages.*

PLAYERS. Two to ten; best for five to eight. More than eight can play only Stud Poker. In all forms of Poker, each plays for himself.

CARDS. A regular pack of 52, occasionally with the addition of the joker. The cards rank: A (high), K, Q, J, 10, 9, 8, 7, 6, 5, 4, 3, 2. The ace also ranks low in the sequence

85

5-4-3-2-A. The joker, when used, is a wild card (see below).

Poker is almost invariably played with poker chips of various colors, each color having a different value.

THE DEAL. In every form of Poker the cards are dealt one at a time, in clockwise rotation, beginning with the player at the dealer's left. Usually each player receives five cards, but in various forms of the game more cards are dealt, and often some are dealt face up and some face down. These will be described under the separate forms of Poker.

The first dealer is determined when one player takes a pack of cards and deals it around, face up, until a jack falls to one player, who becomes the first dealer. Thereafter the deal rotates from player to player to the left.

THE PLAY. Poker is a game of betting as to which player holds the best hand. All bets made by all players go in a pile of chips called the *pot,* in the center of the table. The object of the game is to win the pot. The pot may be won in either of two ways: (a) After all players have had full opportunity to bet, there is a *showdown* in which the hands are shown and the best hand wins. (b) If a player makes a bet that no other player is willing to meet, that player wins the pot without showing his hand; for no one may compete for a pot unless he is willing to meet the highest bet made by any other player. This introduces the factor of *bluffing,* betting on a weak hand in the hope that all other players will drop out.

RANK OF POKER HANDS. The following combinations of cards have value in every form of Poker. They are listed in order from highest to lowest.

1. *Straight flush*—five cards in sequence in the same suit. As between two straight flushes, the one headed by the highest-ranking card wins: A-K-Q-J-10 (called a *royal flush*) beats K-Q-J-10-9, and 6-5-4-3-2 beats 5-4-3-2-A. The royal flush is the highest standard hand, but when wild cards are used "five of a kind" is the highest.

2. *Four of a kind*—any four cards of the same rank. As between two such hands, the four higher cards win. Four of a kind beats a full house or any lower hand.

3. *Full house*—three of a kind and a pair. As between two full houses, the one wins whose three of a kind are composed of the higher-ranking cards. A full house beats a flush or any lower hand.

4. A *flush*—any hand of five cards all of the same As between two flushes, the one containing the hig ranking card wins. If these two cards tie, the next-highest ranking card decides; if these two cards tie, the third-highest-ranking card, and so on down to the last card, so that ♠ A-Q-10-9-3 beats ♡ A-Q-10-3-2. A flush beats a straight or any lower hand.

5. A *straight*—any five cards in sequence but not all of the same suit. As between two straights, the one with the highest-ranking card at the head of the sequence is the winner, the highest possible straight being A-K-Q-J-10 and the lowest possible straight being 5-4-3-2-A. A straight beats three of a kind or anything lower.

6. *Three of a kind*, such as three sixes, with two unmatched cards. If two players each hold three of a kind, the higher-ranking three of a kind wins. This hand beats two pairs or anything lower.

7. *Two pairs*—two cards of any one rank and two cards of any other rank, with an unmatched card. As between two such hands, the one containing the highest-ranking pair is the winner; if these pairs are the same, the hand with the higher of the two other pairs is the winner; if the two hands contain the identical two pairs, then the higher-ranking unmatched card determines the winner. Two pairs beat any hand with only one pair or with no pair.

8. *One pair*—any two cards of the same rank. A pair is dealt to a player about twice in every five hands he holds. As between two hands that have one pair each, the pair composed of the higher-ranking cards wins. If both hands have the same pair, the highest of the three unmatched cards determines the winner; if they are the same, the next-highest; and if they are the same, the higher as between the third unmatched cards in the two hands. A hand with only one pair beats any hand which contains no pair and no one of the combinations described in the preceding paragraphs.

9. *High card.* About one out of two hands that a Poker player holds will consist merely of five unmatched cards. As between two hands of this nature, rank is decided by the rank of the highest card, and if necessary by the next-highest, and so on, as described in paragraph 4 above.

Hands identical in all respects tie; the suits of which the hands are composed never make any difference.

WILD CARDS. A joker added to a pack, or any rank or group of cards (usually deuces), may be designated in advance to be *wild*. The holder of a wild card may cause it to stand for any other card he wishes. Except by special house rules: (a) A wild card ranks exactly the same as the natural card it replaces; and (b) a wild card cannot stand for a card the player already holds, so that there cannot be, for example, a "double-ace-high" flush.

The bug is the joker given restricted wild-card use: It may represent an ace, and it may be used to fill a straight flush, flush, or straight. Therefore two aces and the bug are three aces, but two kings and the bug are merely a pair of kings with an ace.

When wild cards are used, five of a kind are the highest-ranking hand. Ties become possible between identical fours of a kind, full houses, or threes of a kind. In such cases the rank of the other cards in the hand determines the winner.

ROTATION. In Poker the turn to do everything passes from player to player to the left. The cards are dealt in this way; the turn to bet goes from player to player in rotation. No player should do anything until the player on his right has acted.

RULES OF BETTING. Betting is done during periods of the game called *betting intervals*. The number of betting intervals depends on what form of the game is being played; for example, in Draw Poker the first betting interval occurs when each player has been dealt his full five cards, and in Stud Poker it occurs when each player has been dealt two cards.

In each betting interval, some player has the first right or duty to bet. Usually there is some minimum and some maximum amount, agreed upon in advance, that he may bet. The proper way is for him to place in the pot the number of chips he bets and at the same time announce the number of chips he is betting. When the designated player has bet, each player in turn after him must do one of the following three things:

1. *Drop* out of the pot (also known as *passing*), which means that he discards his hand and may no longer win the pot. A player may thus drop at any time, and when he drops all chips he may have put into the pot previously are forfeited to the pot and will eventually go to the winner of it.

2. *Call,* which means that he puts in exactly enough chips to make his total contribution to the pot precisely the same as the greatest number of chips put into the pot by any other player. This is also known as *staying in.*

3. *Raise,* which means that in addition to enough chips to call he puts in an added amount and now has put in more chips than any other player. The excess is the amount by which he raises, and every other player must either put in as many chips as he, or must drop and forfeit the pot.

For example, a player opens the pot by betting three chips. The next player may call by putting in three chips; he may raise by putting in more than three chips. If he puts in four chips, he has raised one chip; if he puts in six chips, he has raised three chips, and so on. He may not raise by more chips than the limit established for the game. If the second player does raise three chips, and all the other players drop, the player who opened may stay in by putting three more chips in the pot; for then he will have put in precisely as many chips as the second player.

Betting of this nature continues until all the bets are *equalized.* The bets are equalized when the turn comes around to the player who in his turn made a higher bet than anyone previous to him, and when every intervening player has either exactly called that bet, or dropped.

In many forms of Poker, a player is permitted to *check.* Originally this meant that he made the minimum bet, a chip of such low value that it was hardly worth while putting it in the pot. So when a player checks, it means he has made "a bet of nothing" and each player in turn after him may also check—in effect calling the bet—until any player makes a genuine bet. Thereafter, each player in turn must call, raise, or drop.

For example, assume a seven-hand game and call the players, "A", "B", "C", "D", "E", "F", and "G". "G" is the dealer, so "A" is the eldest hand. Following the deal, "A" and "B" check. "C" opens for five chips (that is, he bets five chips). "D" raises five chips (that is, he puts in ten chips, five to call and five to raise). "E" drops. "F" stays in, putting in ten chips to call. "G" raises ten chips, meaning that he puts in twenty chips in all. "A", who checked on the first round, now has the right to enter the betting; but he drops. "B", who has the same right, puts in twenty chips and calls. "C" calls, putting in fifteen chips (since he put in five chips previously, these fifteen make his total contribution twenty chips, the greatest amount put in by any other player). "D" raises ten more chips, putting in twenty; now he has put in thirty chips altogether. "E", who dropped previously, has no option; once a player drops, he is inactive from that time on. "F", who put in ten chips before, could call by putting in twenty more; but instead he drops, forfeiting the ten chips he put in before. "G" puts in ten chips, making his own total contribution thirty chips, and thus calling the bet. "B" and "C" each put in ten chips, and as in the case of "G" this makes their total contribution the same as any previous player's and means that they both call the previous bet.

Now, of the seven players, three have dropped and the other four have each put in thirty chips, and the turn has come around to "D" again. The bets have been equalized, and "D" may not bet again. This "betting interval" is ended.

Any player who drops out becomes *inactive;* from that time on, the turn to act still passes in rotation from one player to the other, but only from active player to active player.

LIMITS. Most Poker games are played with a limit of anywhere from five to ten chips. Other popular forms of determining a limit are:

Pot Limit. The player making the first bet in any betting interval may bet as many chips as there are in the pot at the time. Any player after him in the same betting interval may raise by as many chips as there are in the pot after he calls. That is, he may announce his intention to raise by "the size of the pot"; then put in enough chips to call the previous bet; then count the pot and match it for a raise.

When playing with a pot limit, some maximum should nevertheless be set for the highest possible bet or raise. Otherwise, in a seven-hand game, this might happen: The *antes* make 7 chips. The opener opens for 7. The next player puts in 7 to call; now there are 21 chips in the pot, and he raises 21. The third player must put in 28 chips to call, and may now raise 70 chips. This means that the fourth player would have to put up 98 chips merely to call, and could then, if he wished, raise 238.

Table Stakes. A more popular way of playing with a

variable limit is to let each player's limit be the number of chips he has at the time. For example, players "A", "B", and "C" are competing for the pot; "A" has a stack of 160 chips, "B" has 110 chips, "C" has only 40. "C" can call any bet made by "A" or "B" for his 40 chips; "B" can call any bet made by "A" for his 110 chips. "A" therefore has 50 chips which he cannot use in this pot.

Suppose "B" bets 70 chips. "C" calls it for 40, that being his limit. "A" calls the entire bet, but does not raise. In the showdown the highest hand takes the main pot, but the side pot—the extra 30 chips each put up by "B" and "A"—go to whichever of them has the higher hand.

When playing with table stakes, no one may add to the chips he has on the table after the deal begins, but between deals he may add as much as he wishes. No one may reduce the number of chips he has on the table until he leaves the game, unless the banker's supply of chips is exhausted and he must buy back chips to supply other players.

ARRANGING THE GAME. In addition to the table and chairs necessary to seat all the players comfortably (specially built Poker tables are circular, usually felt-covered, and have pits for holding the players' chips), and at least one pack of playing cards, the only essential equipment for the game is a set of poker chips. The poker chips should be in at least three colors, white, red and blue; there should be enough of these chips for every player to have an ample supply.

One member of the game is selected as the banker. He may be the host, or a player chosen by lot. At the start, all the chips are the banker's property. He sells or issues them to the players, the same initial amount to each player, and keeps a record of the number of chips each player has taken. The white chip is always the basic unit; each red chip is worth five whites, and each blue is worth ten whites. When in the course of a game a player runs out of chips, he should replenish his supply by purchasing an additional "stack" from the banker; he should not borrow or buy from other players. Each stack purchased should be precisely of the same amount as the original issue. If the banker's supply needs replenishment, he should redeem one or more stacks from players who by their winnings have an excess.

At the start of the game, any player picks up the cards,

shuffles them, and deals them out face up to the players, one by one, in rotation, until any player gets a jack. That player is the first dealer.

Except that the banker is given first choice of seats, usually no one in a Poker game cares where he sits. Each takes the seat nearest him. If there is any disagreement, the banker shuffles a pack and deals one card to each player, face up; of these cards, the highest-ranking sits at the dealer's left, next-highest at his left, and so on. In the course of a game a player may demand a reseating at any time, except that there may not be more than one reseating per hour.

The exact procedure in the game then depends upon which form of Poker has been selected. Most popular is Draw Poker, and that will be described first.

Draw Poker

In Draw Poker each player is dealt five cards, face down. The undealt cards are set aside for later use and there is a betting interval. Then each active player in turn may discard one or more cards, if he so wishes, and the dealer gives him replacement cards from the top of the pack. There is another betting interval, followed by a showdown in which the highest hand among the active players wins the pot.

In the first betting interval, the eldest hand (player at dealer's left) has the first turn to bet. He may either check or bet; and if he checks, each player after him has the same options, until any player *opens* by making the first bet. Thereafter each player in turn must call, raise, or drop, until the betting interval is over.

In the most popular form of Draw Poker, called *Jackpots,* a player may not open unless he has a pair of jacks or any better hand. In another popular form, called PASS AND OUT, a player may open on anything but in each turn must either bet or drop; there is no checking.

In both of these forms of Draw Poker, it is customary for each player to ante one white chip (chip of lowest value) before the deal. If no one opens, everyone antes again and there is a new deal by the next dealer in turn.

The draw begins when the bets have been equalized. The dealer picks up the cards left over from the original deal.

The first active player to his left may discard one or more cards, naming the number he discards, and the dealer gives him that number of cards from the top of the pack. If a player does not wish to discard and draw, he knocks on the table or otherwise signifies that he is "standing pat." When the first active player to the dealer's left has exercised his right to draw, the next active player in turn to the left discards and draws, and so on until the dealer (or, if he has dropped, the active player nearest his right) has drawn. Now another betting interval begins.

The player who opened has the first turn to bet. He may either bet or check. If he checks, the next active player to his left has the same options. If the opener has dropped, the active player at his left has the first turn to bet. Once a bet is made, each active player in turn thereafter must either drop, or call, or raise, until the bets are again equalized. When the bets are equalized (or when every player has checked) the second betting interval is ended.

The showdown follows the second betting interval. Every player who has not previously dropped must place all five of his cards face up on the table. It is helpful if each player announces the value of his hand as he does so, as by saying "Three sixes," or "Kings up" (meaning two pairs, the higher of which is a pair of kings), but such announcement is not required. If a player does announce his hand and has more or less than the values he announces, he need not stick by his announcement. It is a tradition of Poker that "the cards speak for themselves." A player may announce three of a kind when in fact he has a full house, and at any time before the pot is actually gathered in by another player he may correct his announcement. A player may not throw away his hand without showing it simply because a previous player has announced a higher-ranking hand; every player who is "in on the call" must expose his full hand face up on the table in the showdown.

When the hands are shown in the showdown, the player showing the highest-ranking poker hand takes in the pot, all the cards are assembled and reshuffled, the players ante for the next pot, and there is another deal by the next dealer in rotation.

OPTIONAL HANDS. In some Draw Poker games, hands other than the standard ones are counted in the showdown.

What combinations of cards are so counted depends upon the locality in which the game is played and the preferences of the players. The most popular are listed here:

A *big tiger* is a hand in which the king is the highest card, the eight is the lowest card, and there is no pair; a *little tiger* is a hand in which the eight is the highest card, a three the lowest card, and there is no pair; a *big dog* is a hand in which an ace is the highest card, a nine is the lowest card, and there is no pair; and a *little dog* is a hand in which a seven is the highest card, a deuce is the lowest card, and there is no pair. A big tiger beats a little tiger; either tiger beats a dog; and a big dog beats a little dog. All these hands beat a straight but lose to a flush.

When it is necessary to break a tie as between big tigers, little tigers, big dogs or little dogs, the rules are the same as for breaking ties between any two hands which contain no pair or better.

OTHER FORMS OF DRAW POKER

BLIND AND STRADDLE, also called BLIND OPENING, BLIND TIGER, TIGER, and by other names, including ENGLISH POKER, AUSTRALIAN POKER, and SOUTH AFRICAN POKER, is a relatively early form of Draw Poker and is still much played.

There is no ante by each player, though the first bet, which will be called the "blind" here, is often called the ante, and in many games the dealer antes one chip, which does not count as a bet. Before the deal, eldest hand must put up one chip as a blind bet; the player at his left must put up two chips as a blind *straddle;* and each player in turn thereafter may, but need not, double the last previous blind bet as an additional straddle. Usually a limit is placed on straddles, so that there may be no more than three straddles, and the largest blind bet before the deal is eight chips.

Five cards are then dealt to each player, and the players look at their hands. The player to the left of the last straddler must either place a voluntary bet of double the amount of the last straddle, or must drop out; there is no checking, and no player is permitted to stay in the pot without betting, or calling if there has been a bet previously. When the turn comes around to the ante (eldest hand) again, he may count the amount of his blind opening in figuring how many chips he need put in to call or raise; the same is true of the obligatory straddler and any voluntary straddler.

When all bets have been equalized, there is a draw, and then the active player nearest the left of the dealer must make the first bet in the second betting interval (or, of course, may drop). When the bets are equalized in this betting interval, there is a showdown.

STRAIGHT DRAW POKER is the game described above as Pass and Out. It is also called PASSOUT, BET OR DROP, and by other names. Each player in turn, in both the first and second betting intervals, must make a bet (anywhere from the minimum of one white chip up to the limit) or must drop. A player need not have a pair of jacks or better to make a bet of more than one white chip. (In some places, checking is permitted in the second betting interval but not in the first.) This was the earliest form of Draw Poker.

Stud Poker

Stud Poker is the principal form of Open Poker, in which each player has some of his cards face up. The basic form of Stud Poker is now called FIVE-CARD STUD to distinguish it from SEVEN-CARD STUD (described below), which has become at least as popular.

In Five-Card Stud, the dealer gives each player a facedown card, called the *hole card,* and then a face-up card. Each player looks at the face of his hole card but does not show it. Here the deal is interrupted for a betting interval; but from this point on, all cards are dealt face up.

In the first betting interval, the player who was dealt the highest-ranking face-up card must make a bet (if there is a tie for highest-ranking face-up card, the player who first received his card must bet first). After the high-card bets, the betting interval continues until the bets are equalized. A player may drop out at any time, as in any other form of Poker.

The dealer picks up the remainder of the pack and gives each active player another face-up card, and there is another betting interval, commencing again with the player who has the highest poker combination showing. A pair, of course, outranks any combination that does not include a pair; and of two pairs, the higher one outranks the other. If there is no pair, the high card showing determines precedence, and if there is a tie for high card, the second card controls the order, with final determination left to proximity in rotation to the dealer, as in the case of the first card. However, checking is allowed after the first round, and there need be no betting if all active players check.

In the same manner, a third round of face-up cards is dealt to each active player, there is a betting interval, and a final round of face-up cards is dealt to each active player, so that eventually each player has five cards. After a final betting interval, each player who has not dropped turns up his hole card for the showdown.

A player who drops must "fold his hand" by turning down all his face-up cards. It is poor etiquette for a player who drops to reveal his hole card.

Seven-Card Stud

Each player receives two cards face down and one card face up, and there is a betting interval. On each subsequent round of dealing, each active player receives a face-up card until he has four face-up cards (and, of course, two face-down cards) with a betting interval following the dealing of each face-up card all around. Finally a third face-down card is dealt to each player, there is a final betting interval, and each player who has at least called the final bet turns his three hole cards face up, selects any five of his cards to be a poker hand, and there is a showdown.

This game is often called Down-the-River, Seven-Toed Pete, and by other names.

Six-Card Stud Poker (which is identical with Five-Card Stud Poker except that after the fourth face-up card and the fourth betting interval each player receives a second face-down card, followed by a final betting interval), and Eight-Card Stud Poker (which is the same as Seven-Card Stud except that after the seventh card is dealt and there is a betting interval, an eighth card is dealt face down to each active player and there is a final betting interval), are also played, but not so often. In each case, the player selects five of his cards to represent his poker hand in the showdown.

OPTIONAL HAND. A *four-flush* is a hand with any four cards of the same suit. In Stud Poker, it is occasionally ruled that a four-flush beats a pair, though it loses to two pairs. In Draw Poker, it is often ruled that a player may open on a four-flush, but if he does not improve it, it is simply ranked as a hand with no pair.

High-Low Poker

Almost any form of Poker may be played "high-low." There is no difference in the original deal and betting, but in the showdown the highest-ranking poker hand and the lowest-ranking poker hand divide the pot equally. If it cannot be divided equally, the high hand receives any odd chip that is left over.

SEVEN-CARD HIGH-LOW STUD. A player may select any of his cards to compete for the high end of the pot and a different five cards to compete for the low end, and therefore may win both ways. Often *declarations* are played: After the final round of betting is finished but before the showdown, each player in turn must declare whether he is trying for high, for low, or for both. He may win only the part of the pot for which he declares. If a player declares for both high and low he must at least tie each way or he receives nothing.

Lowball

This is Draw Poker except that there are no minimum requirements for opening the pot and in the showdown the lowest-ranking poker hand, instead of the highest, wins the pot.

In Lowball, the ace ranks low only, never high. Straights and flushes do not count. The "bicycle"—5-4-3-2-A—is the lowest possible hand, whether it is composed all of one suit or of two or more suits. Since aces are low, a pair of aces ranks lower than a pair of deuces.

Very often Lowball is played in connection with regular Draw Poker. If a deal of Draw Poker is passed out, eldest hand picks up the turn again and Lowball is played. A player may check if he wishes, but if no one bets there is still a showdown after the dealer has spoken the second time, and the lowest-ranking hand takes the antes. This game is sometimes called JACKS BACK.

Dealer's Choice

Most Poker games played casually by friendly social groups are "Dealer's Choice" games, under the following rules:

1. Each dealer, as his turn comes, may state the game which will be played—Draw Poker, Stud Poker, or any form of either game.

2. If any card is to be wild, the dealer may designate that card or cards.

3. The next dealer in turn is not bound by the previous dealer's choice. If a selected game is one which may be passed out, in the case of a passed-out hand the same dealer deals again.

4. A dealer is not limited to the most common forms of Poker, those that have previously been described in these pages. He may select any of the games described in the following pages, or any game of his invention or knowledge which is simple enough to be described and understandable to the other players without too great loss of time.

Spit in the Ocean

Each player antes. After each player has received four face-down cards, as in Draw Poker, the dealer places one card from the top of the pack face up in the center of the table. This card is wild, and all other cards of the same rank are wild. Each player may use this card as part of his hand. There is a betting interval, followed by a showdown.

VARIATION 1. Instead of one card, the dealer places three cards face up in the center, and each player may select any one of these cards to be the fifth card in his hand and to be wild, together with every other card of the same rank in his hand.

VARIATION 2. The dealer places only one card in the center, but after the betting interval each player turns up any one card from his hand and there is another betting interval; then a second card and a betting interval; and so on, until when each player turns up his last face-down card there is a showdown.

Shotgun

The deal and draw are as in Draw Poker, except as follows: After each player has received three cards, the deal is suspended for a betting interval. Each player receives another face-down card, and there is another betting interval. Each player receives a fifth face-down card, and there is another betting interval. Then there is a draw, as in Draw Poker, followed by a final betting interval. At the end of the final betting interval, the players still in the pot show their hands.

Mexican Stud

There is no difference between this game and Five-Card Stud Poker (page 95) except that all cards are dealt face down. After each card is dealt, each player may turn up one of his cards and leave any card he pleases face down as his hole card.

High-Low Stud Poker

Five-Card Stud Poker is played with the high and low hands splitting the pot at the end. Before the last card is dealt to each player he may turn up his hole card and receive his last card face down.

Baseball

Seven-Card Stud is played, with all ninespots wild and with any three in the hole wild, and with these special rules:

1. The first player who is dealt a threespot face up must decide either to drop out of the pot, or to "buy the pot" (pay a forfeit to the pot equivalent to the number of chips already in the pot) and stay in. If he does buy the pot, from that time onward all threes are wild whether in the hole or not.

2. If a player is dealt a four, face up, he may either keep it or discard it and have it replaced by another card. A four dealt face down has no special significance.

In either case, a player must make his decision (and make the required contribution, if any, to the pot) before another card is dealt. A card dealt in the meantime is dead.

Cincinnati

After giving each player five cards as in Draw Poker, the dealer places five cards face down in the center of the table. There is a betting interval as in Draw Poker.

The dealer then turns up one of the center cards, and there is another betting intervals; then the second, third, fourth and fifth of these cards, with a betting interval after each.

After the last betting interval there is a showdown in which each player selects any five cards from among the cards dealt to him and the cards on the table to be his poker hand.

Criss-Cross

This game is no different from Cincinnati except that the center cards are laid out in the shape of a cross. The card in the center of the cross is turned up last. This card is wild, and so is any other card of the same rank. Each player must select his poker hand from among his own five cards plus either row of three cards in the cross.

Three-Card Poker

Each player receives three cards, all dealt face down, but the deal is interrupted after each round for a betting interval. After the dealing of the third card and the third betting interval, there is a showdown in which three of a kind is the highest hand; then come a three-card straight flush; a three-card flush; a three-card straight; a pair; and high card as among three otherwise unmatched cards.

This game is also played high-low, with the ace ranking high in a high hand and low in a low hand. Usually declarations are required (see page 97).

Two-Card Poker

Each player receives two cards, face down. There is one betting interval and a showdown. Straights and flushes do not count, a pair being the highest hand and high cards determining the rank as among hands with no pair.

This game is usually played with wild cards, either deuces or "one-eyes" (the jacks of spades and hearts, and the king of diamonds). It is often played high-low, with the ace ranking high in the high hand and low in the low hand. Usually declarations are required (see page 97).

Butcher Boy

All cards are dealt face up. When any player receives a card which is of the same rank as a card previously dealt, it is transferred to the hand of the player who received the card of that rank previously. There is a betting interval, with the player to whom the card was transferred having the first right to bet. When the betting interval is ended, the deal continues, the first card going to the player who would have received the last card.

Butcher Boy is usually played with high and low splitting the pot. There is no decision until any player has four of a kind, whereupon he takes half the pot. The other half goes to the low hand. Since not all players have exactly five cards, low hand is determined as follows: A player with more than five cards may select any five to be his low hand. A player with fewer than five cards is deemed to have the lowest card in the pack to make up each gap; for example, a three-card hand 8-5-4 is treated as 8-5-4-double 2 (not a pair of deuces) and beats a natural 8-5-4-3-2 for low.

Put and Take

This is often played in Dealer's Choice Poker games, though some bar it because the dealer has a great advantage.

Each player antes one chip. The first dealer is selected by lot, and thereafter the deal rotates. The dealer takes no cards, but gives each player except himself five face-up cards, dealt one at a time.

The dealer then turns up five "put" cards, one at a time. As each card is turned up, any player whose hand contains a card of the same rank must put into the pot a certain number of chips: one chip if it is the first card turned up, two if it is the second, four if it is the third, eight if it is the fourth, and sixteen if it is the fifth. A player having two or more cards of the rank in his hand must put up for each.

The dealer then turns up five "take" cards, and for each card a player having a card of the same rank in his hand takes from the pot one chip on the first card, two on the second, four on the third, eight on the fourth, and sixteen on the fifth. Again, if he has two or more cards of the same rank in his hand, he takes the full number of chips for each.

If there are any chips left in the pot, the dealer takes them. If the pot does not have enough chips to supply what the players are entitled to take, the dealer must make good. The dealer has an advantage because of the original antes.

Red and Black

In betting and settlement, Red and Black is the same as High-Low Poker; but it is not the rank of poker hands which decides the result. All red cards have a "plus" value, and all black cards a "minus" value. Aces count 1 each, face cards 10 each, other cards as many points as the numbers showing on their faces. If a player has ♡ K Q ◇ 7 ♠ 9 ♣ 4 he is "plus 14," because he has 27 points in plus cards and 13 points in minus cards.

There is a deal of five cards and a betting interval as in Draw Poker; then a draw and another betting interval, followed by a showdown in which the highest hand and the lowest hand divide the pot. Theoretically, of course, the "highest" hand can be the lowest minus, or the "lowest" hand can be the smallest plus.

IRREGULARITIES IN POKER

SHUFFLE, CUT. Any player may shuffle, but the dealer has the right to do so last. The cards must be shuffled at least three times. The dealer must offer the cards to the player at his right and that player must cut them. No fewer than five nor more than forty-seven cards may be lifted off the pack in cutting.

NEW DEAL. Any player who has not intentionally looked at the face of his first card and who has not received his second card may call for a new deal if the rules of the shuffle and cut were not fully observed. It is a misdeal, the dealer loses his deal and the next player in turn deals, if, at any time before the pot is gathered in, the pack is proved to be incorrect (to have the wrong number of cards, or a duplication of cards); or if more than one card is improperly exposed in dealing and if the misdeal is demanded by a player who receives such an improperly exposed card and who has not intentionally looked at the face of any other card dealt to him; or if more than two players receive an incorrect number of cards.

INCORRECT HAND. If two players have incorrect hands, one having a card too many and another having a card too few, the dealer may correct it by drawing from the hand with too many cards and giving the excess to the hand with too few. If only one player has an incorrect number of cards, and announces the fact before he looks at any of them, the dealer must correct his hand by drawing the excess from a hand with too many cards and restoring it to the top of the pack; or by supplying a short hand with a card or cards from the top of the pack.

However, a player who has too many cards and has intentionally looked at any of them has a dead hand and must drop out. The player who has too few cards and has intentionally looked at any of them may play on, but must play throughout with a short hand and cannot make a straight, flush, or straight flush.

CARD EXPOSED IN DEALING. Cards exposed prior to the betting interval are dealt with under the paragraph "New Deal" above.

In Draw Poker, if a card is exposed in the draw, the player due to receive it must take the first such card but may not take any subsequent exposed card. Such cards exposed in the draw are placed with the discards. The draw is continued until all other players are satisfied. The player whose cards were exposed may then receive cards from the top of the pack to satisfy his requirements; or may require that the remainder of the pack, together with all discards except his own (and the discards of the opener, if they have been kept separate) be shuffled by the dealer, and cut by him, before the remainder of his draw is dealt to him.

In Stud Poker, if the dealer prematurely exposes a card to be dealt for the next round of dealing, that card is placed with the discards. Other players may receive the cards they would have received if no irregularity had occurred, provided this is possible. The players who would have received the cards exposed then receive their cards from the top of the pack.

PLAYER DEALT OUT. If the dealer omits a player in dealing, he must give his own hand to that player. If he omits more than one player in dealing, his own hand (if any) goes to the player omitted nearest his left, and no other player has any recourse.

If the dealer improperly gives a player a card face up instead of face down, that player has no immediate recourse but the dealer must give him his next card face down. This remedy may continue without penalty on the part of the dealer, unless it is repeated until and including the player's fourth face-up card. At that point the player may, if he wishes, withdraw from the pot all chips he has put in and the dealer must pay a penalty to the pot equivalent to the number of chips withdrawn. If the player chooses to play with all his cards face up, and to withdraw no chips from the pot, the dealer is not subject to penalty.

BET OUT OF TURN. No chips once placed in the pot may be removed from the pot except as provided in the preceding paragraph. If a player bets out of turn, his bet is void, his chips remain in the pot, and the player in proper turn may act. When the offender's turn comes, he may use the chips he put in to call the preceding bet, if they are sufficient to that purpose; and he may add to them sufficient chips to call the preceding bet, if necessary; but he may not raise.

even if his out-of-turn contribution to the pot was more than is required to call.

DROPPING OUT OF TURN. A player may drop without waiting for his turn if there is only one other player in the pot. If there is any other player in the pot, and he drops out of turn, when his turn comes he must call any bet made by any player before him, but his hand is dead and cannot win the pot.

INCORRECT NUMBER OF CARDS. If a player has too many or too few cards and the error is not corrected as provided above: a player with too few cards may compete for the pot, but cannot make a straight, flush or straight flush; a hand with too many cards is dead and cannot win the pot.

INCORRECT ANNOUNCEMENT. A player who announces a bet and does not put in enough chips to conform to the announcement must on demand supply enough chips to call, if so many chips were not previously put into the pot; and may not raise, and if he put into the pot enough chips to raise but not enough to conform to his announcement he is deemed to have called and any additional chips are forfeited.

INCORRECT DRAW. A player who is given by dealer the wrong number of cards (any number of cards not conforming to his discards) and who looks at any of them cannot have his draw corrected. If the result gives him too few cards, he may play on. If the result gives him too many cards, his hand is dead. If he has not looked at any of the cards, he may demand a correction by the dealer.

DRAW OUT OF TURN. A player may not draw if he has permitted a player to his left to draw out of turn. He may stand pat on the cards originally dealt to him, unless he has discarded. If he has discarded, his hand is dead.

ERROR IN OPENING. The opener is permitted to split his openers (for example, to discard a queen from Q-Q-J-10-9 and draw one card to a straight) without announcing the fact. He may place his discard in the pot so that it cannot be shuffled up with other discards and so that he can reclaim it to prove that he had openers.

If the opener cannot prove to the satisfaction of other players that he held openers, his hand is dead and cannot win the pot. Any chips he has placed in the pot are forfeited. If no one has called his bet, the antes plus his opening bet remain in the pot for the next deal. If his bet has been called, his own hand is dead but play continues.

The opener's hand is dead if he has more than five cards, and the penalty is the same as though he lacked openers. If no one calls his bet, he need show only enough cards face up to prove he had openers, and the remainder of his hand face down to prove that he had no more than five cards.

ETHICS AND ETIQUETTE

Each group of Poker players is likely to set its own standards of ethical behavior, and a stranger in the game is well advised to learn what these standards are, so he will not be thought unsporting.

Old-fashioned Poker players feel that so long as a player does not actually cheat, he should not be bound by any code of ethics. Most players feel, however, that there is a limit beyond which one should not venture in misrepresenting his hand.

One may misrepresent his hand in a bantering way, as by saying, "Go ahead and call me; you know I'm always bluffing," or words to that effect, when in fact he has a good hand.

It is not unethical to bet on a sure thing, nor is it unethical to check with a strong hand, intending to raise if anyone else bets.

One should not intentionally break the rules of the game, even when willing to pay the penalty.

Partnerships are contrary to the spirit of the game, and even when husband and wife are in the same game they should treat each other as opponents in the play.

It is not unethical to draw one card to four of a kind, even though the draw cannot improve the hand. (And if a player is lucky enough to hold four of a kind, what does he care what the ethics are?)

STRATEGY OF POKER

To become a good player, one must:

1. Learn the poker hands thoroughly.
2. Learn the relative values of the hands—what sort of hand may be expected to win the pot.

3. Learn how many cards it is best to draw to the various poker combinations.

4. Learn the odds against winning with any particular hand, and how to figure the odds offered "by the pot."

5. Observe the other players in the game, to learn their habits and to read their probable strength or weakness from their actions and mannerisms; and at the same time avoid giveaway mannerisms of one's own.

The relative values of the hands depends on how many players are in the game (or how many are in the pot, for if there are seven players in the game but two have dropped, the circumstances are precisely the same as if there were five in the game and none had dropped). The value of the hand depends also upon what betting there has been: A pair of aces may be an excellent holding when all the other players have checked, but is not worth much if two or three players have already raised, for their raises advertise their holding of strong hands.

In general, one should appraise his hand as follows in a seven-player game:

When one is dealt a straight or any better hand, he will almost always win the pot and it will pay him to bet or raise even if two other players have previously raised.

When one is dealt three of a kind, he will usually win the pot, and he should raise even if another player has previously raised; but he should only call if two players have previously raised.

When one is dealt two pairs, it is about 2 to 1 that he has the best hand before the draw; but at the same time it is 11 to 1 that he will not improve his hand in the draw. Especially if the higher of his two pairs is anything less than queens, he is in danger of losing the pot to another player who will draw three cards to a pair, and improve. For this reason, it is wise for a player with two pairs to raise immediately. The raise usually drives out some players who might otherwise stay and improve their hands.

When one is dealt a pair of aces, it is odds-on that no other player has as good a hand. A player holding aces or any better hand should open the pot in any position and should stay in even if the pot has been raised.

A pair of kings has an even chance of being the best hand when only five or six players remain; a pair of queens, when only four players remain. Holding one of these hands, one should open the pot against the stated number of players but should usually drop if the pot is raised. The last three players at the table, after the first four have checked, may safely open the pot on a pair of jacks.

When another player has opened the pot, it must be remembered that he has at least jacks and probably has an even better hand. It is seldom wise to stay in without a pair of queens or better, except (a) when four or five players have stayed in and there is no danger that anyone will raise; or (b) when you have a straight or flush possibility and the pot is large enough to warrant drawing to it.

A four-flush offers nine chances in forty-seven to make a flush. This means that the odds are more than 4 to 1 against you when you draw one card to a four-flush. If there is at least four times as much money in the pot as you have to put in, such a hand is worth playing. If there is anything less in the pot, the hand should be dropped. Likewise with a double-ended straight (any four cards in sequence, except A-K-Q-J or 4-3-2-A): The odds are 5 to 1 against filling it, and the pot must offer at least that much to make playing worth while. A combination such as A-K-Q-J, 4-3-2-A, or 7-6-4-3 ("inside" straight) is almost never worth playing; the odds are 11 to 1 against filling it.

DRAW POKER. When drawing to a pair, discard three cards and hold only the pair. To keep an ace or other high card as a "kicker" seriously decreases the chances of improving. For example, holding

it would be unwise to hold the two nines and the ace and draw only two cards. This maneuver has little value as a bluff—it is unlikely to make anyone think you hold three of a kind, unless you follow through on the bluff all the way by raising heavily before the draw and betting after the draw, and this is a losing game in the long run.

Likewise, when you hold three of a kind it is best in most cases to throw away both the odd cards and draw two. The only exception is when you have raised before the draw and it seems that another player has two high pairs. If you draw two cards, he may refuse to call a bet. If you hold either of your odd cards and draw only one, he may call.

A player who has opened with a hand like this:

or with a pair and a four-flush, like this:

is often tempted to "split his openers" and draw one card to his straight or flush possibility. However, unless there is enough in the pot to offer 4-to-1 or 5-to-1 odds respectively, it is usually better to draw to the pair. The only exception is when the opener has a four-card straight flush possibility, in which case it is advantageous to split the openers and draw one card. The odds are only 2 to 1 against improving if the straight flush is open at both ends, and 3 to 1 if it is open at only one end.

STUD POKER. Since there is no draw to the original five cards, the average winning hand is lower than in Draw Poker. The player decides on his action after seeing all but one card in every other hand, and is in a better position to judge whether or not to play, or to raise.

Usually a player should drop out when his cards, including his hole card, are beaten by the showing cards of any other player. If another player shows a pair, one should not stay in without a higher pair.

With a concealed pair (a pair which includes the hole card) raise immediately. With an open pair, bet the limit immediately. (In both cases, assuming that no other player shows a higher pair.)

It is seldom wise to bet against a player whose hole card may give him a hand you cannot possibly beat.

DEUCES WILD. This is a much maligned game. Most people think of "deuces wild" as the afternoon diversion of silly women who do not even know the rank of the poker hands. Actually, Deuces Wild is at least as scientific a game as regular Draw Poker.

The considerations in the two games are about the same except that two pairs are almost valueless in Deuces Wild. A straight will win more often than not, but is not worth more than one raise.

It is usually advisable to open on any hand containing a deuce; one should also open on a pair of aces. Two low pairs should be opened only by the last two players in turn, after all others have checked; they should be thrown away or split if any other player opens. A sequence of three cards plus a deuce should be played even if the pot is small at the time.

Do not raise before the draw with less than three aces (including at least one deuce), or a pair of deuces.

If your hand contains two deuces, draw three cards to them unless you also have an ace, in which case hold the ace.

FREQUENCY OF POKER HANDS

	52-CARD PACK (*Nothing Wild*)	53-CARD PACK (*With Joker*)	52-CARD PACK (*Deuces Wild*)
HAND			
Five of a kind	0	13	672
Royal flush	4	24	484
Straight flush	36	180	4,072
Four of a kind	624	3,120	30,816
Full house	3,744	6,552	12,672
Flush	5,108	7,804	13,204
Straight	10,200	20,532	66,236
Three of a kind	54,912	137,280	355,056
Two pairs	123,552	123,552	95,040
One pair	1,098,240	1,268,088	1,222,048
No pair	1,302,540	1,302,540	798,660
Total combinations	2,598,960	2,869,685	2,598,960

NOTE: These are the chances of being dealt such combinations in the original five cards. The exact odds against a particular hand are determined by deducting the number of combinations from the total combinations, then dividing the larger number by the smaller. For example, the odds against being dealt three of a kind with a 52-card pack, nothing wild, are 2,598,960 minus 54,912, or 2,544,048, divided by 54,912, or about 46 to 1.

RED DOG

This is a favorite game for social groups who want a betting game in which the action is fast and the demands on brainwork not too great. Though classed as a gambling game, Red Dog is seldom played for high stakes. It is called also HIGH-CARD POOL.

PLAYERS. Two to ten.

CARDS. A regular pack of 52, ranking A (high), K, Q, J, 10, 9, 8, 7, 6, 5, 4, 3, 2. Poker chips or similar counters are used.

THE DEAL. Five cards are dealt to each player, one at a time, face down. First dealer may be decided in any way and the deal rotates. If more than eight play, each receives only four cards.

THE PLAY. At the start, each player antes one or any other agreed number of chips to form a pool. The object of the game is to beat the top card of the pack (cards remaining undealt) by having a higher-ranking card of the same suit. All bets are made against the pool.

Eldest hand has the first turn. He may bet from one chip up to the number of chips in the pot at the time (the latter is called "betting the pot"). After he has named his bet and put the proper number of chips in front of him, the dealer turns up the top card of the pack. If the player can show a higher-ranking card of the same suit, he does so and takes back his bet together with the same number of chips from the pot. If the player cannot beat the top of the pack, the chips he bet are added to the pot and he shows his entire hand face up. He then discards his hand, face down, and the turn to bet passes to the player at his left.

A player may pay a forfeit of one chip to the pool instead of betting. Then he discards his hand without showing it.

When there are no more chips in the pot at any time, each player antes again and the game continues. The pot can never have too little to pay off a bet, for the maximum bet is the size of the pot.

IRREGULARITIES IN RED DOG

A hand with too many cards is dead, but a hand with too few cards may be played. However, the holder of a short hand may discard it without either betting or paying a forfeit.

There is no misdeal.

When, at any time after the deal is completed, the top card of the pack is found to be exposed, it is discarded and the game continues.

A bet paid to the pot in error cannot be corrected. A bet collected from the pot in error may not be corrected after the next player in turn has bet and a card has been turned from the pack for him.

STRATEGY OF RED DOG

Intelligent betting is simply a matter of counting cards to discover whether the chance of winning is better than the chance of losing.

If you are the first bettor, there are forty-seven cards whose location you do not know. The top card of the pack is equally likely to be any one of them. Suppose you hold:

There are three hearts, seven diamonds and thirteen clubs that you cannot beat. This makes twenty-three cards out of forty-seven, leaving twenty-four cards that you can beat. The odds are 24 to 23 in your favor—practically an even bet.

If you were the second bettor and the first bettor had bet and lost, holding ♠ 10 ♡ Q ♣ J 8 2, and the ◇ 9 was turned up from the pack, you could eliminate five of the cards that originally you counted as losers—the ♡ Q, ◇ 9 and three clubs. Now there are forty-one unknown cards, of which there are only eighteen you cannot beat (two hearts, six diamonds, ten clubs). The odds are 23 to 18 in your favor.

RUMMY

At some time *after 1850 a Spanish game,* Conquian, *crossed the Mexican border into the southwestern United States and became* Coon-Can. *This game combined two ideas: scoring by melding, and scoring by "going out" (getting rid of all cards in the hand). American players began to develop the crude* Coon-Can *in two directions, both of which were called* Rum *or* Rummy. *One direction was to emphasize going out, leading to (basic) Rummy, Knock Rummy, Gin Rummy, etc. The other direction was to emphasize melding, leading to Five Hundred Rum, Canasta, Samba, etc. Until about 1910, Rummy was a "minor" game. Then its growth become phenomenal. By 1935, as indicated by a survey, more persons knew the rules of Rummy than of any other card game. One member of each line of development enjoyed a nationwide boom as a "fad game"—Gin Rummy after 1940, and Canasta after 1949. The original game survives in* Panguingue.

Players. From two to six, each playing for himself.

Cards. A regular pack of 52. In each suit the cards rank: K (high), Q, J, 10, 9, 8, 7, 6, 5, 4, 3, 2, A (low).

The Deal. Cards are distributed one at a time to the left (clockwise), beginning with the opponent at left of the dealer. Each player receives: with two players, ten cards;

with three or four players, seven cards; with five or six players, six cards.

STOCK AND DISCARD PILE. The undealt remainder of the pack is placed face down in the center of the table, forming the *stock*. Its top card is turned face up and placed beside it; this *upcard* is the beginning of the *discard pile*. (The term "upcard" is also applied to the top of the discard pile, after the pile has grown to two or more cards.)

MATCHED SETS. The object of play is to form the hand into sets (also called melds, spreads, etc.). There are two kinds of sets:

(a) *Groups.* Three or more cards of the same rank, as ♠ 9 ♡ 9 ♣ 9.

(b) *Sequences.* Three or more cards of the same suit, in sequence of rank, as ♢ Q ♢ J ♢ 10. In basic Rummy, an ace may not be ranked above the king to make a sequence such as A-K-Q or 2-A-K.

THE PLAY. Opponent at left of the dealer plays first, and the turn to play passes continuously to the left (clockwise). In his turn, each player must adhere to the following order:

(a) *Draw.* He must begin by drawing one card: the top of the stock or of the discard pile.

(b) *Meld.* He may then, if he pleases, place any number of cards from his hand face up on the table, provided that they form proper matched sets or proper additions to sets already on the table (*laying off*).

(c) *Discard.* He must end his turn by placing one card from his hand face up on the discard pile, except that he need not discard if he has melded all his remaining cards.

LAYING OFF. A player may *lay off* cards from his hand on melded sets—the fourth card of the same rank on a group, or additional cards in suit and sequence on a sequence. He may lay off on sets melded by his opponents, as well as on his own melds.

GOING OUT. When any player melds all cards remaining in his hand, he thereby *goes out* and wins the deal. Play ceases and the deal is scored. If no player goes out by the time the stock is exhausted, the discard pile is turned face down (without shuffling) to form a new stock, and play continues.

SCORING. When a player goes out, each other player pays the winner for the points left in his own hand, counting each ace 1, each face card 10, each other card its index value. (All cards are paid for, even those in matched but unmelded sets.)

A player is said to *go rummy* if he melds his entire hand in one turn, having made no previous meld. In such case, the losers must pay him double.

IRREGULARITIES IN RUMMY

NEW DEAL. There must be a new deal by the same dealer if a card is exposed in dealing, or if a card is found faced in the stock during the deal, or if the dealer gives any hand the wrong number of cards.

INCORRECT HAND. If, after play has begun, a player is found to have an incorrect hand, he must rectify it in course of play: by omitting one or more successive draws, if he has too many cards, or by omitting one or more successive discards, if he has too few. In any turn when he begins with an incorrect hand, he may not meld.

DRAWING TWO CARDS. If a player inadvertently draws two cards from the stock and sees both, he must keep the correct top card; the other is placed face up on the stock. The next player in turn may draw the faced card; if he draws from the discard pile instead, the faced card is then buried face down in the middle of the stock.

PLAY OUT OF TURN. If a player draws out of turn and discards before the error is noted, it stands as a proper turn and the opponent at his left plays next.

If a player draws from the stock out of turn and the error is noticed before he discards, he must keep the drawn card; the turn reverts to the proper player; the offender then begins his next proper turn without drawing.

If a player draws from the discard pile out of turn and the error is noted before he discards, he must replace the card.

If a player melds after drawing out of turn and the error is noted in time, he must retract the melded cards.

DISCARDING TWO CARDS. If a player discards two cards, and the error is noted before the next player has ended his turn, the offender must retract one of the cards. (He may choose, unless the next player has drawn one of the two.) If the error is first noticed at a later time, the offender must rectify his hand as under Incorrect Hand above.

INCORRECT MELD. If a player lays down cards that do not in fact form a proper set or proper additions to a melded set, he must retract all the incorrect cards on demand, if made before the cards have been gathered for the next shuffle.

Contract Rummy

This game is also called LIVERPOOL RUMMY, KING RUMMY, or ZIONCHECK. As in basic Rummy, the sole object is to form matched sets, but these must conform to a rigid schedule. Another popular game on the same principles is Continental Rummy, described later.

PLAYERS. Best for five to eight.

CARDS. Three regular packs of 52 shuffled together, plus two jokers, making 158 cards in all. (Fewer than five players should use only two packs plus two jokers.) The cards rank as in Rummy, except that the ace may be high in the sequence A-K-Q or low in the sequence 3-2-A.

THE DEAL. A game comprises seven deals. In each of the first four, each player receives ten cards. In each of Deals 5, 6, 7, each player receives twelve cards. As in Rummy, the rest of the pack becomes the *stock* and an *upcard* is turned beside it.

THE CONTRACT. Matched sets, groups and sequences, are the same as in Rummy (page 114), but a player's first meld must satisfy the contract. The list of contracts varies in different localities; the following is the one most generally adopted:

Deal 1: two groups
Deal 2: one group and one sequence
Deal 3: two sequences
Deal 4: three groups
Deal 5: two groups and one sequence
Deal 6: one group and two sequences
Deal 7: three sequences, with a complete hand

THE PLAY. The play follows the rules of Rummy, with the following differences.

If the in-turn player does not wish to draw the discard, he must so state; then another player may take it. If two or more wish it, it goes to the one nearest the left of the in-turn player. A player who thus obtains the discard out of turn must also draw the top card of the stock, but does not discard, since his play does not constitute a turn. After the discard is taken (or refused by all) the in-turn player draws from the stock and proceeds with his turn.

A player's first meld must be the precise melds called for by the contract. Further, until Deal 7 each meld of the contract must be three cards only, no more. At his next and all subsequent turns after melding the contract, the player may lay off on any melds, his own and other players'; he may not meld any new sets of his own. For Deal 7, the entire hand must be formed into only three sequences, at least one of which must therefore include more than three cards.

The jokers are wild. A joker may be melded as part of a set, the owner stating its intended rank and suit. Any other player having a natural card of this rank and suit may later, in turn (and provided that he himself has melded the contract), trade it for the joker. A joker thus received may be laid off anywhere in the same turn.

GOING OUT. When any player gets rid of all cards in his hand, play ends. If none goes out by the time the stock is exhausted, the discard pile is shuffled and turned face down to form a new stock.

SCORING. At the end of play, each player counts the total value of cards in his hand, and that amount is charged against him on the score sheet. Each ace or joker counts 15, each face card 10, each other card its index value. At the end of the game, seven deals, the player having the lowest accumulated score is the winner. (In some circles, the hand going out receives a bonus and there are elaborate provisions for special contingencies such as melding no wild card, going out without a draw, etc.)

Continental Rummy

This was at one time the most popular form of Rummy in women's afternoon games, until in 1950 it lost out to Canasta. It is akin to Contract Rummy in requiring that certain combinations be melded but each deal, not a series of deals, is a game.

PLAYERS. Any number up to twelve; usually five to eight.

CARDS. Two or more regular 52-card packs plus one joker per pack: for six to eight players three packs, for nine to twelve players four packs. The cards rank as in Contract Rummy, with ace high or low. All deuces as well as all jokers are wild.

THE DEAL. Each player is dealt fifteen cards, three at a time. The next card is turned up to found the discard pile, and the undealt cards are the stock, as in other Rummy games.

MELDING REQUIREMENTS. Only sequences count. To go out, a player must meld his entire hand and it must be one of the following combinations:

Five three-card sequences; or
Three four-card and one three-card sequences; or
One five-, one four-, and two three-card sequences.

THE PLAY. In each turn a player may take the top discard or top card of the stock and must then discard one card. There is no melding until a player can go out.

SCORING. The player who goes out collects from each other player: 1 for going out; 1 for each deuce and 2 for each joker he melds; 10 if he uses no deuce or joker; 7 for going out on first turn; 10 for going out on a first turn without drawing; 10 for having all fifteen cards in one suit. In appropriate cases a player may collect for two or more of these.

IRREGULARITIES. A player who claims to go out when he cannot legally do so must expose his whole hand and leave it exposed until he or some other player goes out.

STRATEGY. Draw and pray. Taking of previous discards by the left-hand opponent may yield clues as to cards it is unsafe to throw to him, and draws from the discard pile by other players may be a guide to the best two-card possibilities to hold, but usually one must sacrifice safety in discarding to the primary object of completing his own hand.

Knock Rummy

This form of Rummy introduced a new principle: Matched sets do not count against a player whether he has melded them or still has them in his hand. Knock Rummy was very popular in its time, but it grew into Gin Rummy, which has almost entirely replaced it. The rules of basic Rummy (page 104) are followed except as follows:

There is no melding. The object is to reduce *deadwood* (unmatched cards), but matched sets are kept in the hand, not laid on the table.

A player may *knock* in any turn; to knock is to declare the play ended, and it is usually signaled by an actual knock on the table. All players then expose their hands, arranged in matched sets with deadwood segregated. If the knocker has the lowest count of deadwood, he collects the difference in count of unmatched cards from each other player. If any other player ties the knocker, he collects as the winner. If any other player has a lower count, he supplants the knocker as winner, and the knocker must pay him 10 extra for *undercut*. If more than one player undercuts the knocker, each collects the extra 10 from him; lowest count collects from the others, or tying players divide the winnings (each loser paying only singly to the low count).

If the knocker lays down a rummy hand (no deadwood), he collects an extra 25 from each other player, even from a player who also has a rummy hand. (This bonus cannot be collected by a player who wins by undercut.)

It is usual to rank the ace only as low, in sequence with the two but not with the king. In some circles, other players are permitted to lay off on the knocker's matched sets (but not on each other's).

Five Hundred Rum

Five Hundred Rum was one of the earliest Rummy games to give scoring values to the melds. It is sometimes called MICHIGAN RUM or PINOCHLE RUMMY.

PLAYERS. From two to eight, each playing for himself. Four sometimes play a partnership game.

CARDS. A regular pack of 52 when four or fewer play; two packs shuffled together, with five or more. The cards rank as in Rummy, but with ace either high in A-K-Q or low in 3-2-A.

THE DEAL. In two-hand, each player receives thirteen cards. With three or more, each player receives seven cards. The cards are dealt one at a time. As in Rummy, the rest of the pack becomes the *stock* and an *upcard* is turned face up beside it.

THE PLAY. The rules of play (plus the additional rule below) are as in Rummy, and the same object is in view—to form the hand into matched sets, groups, or sequences. The sets are melded as in Rummy.

A player in turn may draw the top of the stock or the top of the discard pile; but he has a third option: he may take a batch of two or more cards from the top of the discard pile (even the whole pile), provided that he melds the bottom card of the batch. He may meld this card by laying it off on a prior meld, or by combining it with cards from his hand in a new set, or even by combining it with cards wholly from the batch taken, in a new set.

As in Rummy, a player may lay off additional cards on any melded sets—opponents' as well as his own. But he should keep such laid-off cards in front of himself, so as to score them for himself. When a card could be laid off on either of two sets (a group and a sequence), he must state his choice, since this may affect the places open for future layoffs.

Play ends when any player gets rid of the last card in his hand. (The player going out need not make a final discard; he may meld all his remaining cards.) If none has gone out by the time the stock is exhausted, play continues so long as each successive player draws from the discard, but ends as soon as one player cannot or will not draw.

SCORING. The card values are as in Rummy except that an ace counts 1 only when melded in a low sequence, A-2-3. In all other circumstances, it counts 15.

At the end of play, each player totals the point values of his melded cards. From this amount he subtracts the total of cards left in his hand (including cards matched in sets), counting each ace 15. The difference, plus or minus, is entered in his column of the scoresheet, and a running total is kept of each player's score.

The player first to reach a total of plus 500 or more wins the game. Settlement is made on the differences of the final scores.

There is no bonus for going out and none for winning a game—all scores accumulate from melding alone.

IRREGULARITIES. The rules of Rummy apply, with one addition: If a player takes a batch from the discard pile and then finds he cannot meld the bottom card, he must return all the cards and draw from the stock. The discard pile (if the cards have become mixed) is reconstructed by majority opinion of the players.

This rule is superfluous if the customs of the game are followed. By custom, a player taking a batch first detaches it from the pile, without mixing the order, and leaves it on the table for inspection. The other players are entitled to "a good look." The player picks out the bottom card and melds it, before adding the rest of the batch to his hand.

STRATEGY OF FIVE HUNDRED RUM

At the beginning, the prime object is to acquire as many additional cards as possible. In early discarding a common stratagem is to "salt" the discard pile by cards from combinations or even matched sets, to pave the way for capturing a batch of subsequent discards. Much judgment goes into the question of how long to wait before making the capture—another player may "dig in" first.

In early play, do not meld any more than you must in order to capture from the discard pile. Presently comes a time when there is danger that some other player may go out; you must then unload all you can. Since your melds may enable another player to unload or even go out, try to delay unloading to the last moment of safety. You can often avoid panic unloading by keeping track of discards taken by other players, among which will be odd or dead cards that must probably be discarded before the hand can possibly go out.

In early discarding, the natural tendency is to avoid adding a card to the pile that makes a pair or near-sequence with another already there. If the pile is large, your hand may have no safe discard. Then, usually, match a card near the top of the pile, rather than one far down. After general unloading has begun (when one player "cracks" the others usually unload too), the danger in discarding is much less, for the general aim is now to go out and a player will seldom dig deep for a new meld.

Persian Rummy

This game has, of course, no connection with Persia; the name was bestowed fancifully.

The game is a four-hand partnership elaboration of Five Hundred Rum, the rules of which apply with the following modifications.

One regular pack of 52 is used, plus four jokers. The jokers are not wild but form an additional rank that may be melded in groups like the other ranks, but never in sequences. The ace ranks only high, above the king. In point value, a joker is 20, an ace 15. A group of four of a kind, if melded all at once, is closed up face down and counts double.

Unmelded cards taken from the discard pile are not added to the player's hand but are left face up on the table for inspection. They still belong, of course, to the player who captured them.

A game comprises two deals. When a player goes out his side scores a bonus of 25. The side with the higher total for the two deals scores a bonus of 50. If no one goes out by the time the stock is exhausted, play *must* continue so long as each player in turn can legally draw from the discard pile.

The partnership feature affords considerable scope for skill in partnership co-operation. Devotees have devised elaborate systems of signals in discarding.

GIN RUMMY

Gin Rummy *was invented in* 1909 *by Elwood T. Baker of New York, as an improvement on Knock Rummy. He called it "gin" because the parent game was then called "rum," another alcoholic drink. Gin was very popular in the* 1920's, *lost favor for some years, and then about* 1940 *became a fad game among the movie colony in Hollywood, where it was first called Gin Rummy. It is now perhaps the most-played two-hand card game. An effort was made to have official laws for Gin Rummy, as for Bridge, but players did not accept the committee's proposed scoring, adopting instead the scoring given below.*

Players. Two. Three or four often participate in rotation, but only two play at a time.

Cards. A regular pack of 52. The cards rank as in Rummy, K high, A low only. Face cards count 10 each, aces 1 each, other cards their index numbers.

The Deal. Each player receives ten cards, dealt one at a time. As in Rummy, the rest of the pack becomes the *stock* and its top card is turned over as the *upcard.*

Players draw for first deal; the player drawing the higher card may deal first or require opponent to do so. Thereafter, the winner of each hand deals the next. The winner of a game deals first in the next game.

THE PLAY. Nondealer may begin play by taking the up-card. If he refuses it, dealer may take it. If both refuse the upcard, nondealer draws the top card of the stock. Play proceeds as in Rummy, and the object is the same—to form matched sets of three or more cards, groups or sequences. However, the sets are not melded—the player keeps all ten cards in his hand.

KNOCKING. Cards in hand that are not formed in matched sets are called *deadwood*. A player may legally *knock* whenever the total of his deadwood is 10 points or less. To knock is to end the play with a showdown. The player may knock after drawing in turn, but before dis-carding. Usually he raps on the table, but he may simply make the final discard face down. He then spreads his ten cards face up on the table, arranged in his intended matched sets and with the deadwood clearly segregated. His oppon-ent does the same.

LAYING OFF. Opponent of the knocker is entitled to lay off (add matching cards) what cards he can on the knock-er's sets, provided that the knocker has not laid down *a gin hand*—having no deadwood.

SCORING. If the knocker has a lower count of deadwood than his opponent, he scores the difference. The score is kept on paper. Each time a player wins a hand, the points won are added to his previous points won, the new total is written down, and a line is drawn under it. (See illustra-tion.)

Gin Bonus. If the knocker lays down a gin hand (count of zero) he scores all of opponent's deadwood (if any) plus a bonus of 25 points.

Undercut. If the opponent has an equal or lower count of deadwood, he scores the difference if any plus a bonus of 25 for *undercut*. However, a gin hand cannot be undercut, nor can the opponent win the bonus for gin—this can be scored only by the knocker.

Game Score. The player who first reaches a total of 100 or more wins a game and receives a bonus of 100. To each player's score is then added 25 points (called a *line* or *box* bonus) for each hand he won during the game.

Shutout. If the loser has not won a hand during a game, the winner scores a shutout (called also whitewash, schnei-der, skunk, etc.). The winner's score, including the game bonus of 100, is doubled. The line bonuses, however, are not doubled, unless the players agree in advance to double them.

DRAWN GAME. If only two cards remain in the stock and neither player has knocked, the game ends in a draw: The final discard may not be taken. The same dealer deals again.

ILLUSTRATION OF GIN RUMMY SCORING

First hand: YOU knock with 6. HE has 19. You score 13.

Second hand: HE goes gin—knocks with 0. You have 24. He scores the 24 + 25 points gin bonus, 49 in all.

Third hand: HE knocks with 8. You have 9. He scores 1, giving him a total of 50.

Fourth hand: YOU knock with 10. HE has 27. You win 17 and your new total is 30.

Fifth hand: HE knocks with 4. YOU also have 4. You score 25, the undercut bonus. Now your score is 55.

YOU	HE
13	49
30	50
55	
87	
118	
118	
75	
100	
293	
50	
243	

Sixth hand: YOU knock with 7. HE has 39. You win 32, and your new total is 87.

Seventh hand: YOU go gin. HE has 6, so you score 6 + 25, adding 31 to your score. This puts you over the 100 mark with a total of 118, and gives you game. You have five boxes, a total of 125 points at 25 each; he has two boxes, worth 50 to him; so you write down 75 more points for boxes. You add 100 for winning the game. Your grand total is 293; his is 50. So your winnings for the game are the difference in score, or 243 points net.

IRREGULARITIES IN GIN RUMMY

NEW DEAL. There must be a new deal by the same dealer if a card is found faced in the pack or is exposed in dealing, or if at any time both players are found to have an incorrect number of cards.

INCORRECT HAND. If (after play has begun) one player is found to have too few or too many cards, his opponent may require a new deal or may allow play to continue. In the latter case, the offender must correct his hand by discarding without drawing, or drawing without discarding, a sufficient number of times. He may not knock until the next turn after his hand has been corrected.

If the opponent is found to have an incorrect hand after a knock, he is charged 10 for each missing card, or all his cards (if more than ten) are counted; in either case, he cannot score for undercut. (If knocker's hand is incorrect, see *Illegal Knock* below.)

EXPOSED CARD. If in drawing a player sees any card to which he is not entitled, all such cards must be placed face up on the table. The offender may knock in his current turn only if he has a gin hand. Otherwise, play continues, and the nonoffender may in each succeeding turn take one of the exposed cards (or the top of the discard pile); after the first occasion when he draws from the stock instead, the right to draw from the exposed cards goes to the offender; and after the offender has first drawn from the stock instead, any remaining exposed cards are inserted at random in the stock.

A card found faced in the stock (after play has begun) must be shuffled back into the stock. There is no penalty against a player for exposing a card from his hand.

ILLEGAL KNOCK. If the knocker is found to have a deadwood count of more than 10, opponent may accept the knock, or may require the offender to play on with his whole hand exposed. If the knocker is found to have an incorrect number of cards, opponent may demand a new deal, or may require the offender to play on with his hand exposed and to correct it by drawing without discarding or discarding without drawing. If the knocker can make his claim good by rearranging his cards into different sets, he may do so.

LOOKING THROUGH DISCARD PILE. The players may agree in advance that looking through the discard pile will be permitted. In the absence of such agreement, the discard pile must be kept squared so that only the top card is readable; a player who spreads it and so sights a covered card loses his next turn, opponent then having two turns in succession.

STRATEGY OF GIN RUMMY

As a rule, to which justifiable exception is rare, draw from the discard pile only to complete or add to a set, not to form a *combination* (two cards that may become a set).

Usually aim to form two matched sets plus three or four (or fewer) unmatched low cards—time often prevents the formation of three sets. Therefore save low cards (aces, twos, and threes, sometimes fours) on general principle. In early discarding, as a matter of necessity, both players often unload face cards. A high pair in the original hand thus has a good chance to be filled; however, keen judgment is required as to how long to keep such a pair. After five or six turns, you must usually reduce your deadwood for safety.

Knock as soon as you can, except in rare cases when you have reason to fear undercut. There are few situations that justify trying for gin when you are able to knock.

Ultimate skill in the game lies in keeping track of the discards, not only to know which of your own combinations are fully "alive" but also to deduce what combinations your opponent is holding. For example, ♠ J - ♡ J lose half their value if a jack has been discarded; they gain value if ◇ 10 and ◇ Q or ◇ K have been discarded, for then the opponent can have no use for ◇ J and is likely to discard it if he draws it. An "interlocking" combination such as ♠ 9 ♡ 9 ♣ 8 ♣ 7 can be filled by only three cards; if it were ♠ 9 ♡ 9 ◇ 7 ♣ 7 or ♠ 9 ♡ 9 ◇ 7 ◇ 6 it could be filled by any of four cards.

Oklahoma Gin

This should not be confused with the game called Oklahoma, which is a Rummy game dissimilar to Gin Rummy.

In Oklahoma Gin, the first upcard determines the minimum count on which a player may knock. If it is a face card or ten, one may knock with 10 as usual; if it is a spotcard, one needs its number or less; if it is an ace, a gin hand is required. If the upcard is any spade, scores for that hand are doubled (not including the line bonus).

Hollywood Gin

Hollywood Gin is a method of scoring Gin Rummy so that in effect three games are played simultaneously. A player's first win is entered only in his column of Game 1; his second win is entered in both Game 1 and Game 2; his third and subsequent wins go into all three games. The three games are terminated and scored separately. When a game ends, no further scores are entered in that game. When the third game ends, a new series is begun.

GAME 1		GAME 2		GAME 3	
YOU	HE	YOU	HE	YOU	HE
17	26	8			
25					

Illustration of Scoring: YOU win the first hand, scoring 17. This is entered to your credit in Game 1. YOU win the second hand, scoring 8. Now you have a score of 25 in Game 1 and a score of 8 in Game 2. HE wins the third hand, scoring 26. HE scores this in Game 1, so the score in that game is now 26 to 25 in his favor, but he scores nothing in Game 2, since this is the first hand he has won.

Gin Rummy for Three

The usual method of three-hand Gin Rummy play is "chouette." Cards are drawn; lowest card sits out first. Highest card marks the man "in the box," a lone player against the other two in partnership. Second-highest is captain of his side; he may obtain advice from the sit-out player, but may make all decisions. If the man in the box wins the game, he retains his position, while the other two exchange roles. If the man in the box loses, he sits out next; the captain who defeated him goes into the box, and the previous sit-out becomes the new captain.

Gin Rummy for Four or More

Four-hand Gin Rummy is usually played in two fixed partnerships. Let us suppose that A and B are partners against C and D. Two packs are provided; each is dealt; A plays against C and B against D. For the second deal, A plays against D and B against C. The game continues in the same way, the oppositions alternating.

After each hand, the scores (plus or minus) made by the two members of a partnership are netted to determine which side won the deal, and only the net is scored. For example, A wins 26 from C but D wins 20 from B; A-B win the hand by 6. When a hand ends, the players of that hand may advise their respective partners in the unfinished hand.

This same system is followed for even numbers of players, split into two partnerships, up to about twelve players, beyond which it becomes unwieldy.

CAROUSEL

CAROUSEL may be played by two, but is more exciting with three or four. With two players, use a regular pack plus one joker; with more than two, use two packs plus two jokers. The jokers are wild, and count 25 each if left in the hand. Other cards count as in Gin Rummy.

Deal ten cards to each player. Beginning with the player at dealer's left each in turn must draw at least one card from the stock. He may then meld or lay off if he can and if he pleases. If he does not meld, he must draw a second card, and again may meld if he wishes; if not, he must draw a third card, and then his turn ends. He may not meld after taking the third card.

There is no discarding. The object of play is to reduce one's deadwood to 10 points or less by melding, and the first to do so wins the deal.

Melds may comprise sequences, or groups of three or four of a kind. No group may contain two cards of the same suit. All melds on the table are common property, and a player in his turn may rearrange the cards in any way he pleases, so as to absorb additional cards from his hand, so long as he leaves all the sets valid in form. A joker may be specified to be any card to complete a set, and it may be moved about and renamed at the pleasure of the in-turn player. This player may continue to add cards to the table so long as he can find place for cards from his hand; his turn ends only when he states that he is finished, but having melded one or more cards he may not draw again from the stock in that turn.

Having 10 points or less in deadwood, a player may knock when it comes his turn to play, before drawing any card from the stock. Play ends at once. No additional cards may be laid off. All players show their hands, and the one with the lowest count of deadwood collects the counts of all the other players. If the knocker is not lowest, he pays an additional 10 for undercut to the winner. Two or more hands tying for low divide the winnings equally. If a player gets rid of all his cards, he wins the deal at once (in this case, he need not wait one turn to knock) and collects an extra 25 points from each other player, besides the total of deadwood.

The player first to reach a total of 150 wins a game, and scores a game bonus of 100. A player who fails to score at all during a game pays double for shutout.

TUNK

TUNK is a version of Gin Rummy adapted to play by two or more players, up to about five. With two or three, use one regular pack; with four or five, use two packs shuffled together. Deal seven cards to each player, and turn the next card of the stock to commence the discard pile. Only eldest hand, at dealer's left, has option of taking this upcard. Play proceeds as in Gin. Each player in turn must draw the top card of the stock or the top of the discard pile, then discard one card.

The object of play, as in Gin, is to form the hand into matched sets so as to reduce the count of deadwood. Even with two packs, a set of cards of the same rank may not include more than four, and may never include duplicates. Each deuce is wild and may be specified to be of any rank and suit to complete a set; a deuce may not be added to a set of four cards of the same rank. A sequence may be extended as far as the king (high) and ace (low).

A player whose unmatched cards total 5 or less may *tunk* in his turn to play, without drawing. *Tunking* means the same as the commoner term *knocking*. The tunker places his whole hand face up on the table, arranged in sets and with the deadwood segregated from them. Each other player then has one more turn, during which he may *lay off* what he wishes on the tunker's sets, except that no laying off is permitted when the tunker has a complete hand with no deadwood.

The deadwood finally left in each hand is counted and charged against the player. An unmatched deuce counts 25. The tunker suffers no additional loss if he does not have the lowest count. When a player accumulates 100 or more points on the scoresheet, he retires from the game, and the others continue play until only one survivor remains.

If the stock becomes depleted to the point where not enough cards remain for a round of drawing after a tunk, the deal is abandoned without any score.

CANASTA

CANASTA *in its many forms is the most popular game in one of the two main branches of the Rummy family—the branch in which the object is to score points by melding, with "going out" a secondary and usually an unimportant factor. Canasta is the culmination of many minor features tacked onto* FIVE HUNDRED RUM. *It originated in Uruguay, developed in Argentina, reached the U. S. in 1949, and from 1950 to 1952 was the biggest fad in the history of card games. The word* canasta *means basket in Spanish and most likely was suggested by the tray placed on the table to hold the stock and discards. Though variants such as* BOLIVIA *have become more popular than the early forms of Canasta, the original and basic game is described first below. Canasta has "official laws" but few follow them entirely, except in the treatment of irregularities.*

PLAYERS. Four, in two partnerships. The two-hand form, which differs only slightly, is almost as popular. Adaptations have been made for three, five, and six players, but these are little played.

CARDS. Two regular packs of 52, plus four jokers, making 108 cards in all. There is no rank of cards, since sequences do not count, except that in drawing for partners and deal, players usually follow the laws of Contract Bridge.

THE DEAL. Each player receives eleven cards, dealt one at a time. As in Rummy, the rest of the pack becomes the *stock*, and an *upcard* is turned face up beside it to start the *discard pile*.

THE PLAY. As in Rummy, each player in turn to the left must

First, draw a card from the top of the stock or the top of the discard pile;

Second, meld if he can and wishes to;

Third, discard one card face up on the discard pile— except that the discard may be omitted in going out.

The general object of play is to score by melding. The play ends when any player gets rid of the last card in his hand, by melding or discard, or when no card remains that can or must be drawn.

WILD CARDS. All jokers and twos are wild and may be designated to be of any rank for purpose of completing or augmenting melds.

MELDS. A meld comprises three or more cards of the same rank, including at least two natural cards and never more than three wild cards. Wild cards and threespots may not be melded (but see below for black threes). A side may not meld more than one set of the same rank; after a player has melded a set, all additional cards of the same rank melded by him or his partner must be laid off on (added to) this set. A player may in any turn lay off on a set or sets melded by his side; he may never lay off on opponents' melds.

BLACK THREES. A set of three or four black threes without wild cards may be melded by a player in the turn in which he goes out. In all other circumstances, black threes are unmeldable. The discard of a black three compels the next player to draw from the stock—he cannot take the discard pile. On this account the black threes are called "stop cards."

RED THREES. The red threes are bonus cards, not meldable in sets. If a player finds a red three in his original hand, he must at his first turn place the three face up on the table and draw a replacement from the stock, additional to his regular draw. Similarly, if a player draws a red three from the stock, he must place it on the table and draw a replacement. A red three obtained by taking the discard pile must likewise be laid on the table, but in this case it is not replaced.

POINT VALUES. Each card has a point value, as follows:

Each joker	50
Each two	20
Each ace	20
Each K, Q, J, 10, 9, 8	10
Each 7, 6, 5, 4, black 3	5

INITIAL MELD. The first meld made by a side in a deal must meet a certain *initial meld requirement,* that is, the total point values of the melded cards must be not less than a certain minimum. This minimum depends on the side's score at the beginning of the current deal, accumulated from previous deals:

PREVIOUS SCORE	REQUIREMENT
Minus	15
0 to 1495	50
1500 to 2995	90
3000 or more	120

If a player takes the discard pile in making an initial meld, he is entitled to count only the top card (which must be melded) toward the requirement. An initial meld by either member of a partnership releases *both* from the previous limitations on their play ("unfreezes the pack" for both).

TAKING THE DISCARD PILE. When a player takes the top discard, he takes with it the entire discard pile (called the *pack*). He may take the top discard only in the following circumstances.

First of all, the player may take the discard only if he can meld that card in the same turn. He may meld it with other cards of the same rank from his hand to form a new set, or he may lay it off on a set previously melded by his side. (But he may not use it to form a new set wholly of cards found in the discard pile.) Having established his right to take the discard, he then takes all the rest of the discard pile into his hand. With help of these cards, he may then make all the additional melds he pleases.

In the second place, the circumstances under which the discard pile may be taken differ according as the pile is *frozen* or *unfrozen*.

The pile is frozen (a) against one side: before that side has made its initial meld; (b) against both sides: when it contains a red three or a wild card (a red three or wild card having been turned for the upcard, or a wild card having been discarded).

When the pile is frozen, it may be taken only by matching its top card with a natural pair of the same rank from the hand, to form a new set. (However, if the side has already melded a set of that rank, it is not prevented from taking the pile thus, for the "new set" is then laid off on the old.)

When the pile is unfrozen, it may be taken by matching its top card with a natural pair, as above, or with one natural card and one wild card, or to lay off its top card on a set of the same rank, previously melded by his side. (NOTE: Few players now permit any discard to be taken without a natural matching pair.)

CANASTAS. A *canasta* is a melded set of seven or more cards. It is *natural* (or *pure*) when it is wholly formed of natural cards; it is *mixed* when it contains one to three wild cards. The foremost object in play is to build up canastas, for (a) they carry the largest scoring values, and (b) a side is not permitted to go out before it has completed at least one canasta. On completion, a canasta is squared up in a pile, with a red card on top if it is natural, a black card if it is mixed. Natural cards from the hand may be laid off on a canasta; wild cards may be added to it provided that the limit of three wild cards is not exceeded.

GOING OUT. A player goes out when he gets rid of the last card in his hand, ending the play. He may at this time meld three or four black threes, and he need not make a final discard. If no one goes out by the time the stock is exhausted, play continues so long as any hand can take the top discard (of an unfrozen pile) and add it to a previous meld of his side, in which case he is said to be "forced"; or can legally and does take the discard for a new meld. A special rule is that at no time may a player having only one card in his hand take a "discard pile" comprising only one card.

A player goes out *concealed* if he melds his entire hand in one turn, having made no previous meld. He must meet the initial count requirement and meld at least one canasta, if his partner has not already done so.

A player is legally entitled to ask "May I go out, partner?" The partner must respond "Yes" or "No" and the asker is bound by the reply. (As some play, the reply must always be "No" and the question is asked merely to warn partner to meld all he can. The question is illegal and subject to a 100-point penalty if the asker cannot in fact go out, but there is no practicable way of determining this fact.)

SCORING. Score is kept on paper and accumulated. When play ends, each side first reckons its "basic count" from the following table:

For going out unconcealed	100
For going out concealed	200
For each red three (see below)	100
For each natural canasta	500
For each mixed canasta	300

If a side has made no meld at all, its red threes count minus. If one side obtains all four red threes, their total value is 800 (instead of 400).

To its basic count, the side adds the total point values of all its melded cards. From this total it subtracts the point values of all cards remaining in the hands of both partners.

The final net is written on the scoresheet and totaled with the previous accumulation. The side that first reaches 5,000 or more wins a game. There is no bonus for winning a game. Settlement is made on the difference of final totals.

IRREGULARITIES IN CANASTA

INCORRECT DRAW. If a player draws too many cards, he must rectify the error by discarding without drawing in each turn until his hand is correct. If a player discards without drawing, he may be required to take the top card of the stock if attention is called to the omission before the next player has drawn. If a player, in drawing, exposes one or more cards of the stock, he must show them to all other players and replace them on the stock; the first player thereafter who draws from the stock may first shuffle it if he wishes.

EXPOSED CARDS. If (in partnership play) a player exposes one or more cards from his hand, except to make a legal meld, all such cards must be left face up on the table and discarded in successive turns. But the owner is entitled to use such cards in melds, if he can, and validly melded cards are exempt from the discard rule.

INSUFFICIENT COUNT. If for the initial meld a player shows less than the required count, he may validate his meld with additional cards. If he cannot or does not wish to do so, he must retract all cards exposed, and the minimum count for his side is increased 10 points. If an opponent draws before attention is called to the insufficiency, the meld stands as sufficient.

UNDECLARED RED THREE. If a player is dealt or draws a red three, and fails to declare it before the play of the deal ends (provided he has had a turn to play), his side is penalized 500 points.

INCORRECT MELD. If a player makes a meld including more than three wild cards, or attempts to add a wild card to a meld already containing three, he may without penalty use the wild card in a legal meld or discard it; if he returns it to his hand, his side is penalized 100 points. (This penalty applies also if a player retracts an exposed card in process of rectifying an insufficient initial meld.)

STRATEGY OF CANASTA

A hand reduced to less than its original eleven cards early in the play is thereby crippled. Usually avoid early melding except to obtain the discard pile. Try to make the initial meld as economically as possible: Unless you can take the discard pile in the same turn, do not use more than three cards for 50 (as, A A 2), four cards for 90, or six cards for 120.

Above all else in early play, strive to increase the size of your hand. The most likely way to obtain the discard pile is to keep pairs of as many different ranks as possible, plus only as many wild cards as you need to meet initial meld requirement.

Do not hesitate to discard a wild card to freeze the pile, if your opponents have melded and your side has not. Such play is often imperative to prevent them from obtaining the pile repeatedly.

If you are stuck with cards useless to you but probably wanted by the opponents, discard these cards when the discard pile is small or worthless, saving your safe discards (as black threes) for later rounds.

More mistakes are made by hoarding than by squandering wild cards. Usually try to keep even with the opponents in the number of canastas, using wild cards when necessary to complete your own. It is especially important to complete the first canasta of the deal; the side that does that puts added pressure on the opponents.

Two-Hand Canasta

Each player receives fifteen cards. In drawing from the stock, a player takes two cards but discards only one. A player may not go out unless he has completed two canastas.

Three-Hand Canasta

Each plays for himself. Thirteen cards are dealt to each. The game may be played under the rules of four-hand Canasta, but a more satisfactory method is as follows:

In drawing from the stock, a player takes two cards but still discards only one. The first player to take the discard pile becomes the *lone* player and the other two become partners against him for that deal. However, the initial meld requirement of each partner depends on his own score.

Each player has a separate column on the score. The lone player scores his own total. Each of his opponents scores the total made by the partnership. Red threes, however, are scored by each player separately. They count for a partner if either he or the other partner has melded. Two canastas are required to go out. Game is 7,500.

If the discard pile is never taken, each player scores separately. If no one goes out, play ends when the last player to draw from the stock has discarded. If a player goes out before the discard pile is taken, he is the lone player and the other two score together.

Other Forms of Canasta

As Canasta's popularity spread, various features were grafted onto the game, principally these: (a) Three packs with six jokers were used instead of two packs with four jokers. (b) A natural matching pair was always required to take the pack. (c) No card could be added to a completed canasta. (d) A meld could have no more than two wild cards. (e) Sequences could be melded. (f) Wild cards could be melded in certain groups. (g) Much larger bonuses were paid for sequence or wild-card melds or for certain special combinations melded. (h) Two cards could be drawn from the stock in each turn. (i) At least two canastas or other special combinations of seven or more cards were required to go out; . . . and other variations too numerous to mention. From these innovations arose variant games that are often known in the United States by the name of the country in which they originated, for example Bolivia, Chile, Italian Canasta. The principal ones are described below, beginning with the earliest, Samba, which was named and largely constructed by John R. Crawford of Philadelphia.

Samba

CARDS. Three regular packs of 52, plus six jokers, making 162 cards in all.

THE DEAL. Each player receives fifteen cards.

THE PLAY. In drawing from the stock, the player takes two cards, but the discard remains one card.

MELDS. In addition to groups of the same rank, *sequences* may be melded—three or more cards of the same suit and consecutive rank, ranging from ace (high) to four (low). A sequence of seven cards is a *samba,* and is immediately squared up face down, since no more cards may be added to it. No wild card may be used in a sequence.

Not more than two wild cards may be used in a group meld. Natural cards from the hand may be added to a canasta, but the top discard may not be taken for this purpose.

A side may meld more than one group set of the same rank. Either partner may combine such sets for canasta-building. Likewise, sequence melds in the same suit may be combined, when they adjoin properly, provided that not more than seven cards are involved. (Thus, a sequence of four cannot be combined with another sequence of four.)

INITIAL MELD. The game being 10,000, the initial meld requirement is 120 for score of 3,000 to 6,995, and 150 for 7,000 or more.

TAKING THE DISCARD PILE. The pile may be taken only by a natural pair, or (if unfrozen) to lay off the top card on a group or sequence meld of less than seven cards. Note that wild cards cannot help to obtain the pile, and the top card cannot be taken to form a new sequence with cards from the hand.

GOING OUT. A samba is rated as a canasta for the purpose of going out. A side may not go out until it has completed two canastas.

The "concealed hand" of Canasta is abolished in Samba. So is the special rule as to a one-card discard pile.

SCORING. The bonus for going out is 200. Each samba counts 1,500. If all six red threes are obtained by one side, they count 1,000 (instead of 600). Game is 10,000. All other scoring is as in Canasta.

Bolivia

Three or more wild cards may be melded. Sequences may be melded as in Samba. A canasta of wild cards, called a *bolivia,* pays a bonus of 2,500. Game is 15,000. The initial meld requirement never exceeds 150. At least one of two canastas required to go out must be a sequence. A black three left in the hand counts 100 points minus.

Brazilian Canasta

Wild cards and sequences may be melded; a wild-card canasta pays a bonus of 2,000, and sequence canasta a bonus of 1,500, but an uncompleted meld toward these canastas costs 1,000 points when anyone goes out. The discard pile may not be taken to make the initial meld. Game is 10,000, and at 7,000 points the initial meld requires a canasta; at 8,000, a canasta in a total meld of at least 200 points; at 9,000, a natural canasta.

The regular (106-card) Canasta deck is used, only one card is drawn per turn, but two canastas are needed to go out. Thirteen cards are dealt to each player. The pack is always frozen. Game is 8,500, and the minimum meld is 95 when under 3,000; 125 from 3,000 to 4,995, and 155 over 5,000. A canasta may not have more than seven cards. Wild cards may be melded and the bonus is 2,000 for a wild-card canasta, 3,000 if it includes all four jokers, and 4,000 if it is composed of seven deuces. All threes, black as well as red, are bonus cards and are faced as soon as drawn. A side's first three in a color counts 100; its second and third threes in that color, 200 each; its fourth three of a color, 500 (making 1,000 for all four in a color). These scores count against a side that has not completed a canasta.

Oklahoma or Arlington

OKLAHOMA *is a relatively new game; it is similar to Five Hundred Rummy, which is described on pages 119 to 121. In Oklahoma two 52-card packs and one joker are shuffled together, making a 105-card pack. Two to five may play; when four play it may be a partnership game, but Oklahoma is best when each plays for himself. Thirteen cards are dealt to each.*

The object is to meld matched sets of three or more cards, either groups (cards of the same rank in any suits) or sequences in the same suit. The joker and all deuces are wild. Ace is high in A-K-Q and low in A-2-3. The play is the same as in Five Hundred Rummy except that when a player takes the top discard—which he may do only if he immediately melds it with two or more cards from his hand or by adding it to one of his own previous melds—he "takes the pack" (the entire discard pile). The first upcard (but only the first) is available to each player in turn if the player before him refuses it.

A player must announce the exact card a deuce or joker represents in a meld. He may trade for a joker he previously melded, by substituting the natural card it represents, but he may not trade for a deuce.

A group is "closed" when it contains four of a kind (natural or wild cards) and no further card may be added to it.

A player may not discard a queen of spades if he has any other card to discard.

SCORING. Play ends when a player goes out. The player who goes out must make a final discard. Play also ends when a player draws the last card of the stock and discards.

When play ends, the value of each player's melds counts *for* him, and the value of the cards left in his hand counts *against* him, according to the following table:

CARD	IN A MELD	IN HAND
A	20	20
K, Q, J, 10, 9, or 8 (except ♤ Q)	10	10
7, 6, 5, 4 or 3	5	5
Queen of spades	50	100
Deuce, representing K to 8, including ♤ Q	10	20
Deuce, representing 7 to 2	5	20
Joker	100	200

The player who goes out receives a bonus of 100 points.

The first player to reach a total plus score of 1,000 points wins the game and receives an additional bonus of 200 points. If two or more players pass the 1,000 mark on the same hand, the highest score wins. If they tie, they divide the 200-point bonus equally.

After the game ends, a player who has gone out "concealed" on any hand receives an additional 250 points, but these points do not count toward reaching the 1,000-point mark.

To go out concealed, a player must go out by melding every card in his hand, in his second or later turn. A player who goes out on his first turn does not receive the bonus. If he has made any meld in a previous turn, a player can no longer "go out concealed."

STRATEGY

Don't meld too early in the play; after four or five draws your hand may form other combinations that will use more cards.

Usually hold a pair rather than a two-card sequence, as there is a better chance to improve the pair.

As a general rule you take the discard pile when it will give you more points in melds than the point value of the unmeldable cards.

Save an odd queen or a high spade—♤K, ♤J or ♤ 10— even when it is unmatched with other cards. If you draw the ♤Q you cannot discard it, and a matching card will improve your chance of melding it.

When you take the discard pile, before mixing it with your hand count back to remember which cards each other player has thrown.

It is both ethical and proper to throw a card that will put the next player out, if there is a danger that otherwise another player will go out concealed.

Prefer to meld three of a kind rather than four of a kind, using the fourth card in another meld. Four of a kind is a closed meld and you cannot go out by adding to it if you are left with a single card later.

PANGUINGUE

PANGUINGUE, *a game for six to nine players, is the survivor in the direct line of* CONQUIAN, *the ancestor of all the Rummy games. In the western United States many commercial clubs flourish, devoted principally to furnishing their habitués with "Pan" games.*

From its ancestor, Pan inherits the Spanish pack, which is made from the modern 52-card pack by discarding all eights, nines and tens. The seven is in sequence with the jack, and the ace ranks low, below the deuce. No less than eight such Spanish packs are used by the best houses, shuffled together.

Because of the great number of cards, shuffling is a communal enterprise. After the shuffle, the cards are cut in two parts—the *head*, which is used in dealing, and the *foot*, a reservoir plumbed if necessary.

Ten cards are dealt to each hand, five at a time. Preserving the tradition of Conquian, the rotation of deal and play is to the *right*, instead of to the left as in most other games. The balance of the head is placed face down to form the stock, and the top card is turned over beside it to start the discard pile.

As Pan offers less opportunity than any other game of the Rummy family to improve the original hand, every player is first given a chance to drop out of the deal. Each in turn to the right either stands or drops, and the hands of those who drop are collected and put under the foot of the pack. In the Pan clubs, a player who drops has to pay a forfeit, and the forfeits are placed on the foot of the pack. Dropping is therefore called "going on top."

Then, as in all Rummy games, each player in turn to the right draws one card, either the top of the stock or the top of the discard pile, and discards one card. But here the discard may not be drawn to combine with cards from the hand in a new meld; and the card from the stock may not be kept, unless it is immediately melded. Consequently, the card drawn is never put in the hand, and if it came from the stock it is immediately exposed for all players to see. The player's original hand thus never changes, except by subtraction—by discarding after a meld.

A meld, as in all Rummy games, may be either a group of three cards of the same rank or a sequence of three cards in the same suit. (The colloquial term for a sequence is *rope*.) Only three cards may be melded in the original set. But a player may add to his own melds (not to melds of other players).

The regulations in full are as follows:

Any three aces or any three kings, regardless of suits, form a valid set. These ranks are called *non-comoquers*. Any card of the same rank may be added to a non-comoquer set, regardless of its suit. All other ranks are *comoquers*, and a set here must be three cards of different suits or all of the same suit. To a set of cards in different suits may be added other cards of the same rank in any suit. To a set of cards all in the same suit may be added only cards that are the same in suit as well as rank. A sequence may be added to until the limit of the rank is reached, king high or ace low.

Conditions are certain melds for which the player immediately collects from every other active player. In the description below, *valle cards* refers to threes, fives and sevens. The conditions are:

Any group of valle cards in different suits (collects 1 chip). Any group of valle cards in the same suit (collects 4 chips in spades, 2 in another suit). Any group of non-valle cards in the same suit (collects 2 chips in spades, 1 in another suit). Low sequence, 3-2-A; high sequence, K-Q-J (collects 2 chips in spades, 1 in another suit).

In the course of adding cards to his melds, a player may split one meld into two, provided that each remains a valid meld, and may borrow from an amplified meld to make a new one, under the same proviso. *Conditions* made by splitting or borrowing collect as though they were entirely new. Each card added to a condition collects anew for the entire condition.

The first player to meld exactly eleven cards wins the deal. Since the original hand of ten cards cannot be increased, this means that the winner at his last turn draws a card, melds it, and does not discard. A player may meld all his ten cards and have none left; in this case he continues to draw and discard until he draws a card that he can lay off. An important (and exasperating) rule is that if a discard fits with a meld of the in-turn player, he must draw it and meld it on demand of any other player. The object in making this demand is to make it more difficult for the victim to go out. If he holds two cards, which may be a pair, his chances of going out are reduced if he has to break up his pair.

The winning player collects all over again for such of his melds as are *conditions,* plus 1 chip extra from each active player, and he also takes the forfeits put "on top" by the players who dropped from the deal.

IRREGULARITIES IN PANGUINGUE

A player who has an incorrect hand may have it replaced with a new hand before he makes his first play; thereafter an incorrect hand is dead but the holder must make all payments as though he were still in the game. If he has made any collections for conditions, he must return them.

An illegal meld must be made legal when attention is called to it; if he cannot make it legal, the penalty is the same as for an incorrect hand (see the preceding paragraph). No play is final until a player has discarded.

PINOCHLE

PINOCHLE *is the name of a whole family of games, related by origin and having certain basic features in common, but varying widely in form and strategy. The first of the family was undoubtedly the two-hand game first described below; this is almost identical with the French game* BÉZIQUE. *It was developed in the United States probably in the middle of the 19th century. The whole family grew up in the United States—not in Germany, as many persons assume merely because Pinochle games use a German ranking of the cards and took some of their features from German games such as Skat. The basic features common to the whole family are as follows.*

CARDS. The Pinochle pack is 48 cards—two cards, duplicates, of each rank in each of the four suits. In one two-hand form a 64-card pack is used.

RANK OF CARDS. In each suit the rank is: A (high), 10, K, Q, J, 9, (8, 7, if used). When duplicates are played to the same trick (as two aces of spades) the first-played ranks as higher.

147

CARD VALUES. The higher cards have scoring value when won in tricks:

	ORIGINAL COUNT	SIMPLIFIED COUNT
Each ace	11	10
Each ten	10	10
Each king	4	5
Each queen	3	5
Each jack	2	0

(No count for lower cards.)

Winning last trick usually counts 10 points. Under either the original or the simplified count, the total points at stake in the play are thus 250.

MELDS. Certain combinations of cards (melds) have scoring value:

SEQUENCES

A-K-Q-J-10 of trumps (flush)	150
K-Q of trumps (royal marriage)	40
K-Q of any other suit (simple marriage)	20

GROUPS

♠A-♡A-◇A-♣A (hundred aces)	100
♠K-♡K-◇K-♣K (eighty kings)	80
♠Q-♡Q-◇Q-♣Q (sixty queens)	60
♠J-♡J-◇J-♣J (forty jacks)	40

SPECIAL

♠Q-◇J (pinochle)	40
9 of trumps (dix, pronounced "deece")	10

A card may be used in two or three melds, provided that they are of different classes. For example, the same ♠ Q may be used in a marriage, sixty queens, and pinochle. But when a flush is melded, the K-Q do not count separately as a royal marriage.

Additional rules of melding and additional melds are met in some Pinochle games.

Two-Hand Pinochle

This game, once very popular, has lost out almost entirely to Gin Rummy, two-hand Canasta, and to a lesser extent Russian Bank.

CARDS. The 48-card Pinochle pack (page 147); more often, however, a 64-card pack, duplicates of A, 10, K, Q, J, 9, 8, 7 in each suit. When the 64-card pack is used, the game is often called GOULASH; the seven instead of the nine is the *dix;* a 9, 8, or 7 won in a trick has no scoring value.

PRELIMINARIES. Each player draws a card from the shuffled pack spread face down. Lower card deals first. Dealer has the right to shuffle last. His opponent cuts the pack. The cut must leave at last five cards in each packet.

If the game is for 1,000 (or other number of) points, the deal alternates. If each deal is settled as a separate game, the winner of each hand deals next.

THE DEAL. Each player receives twelve cards, dealt three at a time, if the 48-card pack is used; sixteen cards, dealt four at a time, if the 64-card pack is used. The rest of the pack is placed face down in the center of the table as the *stock*. Dealer turns the top card of the stock face up and puts it partly underneath the stock; this *trump card* fixes the trump suit for that deal.

THE PLAY. Nondealer makes the opening lead. The hands are played out in tricks. The winner of a trick draws the top card of the stock; his opponent draws the next; thus the hands are maintained at twelve cards until the stock is exhausted. At all times, a trick is won by the higher trump or by the higher card of the suit led; of identical cards, the one led wins. The winner of a trick leads to the next.

During the early play (before the stock is exhausted) the second player to a trick need not follow suit: he may play any card. In this period the players may score by melding, as below.

MELDING. A player may place face up on the table any of the melds listed on page 134, under certain restrictions:

The holder of a dix may exchange it for the trump card after winning a trick, thus obtaining a higher trump (and also scoring 10). This exchange, and also the meld of the second dix (which is accomplished merely by showing it and scoring 10) may be made in the same turn with any other meld. In all other cases, a player may meld only one combination in a turn. In some games not even the dix is permitted to be scored in the same turn as another meld.

A player may meld only after winning a trick, before drawing from the stock.

A card already on the table may be used as part of a new meld provided that the two melds are of different classes; further, having melded a royal marriage and scored 40, a player may later add the trump A-J-10 and score 150 for flush. But if a flush is melded entire, the marriage does not score separately, nor can a player later add a single king or queen and score the marriage. For each new meld, the player must lay down at least one new card from his hand. If such a card would form two new melds with cards on the table, the player may score only one of them. (E.g., having pinochle on the table, a player melding 80 kings may not also score the spade marriage.)

A combination of four kings and four queens of different suits is colloquially called a "roundhouse." In three-hand Pinochle all eight cards can be melded at once, scoring 240. But the roundhouse is not in the list of proper melds; hence in two-hand Pinochle it must be treated as a number of separate melds, and in whatever order they are put down the owner can amass no more than 220 points from them.

Melded cards are left on the table but remain a part of the owner's hand and may be played in tricks. Care must be taken not to violate the rules of melding: e.g., if a king is played from a melded marriage, the other king may not later be married to the same queen.

LATER PLAY. The winner of the twelfth trick must expose the card he draws (the last face-down card of the stock). The other draws the face-up card, usually the dix previously exchanged for the trump card. Then all melds are picked up and the last twelve cards are played out in tricks. During this time no further melding is allowed. The second player to a trick must follow suit if able, and if void of the suit led must trump if able. When a trump is led, the other must win if able.

SCORING. The scores for melds are accumulated during play. At the end, each player counts what he has won in tricks, according to the card values given on page 148. Winning last trick counts 10. (If the original count is used, the total won in tricks is taken to the nearest multiple of 10.) The scores for tricks are added to the accumulated scores, usually recorded by chips but sometimes on paper.

GAME. The player who first reaches a total of 1,000 points wins a game. At any time during the game, a player may claim that he has reached 1,000, whereupon play ends and the tricks are examined. If the claim is correct, the claimant wins, even though his opponent actually has a higher score. If there is no claim, and both players reach 1,000 as a result of the same deal, they play on to 1,250—and similarly they can play on to 1,500, or 1,750, etc.

Some players prefer to play for a game of 500. Others treat each deal as a separate game and settle at once.

IRREGULARITIES IN TWO-HAND PINOCHLE

EXPOSED CARDS. If dealer exposes a card going to himself, he must accept it. If he exposes a card going to his opponent, the opponent may accept it or require a new deal. If more than one card is exposed in turning the trump card, the stock must be shuffled and dealer's opponent then draws out a card for trumps. If, after play begins, a card is found faced in the stock, the stock is shuffled and play continues.

WRONG NUMBER OF CARDS. Either player, before playing to the first trick, may demand a new deal if he has more or less than twelve cards. If his hand is found incorrect after play has begun, play continues and the error is rectified: A short hand draws extra cards at once from the stock; a long hand omits drawing until correct, and until this time the hand may not meld.

INCORRECT STOCK. If at any time the stock is found short one card, play continues. When only three cards are left, the last player may take either the stock card or the trump card. The remaining card is discarded from that deal, counting for neither player. If it is the stock card, it is shown before being discarded.

LEAD OUT OF TURN. If a player leads out of turn, opponent may either accept it or require that it be withdrawn. There is no penalty.

REVOKE. In the later play, failure to follow suit when able, to trump when so required, or to win a trump lead if able, is a revoke. A player may correct his revoke before he plays to the next trick, otherwise it stands as established. The offender may then score nothing for cards taken in tricks (he does not lose his melds made previous to discovery of the revoke), but play continues to determine the nonoffender's score.

STRATEGY OF TWO-HAND PINOCHLE

At the beginning, save cards for valuable melds, letting go jacks and lower cards. Save for marriages when you can, but try to keep track of what combinations have become impossible or unlikely from opponent's play of the necessary cards. Use tens to capture the lead when you wish to meld. If you wish to retain the lead the lead of a ten is often good, for then opponent cannot win without (usually) impairing his chances for 100 aces or flush.

Having several melds in hand, put down the one having the least cards that you wish to save for other melds. Thereby you make the cards available for play. But put down a royal marriage promptly, in case you later complete a flush.

Toward the end of the early play, give thought to defending against a flush if this possibility is still open to opponent; the method is to lead trumps, so that he cannot win the trick without giving up a vital trump.

Usually you should lead your longest suit and keep leading it. The opponent then is least likely to have cards of the same suit with which he can win tricks and meld.

When feasible, save all trumps and aces to build up a strong hand for the final play.

The best players invariably know all of the last twelve cards held by the opponent. If you are unable to carry so many cards in mind, at least keep count of trumps and aces. In the later play it is usually more important than ever to lead one's longest suit and force the opponent to trump, using one's own trumps only when forced to do so. Last trick goes almost invariably to the hand with the majority of trumps.

With any chance to reach 1,000 in a deal, try to pile up everything you can in melding. Expend trumps and aces liberally for this purpose.

Auction Pinochle

This is one of the best three-hand card games of history (in opportunities for skill) and was once among the most popular forms of Pinochle. It has lost out to Bridge and to various forms of Rummy.

PLAYERS. Though only three are active at a time, the game is best for four; and five may sit at the table and participate. With four, dealer gives himself no cards. With five, he omits himself and the second player to his left.

CARDS. The 48-card Pinochle pack (page 147).

THE DEAL. Each player receives fifteen cards, dealt in batches. Dealer is usually allowed to follow his own preference among many plans: three at a time, or 4-4-4-3, etc. But he must adhere to the plan he commences. After the first round of the deal, three cards are dealt face down on the table, forming the *widow*.

BIDDING. Each player in turn to left of the dealer must make a bid or pass. A player may continue bidding in turn in effort to win the contract, but once he has passed he is out of the bidding.

Each bid is a number of points, a multiple of 10. No suit is mentioned. It is customary to require the player at left of the dealer to open with a compulsory bid; the minimum is usually set at 300, but it is 250 or 200 in various circles. No other player need bid if he prefers to pass.

The highest bidder becomes the Bidder. The other two become Opponents, combining in temporary partnership against him.

THE WIDOW. The Bidder turns the widow face up for all to see. He may then take the cards into his hand. Next he may meld; no other player may do so.

MELDING. The Bidder may put face up on the table all his cards that form proper melds (see page 134). The value of all such melds is totaled as the first item in his (potential) score. A roundhouse (K-Q in every suit) is scored as 240.

The Bidder may change his melds and the trump suit at any time before he has made the opening lead.

CONCESSION. The Bidder may concede defeat before leading. In this event, he loses *single bete* (pronounced "bate"). Or, the Opponents may concede that he will surely make his bid, and then there is no play. One Opponent's concession is not binding on the other.

If the Bidder's melds total as much as, or more than, his bid, his contract is scored as made and there is no play. (The Bidder need not win a trick to count his melds.)

BURYING. If the Bidder needs some points from play to make his bid, and if he elects to play, he buries (discards) any three cards from his hand face down. He must not bury any card he has used in a meld, but he may bury trumps and aces. The buried cards belong to the Bidder after the play, and he counts them along with his tricks. After burying, the Bidder picks up all his melds. He names the trump suit (if he has not already indicated it by melding a flush or by claiming 40 for a royal marriage).

THE PLAY. The Bidder makes the opening lead. He may lead any card, not necessarily a trump. The hands are played out in tricks. A player must follow suit to a lead, if able. If unable to follow to a nontrump lead, he must trump, if able. When a trump is led, he must play higher than any card already in the trick, if able. (He need not overtrump a trump previously played on a nontrump lead.) A trick is won by the highest trump in it, or, if it contains no trump, by the highest card played of the suit led. The winner of a trick leads to the next.

Tricks won by the Opponents are gathered in one pile.

RESULT OF PLAY. The Bidder examines his tricks and buried cards, and totals his count for high cards won. He also scores 10 for last trick, if he wins it. If his count for cards plus his melds equals or surpasses his bid, the bid is made; if his total is less, the bid is defeated—or, as is said, the Bidder goes *double bete*.

SCORING. Though score can be kept on paper, the prevalent method is to settle with poker chips after each deal.

The payments are based on a schedule that varies with the locality; the commonest is as follows:

BID	BASE VALUE
300 to 340	1
350 to 390	2
400 to 440	4
450 to 490	7
500 to 540	10
550 to 590	13

The base value is doubled when spades are trumps.

(A bid as high as 600 is hardly possible; bids over 450 are extremely rare.)

When the Bidder concedes single bete, he pays the base value of his bid to each Opponent. When he suffers double bete, he pays each Opponent (including inactive ones) twice the base value—four times if in spades. When the bid is made, the Bidder collects its base value (doubled in spades) from each Opponent.

THE KITTY. It is usual to maintain a kitty, a common pool of chips. When a player makes a forced opening bid (300, 250, or 200) and concedes single bete without looking at the widow, he pays the base value of his bid only to the kitty. In other cases the kitty neither pays nor collects on bids up to 340. On bids of 350 or more, the kitty collects and pays just as though it were a player.

The kitty is originally formed, and is replenished if necessary, by equal contributions and is divided equally among the players when a session ends.

IRREGULARITIES IN AUCTION PINOCHLE

NEW DEAL. There must be a new deal by the same dealer if any card of the widow is exposed in dealing, or any two cards in players' hands; or if the pack was not properly shuffled and cut and attention is called to the fact before the widow is dealt.

EXPOSURE OF WIDOW. If, before the bidding ends, a player sees a card in the widow, he may not make another bid. If he exposes a card in the widow, there must be a new deal by the next dealer, and the offender must pay to each other player (including the kitty and inactive players) the base value of the highest bid made prior to his offense.

WRONG NUMBER OF CARDS. If a player has too few cards and another player or the widow has too many:

(a) If the error is discovered before the Bidder has properly exposed the widow, the incorrect hands must be rectified.

(b) If it is discovered at any later time, the bid is made if Bidder's hand (and discard, if any) are correct; if it is incorrect, the Bidder loses single or double bete, according to whether he has led.

If the widow is found to have too few cards, there must be another deal by the same dealer.

EXPOSED CARDS. The Bidder is not subject to penalty for exposing cards. If a player exposes one card during the bidding and then becomes an Opponent, the Bidder may require or forbid the lead or play of that card at the offender's first opportunity to play it. If the Opponents expose two or more cards after the opening lead, the bid is made.

BID OUT OF TURN. A bid out of turn is void without penalty, but it may be accepted as regular by the one or two other players still entitled to bid.

IMPROPER BURYING. If, after the Bidder leads, he is found to have buried a card he melded, or to have buried too many cards, he is double bete.

RENEGE. A player reneges if he fails, when able, to follow suit to a lead, play over on a trump lead, trump a plain lead, or play an exposed card as properly required by the Bidder. The Bidder may correct a renege without penalty before he has played to the next trick. An Opponent may correct a renege before he or his partner has played to the next trick, but if the Bidder does not make his bid, the deal is void. Cards played after a renege may be withdrawn if it is corrected.

If a renege is not corrected in time, play ends forthwith. If the offender was an Opponent, the bid is made; if it was the Bidder, he is double bete.

LEAD OUT OF TURN. If the Bidder leads out of turn, there is no penalty but the correct leader may accept it or require it to be withdrawn. If an Opponent leads out of turn, the offense is treated as a renege.

ERROR IN COUNT OF MELD. If an incorrect value was agreed upon for the Bidder's meld, correction may be made at any time before settlement is completed.

STRATEGY OF AUCTION PINOCHLE

In bidding, you may properly expect the widow to improve the playing value of your hand by 20, but do not expect it to fill a needed meld unless you have at least five "places open" (any of five outstanding cards will fill). As Bidder, play the hand rather than concede unless the odds are 2-1 or worse against making. (When spades count double, play a doubtful spade hand if the chances are not worse than even against you.)

In burying, usually discard a weak short holding (three cards or less with no ace). Save your longest side suit entire. Sometimes you may well bury one or two tens, to save them from falling to the Opponents.

The commonest type of hand that you are forced to play as Bidder contains a trump suit of five or more cards, not solid, with a side suit of four or more. After cashing blank aces, if any, open the side suit and continue it at every opportunity. You may eventually force an Opponent to trump, thereby weakening his trump stoppers, and if this is a trick his partner would have won anyhow with a high card, you have escaped a *smear* (or *schmier*). The novice's most frequent error is leading trumps.

As an Opponent, usually try to force the Bidder to trump a plain suit. But sometimes, and especially when the Bidder needs few points, a better plan is to lead trumps. Unless there is a suit with which the Opponents can force the Bidder to trump, they should try to have the trick won by the Opponent who can lead through the Bidder.

The most costly error is bidding on hope rather than cards actually held. The chances of finding a specific card in the widow are:

PLACES OPEN	APPROXIMATE ODDS
1	5 to 1 against
2	2 to 1 against
3	Even
4	3 to 2 for
5	2 to 1 for

Partnership Pinochle

One of the earliest popular Pinochle games was Partnership Pinochle, for four players in two partnerships. The 48-card Pinochle pack was used; twelve cards were dealt to each player, but the last card was turned to fix the trump and then went into the dealer's hand; every player might meld, but unless a side won at least one trick ("to make its meld official") it lost its melding points. The vogue of bidding games, started by Auction Bridge and similar games, caused the original four-hand Pinochle game to be abandoned, but it has survived in PARTNERSHIP AUCTION PINOCHLE, described next; and in the form of DOUBLE-PACK PINOCHLE (page 160) it remains one of the most popular card games.

PLAYERS. Four, in two partnerships. The players sitting opposite each other play as partners.

CARDS. The 48-card Pinochle pack (see page 147).

THE DEAL. Each player receives twelve cards, dealt in batches of three at a time.

BIDDING. Each player in turn, beginning with the player to the left of the dealer, has one chance to bid or pass. All bids must be numbers in multiples of 10, with 100 the minimum bid allowed. No suit is mentioned. The Bidder (high bidder) later names the trump suit for that deal.

MELDING. All four players may meld. The list of basic melds is given on page 134. In addition, double melds have extra value:

Double flush	1500
All eight aces	1000
All eight kings	800
All eight queens	600
All eight jacks	400
Double pinochle	300

Partners must meld separately; they may not pool their cards to build up joint melds. However, their separate melds are totaled and a memorandum is made of the amount. A side does not receive credit for its melds until it wins a trick. (The trick need not contain any counting card.)

THE PLAY. All players next pick up their melds, and the opponent at the left of the dealer makes the opening lead. A hand must follow suit to a lead if able. When a non-trump is led, a hand void of that suit must play a trump, if able. When a trump is led, a hand must, if able, play a trump higher than any already in the trick. A trick is won by the highest trump in it, or, if it contains no trump, by the highest card played of the suit led. The winner of a trick leads to the next.

The object in play is to win cards of scoring value, as given in the table on page 148. Winning the last trick counts 10 points.

SCORING. Each side counts up what it has won in tricks, and to this amount adds the value of its melds (if it has won any trick). Bidder's opponents add this total into their accumulated score. If the Bidder's side won at least the amount of the bid, the number of points bid (not the number made) is added to its running score; if the bid was defeated, this amount is deducted from the side's score.

GAME. The side that first reaches a total of 1,000 points wins a game. It is usual to allow "declaring out." A player may at any time claim that his side has reached 1,000. Play stops and the tricks are examined. If the claim is found correct the claiming side wins, even though the other should have a higher score. If the claim is incorrect, that side loses the game at once.

If both sides reach or exceed 1,000 at the end of a deal, the Bidder's side wins.

IRREGULARITIES IN PARTNERSHIP PINOCHLE

NEW DEAL. There must be a new deal by the same dealer if a card is exposed in dealing; or if the pack was not properly shuffled and cut and attention is called to the fact before the last card is dealt; or if at any time one hand is found to have too many cards and another too few.

BID OUT OF TURN. If a player bids out of turn, the bid is void and his side may not bid again in that deal.

INSUFFICIENT BID. If a player makes an insufficient bid, he must make a sufficient bid and his partner must pass.

EXPOSED CARD. If a player exposes a card except in proper play, the card must be left on the table and played at the first legal opportunity. If the card is still unplayed at the first turn thereafter of the offender's partner to lead, either opponent may name the suit to be led.

If a card is exposed during the bidding, (in addition) the offender's partner must pass.

PLAY OUT OF TURN. If a player leads or plays out of turn, the card is treated as exposed (see above).

REVOKE. A player revokes if he fails, when able, to follow suit to a lead, trump a nontrump lead, or go over on a trump lead. A player may correct his revoke before his side has led or played to the next trick; his erroneous card then is treated as exposed. If not corrected in time, a revoke is established; the offending side then may not score for points taken in play (but does not lose its melds if it has previously won a trick).

Double-Pack Pinochle

This game is now the most popular variant of Partnership Auction Pinochle and follows its rules except as below.

CARDS. A pack of 80: four cards of each rank in each suit: A (high), 10, K, Q, J. (Shuffle together two regular Pinochle packs after discarding the nines.)

THE DEAL. Each player receives twenty cards, dealt in batches, usually five at a time.

BIDDING. The minimum bid is 500. In making a bid, the player may also announce that he holds a flush, or a long trump suit (but he must not name the suit or give other information). In passing before any bid has been made, a player may announce the total value of all (or part) of his melds; such announcement after the auction has been opened with a bid constitutes an overcall of 10 points for each 100 or fraction announced. (E.g., announcing a meld of 120 is an overcall of the previous bid by 20 points; announcing a meld of 240 is an overcall by 30 points.)

MELDS. Besides the basic melds (page 148) the following are allowed, with increased values:

Double aces	1000	Triple kings	1200
(two of each suit)		Triple queens	900
Double kings	800	Triple jacks	600
Double queens	600	Double pinochle	300
Double jacks	400	Triple pinochle	450
Triple aces	1500	Quadruple pinochle	3000
(three of each suit)			

Quadruple aces, etc., count merely as two double melds. Note that there is no increased value for a multiple flush. A side's melds do not count unless it has won a trick (which need not contain a scoring card).

SCORING. The point values of the cards are: 10 for each ace, ten, and king; nothing for queens and jacks. Last trick counts 20. The points in the pack total 500 including last trick.

If the bidding side wins, in melds and tricks, at least what it has bid, it scores all it makes. If the bid is defeated, the amount of the bid is deducted from its score. The other side scores all it makes, in either case.

Game is fixed at various amounts in different circles: 5,000, or 4,550, sometimes 3,550. If both sides might reach game in the same deal, the bidding side counts first.

BÉZIQUE

BÉZIQUE *in France was the principal inspiration of Pinochle, and two-hand Pinochle (page 147) is almost identical with the original Bézique. There have been numerous developments of Bézique, and two of them—* RUBICON BÉZIQUE *and* SIX-PACK BÉZIQUE *or* CHINESE BÉZIQUE *(no connection with Chinese games)—are the only ones still played to any extent. Both are described below, beginning with Rubicon Bézique.*

Rubicon Bézique

PLAYERS. TWO.

CARDS. A pack of 128; four 32-card packs, A to 7 in each suit, ranking A, 10, K, Q, J, 9, 8, 7. Shuffle together four regular packs after discarding all twos to sixes inclusive.

THE DEAL. Each player receives nine cards, one at a time. The rest of the pack is left face down on the table, forming the stock. The winner of each deal deals the next.

THE PLAY. Nondealer makes the opening lead. The cards are played in tricks. Until the stock is exhausted, the second player to a trick need not follow suit—he may play any card. A trick is won by the higher trump, or by the higher card of the suit led. (Of identical cards, the one led wins.) The winner of a trick leads to the next, but first draws the top card of the stock and opponent takes the next card; thus the hands are maintained at nine cards until the stock is exhausted. Cards won in tricks during the early play have no scoring value.

Play begins without a trump suit. But when the first marriage or sequence is declared, its suit becomes trumps for the rest of the play.

DECLARATIONS. A declaration in Bézique is the same as a meld in Pinochle—a combination of cards that scores points when properly placed face up on the table.

Carte blanche may be claimed by a player who is dealt no picture card (king, queen, or jack). He exposes his whole hand before playing to the trick and scores 50. He scores 50 again each time he draws a nonpicture card, but on first drawing a picture card he may no longer score for carte blanche.

Any other declaration may be claimed only after the owner has won a trick and before he draws from the stock. The declarations are:

Sequence (A-K-Q-J-10) in trumps	250
Sequence in a nontrump suit ("back door")	150
Marriage (K, Q) in trumps	40
Marriage in a nontrump suit	20
Any four aces	100
Any four kings	80
Any four queens	60
Any four jacks	40
Bézique (♠Q and ◇J)	40
Double bézique	500
Triple bézique	1500
Quadruple bézique	4500

A player may declare a trump marriage for 40, then later add the trump A-J-10 to score 250 for sequence. But if the whole sequence is declared first, the marriage is lost.

Declarations are faced on the table but remain a part of the hand; the cards may be played to tricks. After playing

a card from a declaration, the owner may score for it again
by declaring a duplicate or equivalent of the played card;
e.g., after playing a king from declared 80 kings, he may lay
down another king and again score 80.

The same card may be used in more than one declaration, e.g., the same ace may serve in both a sequence and
100 aces. But only one declaration may be scored in a turn.
Therefore if a player lays down a card that fits with two
or more declarations, he must specify which he will score at
the moment. The other scores are not lost, however, they
may be scored when he again wins a trick or tricks. E.g.,
four jacks are declared for 40; they include a $\diamond$ J and the
player already has $\spadesuit$ K Q on the table. He says "40 for
bézique to come" and scores it when next he wins a trick.

A deferred score is so credited only if the declaration is
still on the table at that time; if any card essential to it
has been played in a trick, the score is lost.

Multiple béziques may be scored one at a time, i.e., the
first bézique scores 40; if a second is added to it, the player
receives 500. Thus the four béziques melded one at a time
would accumulate 6540 points.

LATER PLAY. After the last two cards of the stock are
drawn, there may be no more declaring. Each player picks
up his cards and the hands are played out. At this time, the
second player to a trick must follow suit if able, and when
void of a nontrump lead must trump it if able. The objects
in play are to win the last trick, counting 50, and to win
brisques—aces and tens—each counting 10.

SCORING. Each player accumulates his score during the
play. It is easiest to draw poker chips from a common pool,
or to use a "Bézique marker" manufactured for the purpose.
Each deal is a separate game. The player with the higher
total receives a bonus of 500. Settlement is made on the
difference of final totals.

The only score counted from the play, usually, is 50 for
last trick. But brisques (of both players) are also counted
when there is a question of winning or escaping *rubicon*.

The loser is rubiconed if his final total is under 1,000. In
such case, the winner scores 1,000 for game (instead of
500), plus the *sum* (instead of the difference) of the two
final totals.

Chinese or Six-Pack Bézique

This game is essentially Rubicon Bézique played with a pack of 192 cards—six duplicates each of A, 10, K, Q, J, 9, 8, 7, in each suit. Each player receives twelve cards, dealt three at a time. The declaration bézique varies; it is:

> ♠ Q and ◊ J when spades are trumps
> ◊ Q and ♠ J when diamonds are trumps
> ♡ Q and ♣ J when hearts are trumps
> ♣ Q and ♡ J when clubs are trumps

Carte blanche counts 250. Besides the declarations listed on page 148, the following count:

Four aces of trumps	1000
Four tens of trumps	900
Four kings of trumps	800
Four queens of trumps	600
Four jacks of trumps	400

Brisques are never counted. Tricks are thrown into a common pile, and the only stake in the play is last trick. The same suit may not be trumps in two successive deals, so if the first marriage declared is in the preceding trump suit it counts only 20 and does not establish the trump.

The bonus for winning game is 1,000. When the loser scores less than 3,000, the winner takes the sum of the final scores but receives no larger game bonus.

STRATEGY OF SIX-PACK BÉZIQUE

The first thought is to declare a marriage and make the trump suit, even if future declaring possibilities are lost and even if weaker in the suit declared than in some other suit.

The object of play is almost entirely to save cards that may turn into declarations. Tens, nines, eights and sevens are almost meaningless. By far the most important cards are the queens and jacks that make bézique. These should never be played until it is absolutely certain that no more béziques can be formed.

Having scored four of a kind, make haste to play one of them so that the same declaration can be scored again.

A player threatened with losing a rubicon does not have to score his declarations.

KLABERJASS

KLABERJASS *means "jack of clubs"—originally the highest trump card in Central European card games. This popular two-hand development, popular also in France as* BELOTTE, *was immortalized in American picaresque literature by Damon Runyon and is known by various names and spellings:* CLOB, CLOBBER, CLABBER, KLAB, KLOB, *etc.—sometimes even by the name* KALABRIÁS, *which actually is a different game, played in Hungary.*

PLAYERS. Two.

CARDS. A pack of 32, A, K, Q, J, 10, 9, 8, 7 in each suit. From a regular pack of 52 discard all twos to sixes inclusive.

In trumps, the rank is: J (high), 9, A, 10, K, Q, 8, 7. The trump jack is called *jass,* pronounced "yahss." The trump 9 is *menel,* pronounced "muh-NELL," and the 7 is *dix,* pronounced "deece." In each nontrump suit the rank is: A (high), 10, K, Q, J, 9, 8, 7.

THE DEAL. Each player receives six cards, dealt three at a time. The next card of the pack is turned face up and placed partly underneath it. This so-called *trump card* proposes trumps for that deal.

BIDDING. Nondealer declares first, saying *pass* or *take* or *schmeiss.* If he passes, dealer may then pass, take, or schmeiss.

If either takes, he accepts the suit of the trump card, thereby becoming the trump *maker,* and play begins forthwith.

The schmeiss is a proposal to abandon the deal; if it is accepted, the cards are thrown in and the next dealer deals; if it is refused, the schmeisser becomes the trump maker at the suit of the turned card.

If both players pass, nondealer may name any other suit as trumps, or may pass. If he passes, dealer has the same options. If both pass a second time, the deal is abandoned.

SERVING. After the trump suit is decided, dealer gives a batch of three more cards to each hand. By custom, he then turns the bottom card of the pack face up. (Thus two cards not in play are known to both players; their identity often affects the strategy of play.)

THE DIX. If the turned card is accepted for trump, either player holding the dix may exchange it for the trump card, thereby obtaining a higher trump. He may not make this exchange after playing to the first trick. (Dealer may delay it until after nondealer has led, but this privilege is often waived as a matter of etiquette.)

SEQUENCES. Three or more cards of the same suit and in sequence have potential scoring value. For the purposes of sequence, all suits rank: A (high), K, Q, J, 10, 9, 8, 7. A sequence of three cards counts 20; four or more count 50.

Only one player is entitled to score for sequence. Therefore nondealer before leading must say "No sequence" or "May I lead?" or "Twenty" or "Fifty"—announcing the value of his best sequence. Dealer then makes appropriate reply—"Lead" or "Good" or "Not good." Further information is given, but only to the extent necessary to establish which player has the higher sequence; this player then exposes and scores the sequence; he may also score any additional sequences he holds. His opponent may score none.

A sequence worth 50 is higher than one worth 20; as between two of the same value, the one with the higher top card wins; as between otherwise equal sequences, a trump beats a nontrump sequence; finally, if the players hold equal nontrump sequences, that of nondealer wins.

THE PLAY. The question of sequence being settled, nondealer makes the opening lead. The hands are played out in tricks. The second player to a trick must follow suit to the lead if able, and if void of a nontrump led must trump if able. When a trump is led, he must win if able. A trick is won by the higher trump, if any, or by the higher card of the suit led. The winner of a trick leads to the next.

BELLA. If a player holds the king and queen of trumps, he may score 20 for them by calling "Bella" on playing the second of the two. The call is not obligatory, and indeed is omitted when this player sees that he is going bete.

SCORING. The object of play is to win specific cards rather than tricks as such. But winning the last trick, called *stich* ("stish"), counts 10.

High cards won in tricks count as follows:

Jass	20
Menel	14
Each ace	11
Each ten	10
Each king	4
Each queen	3
Each jack	2

At the end of play, each player counts what he has taken in tricks, together with any due score for stich, sequence, bella. If the trump maker has a higher total, each player scores his total. If the totals are equal, only the opponent of the maker scores. If the maker has a lower total, he is *bete* and his opponent scores the sum of the two totals.

GAME. The player first to reach a total of 500 wins a game.

IRREGULARITIES IN KLABERJASS

EXPOSED CARD. If a card that would go to nondealer is exposed during the deal, he may accept it or demand a new deal. If dealer exposes a card going to himself, he must accept it.

WRONG NUMBER OF CARDS. If either hand is found incorrect, nondealer—if he has not made his first bid—may decide whether to require a redeal or a rectification. In the latter case, a short hand draws additional cards from the top of the stock; a long hand is placed face down and the opponent draws out the excess cards.

FALSE DECLARATION. If a player asks "How high?" or otherwise obtains unwarranted information about an adverse sequence when he himself has none or when his is already established as high, or otherwise causes his opponent to disclose facts about his hand that could properly have been withheld, the offender loses the deal: Opponent scores all the points in the deal, including bella.

REVOKE. Failure to follow suit when able, to trump when able, or to go over a trump lead when able, is a revoke. A revoke may be corrected without penalty before the next lead; otherwise the offender's opponent scores all the points in the deal, including bella if either player held the K-Q of trumps.

STRATEGY OF KLABERJASS

The normal minimum for a "take" is a hand containing 40 points in high trumps and side aces and tens. But the state of the score and the particular hand often justifies a take on 35 or even 30.

Length in the trump suit is not essential for a take or a make. More vital is the presence or absence of jass. A singleton jass plus a side ace and ten is the "classic take," whereas many four-trump hands lacking jass and menel go bete.

Dealer should obviously shade the minimum for a take when nondealer passes, rather than let his opponent name a new suit. But a good defensive hand—general top strength, or several cards in jacks and nines—should seek to let the opponent name the trump.

The schmeiss is a psychological weapon, used with a hand too weak for a sound take but better at the turned suit than any other. Normally, nondealer should not schmeiss on the first round, for then he may be compelled to become trump maker against a "rockcrusher" in dealer's hand. But this very principle makes the schmeiss in this position a powerful weapon if used sparingly. It can bluff the dealer out of a superior hand.

Never bid in the hope of receiving a specific card in the three served after the bidding. But these cards do add to the strength of the hand (20 points on average), and do justify the expectation that you will receive guards for a singleton menel or ten. That is why such cards are given their face value in the bidding.

SKAT

SKAT *was developed prior to 1818 in Altenburg, Germany, out of two pre-existing games,* TAROK *and* SCHAFKOPF. *The rules of Skat were codified at a congress of more than a thousand players at Altenburg in 1886. German immigrants brought the game to the United States and an American Skat League was founded at St. Louis, Missouri, in 1898. The variant described below,* RAUBER SKAT, *is simpler than the original game and is gradually displacing it.*

PLAYERS. Three. Reckoning leftward (clockwise) from the dealer, they are called: forehand, middlehand, endhand. With only three at the table, the dealer is endhand. But four or five often sit at the table, only three playing at a time; dealer gives no cards to himself (and, in five-hand, no cards to the player second from his right), so the active player nearest the dealer's right becomes endhand.

CARDS. A pack of 32; from a regular pack of 52 all ranks from 2 to 6 inclusive are discarded.

The four jacks are always the highest trumps, ranking: ♣ J (high), ♠ J, ♡ J, ◇ J. A nontrump suit ranks: A (high), 10, K, Q, 9, 8, 7, and this is also the rank of the trump suit (if any) after the ◇ J.

THE DEAL. Each active player receives ten cards, dealt in batches of 3-4-3. After the first round of the deal, two cards are dealt in the center of the table; these are the *skat* (or *widow*).

BIDDING. After the deal is completed, the players bid for the right to name "the game" at which it shall be played. This right belongs initially to forehand; it can be taken from him only by a bid that he is unwilling to equal. Middlehand therefore declares first; he may pass or make a bid. If he bids, forehand may pass and relinquish his right, or may say "I stay" or "Hold," signifying that he holds his right by making an equal bid. Middlehand may raise his own bid repeatedly in effort to overcall forehand.

After these two have settled on a survivor, endhand may bid against the survivor in the same way, winning the right only if he bids higher than the other is willing to go.

The player who finally makes or accepts the highest bid is the Player.

A bid names merely a number of points; it must be the possible value of some "game," but no game or suit is stated in making the bid. The lowest valid bid is 18; the highest practicable bid is around 100, though the scoring value of a game can turn out to be more than 200.

The "Games." There are eight possible games, as follows:

GAME	TRUMPS ARE	BASE VALUE
Diamonds	◇	9
Hearts	♡	10
Spades	♠	11
Clubs	♣	12
Grand	Jacks only	20
Reject	Jacks only	10
		ABSOLUTE VALUE
Simple Null	none	23
Open Null	none	24

Trumps. Whenever a suit is named trumps, the four jacks are nevertheless the four top trumps, as stated previously.

Grand. In this game, the jacks are the only trumps.

Reject. This is a game that may be named only by forehand if both other players have passed without a bid. Jacks are trumps; the skat is set aside; the object of play is to take as few points as possible.

Null. In both Null games, there are no trumps, and in every suit the rank is: A (high), K, Q, J, 10, 9, 8, 7. The Player makes his game only if he takes not a single trick. In Simple Null his hand is concealed; in Open Null he places it face up on the table for the Opponents to see. The values of the Null games, as stated in the table, are absolute (not subject to multipliers, as explained below).

VALUE OF GAME. The "value" of a game (other than Null) is its base value, as given above, multiplied by a factor which is the sum of all due "multipliers." This factor is at least 2 and can go as high as 14. A player cannot know all the multipliers that will apply until the cards are played out; during the bidding, he can only estimate the probable value of his contemplated game.

THE SKAT AND HANDPLAY. Whoever emerges from the bidding with the right to name the game is now called the Player; the other two, who combine in temporary partnership against him, are called the Opponents.

The Player is entitled to pick up the skat, then name his game. Or, he may elect "handplay," in which event he puts the skat aside and names his game without looking at it. But if the Player takes the skat he may not name Null or Reject, in both of which the skat must be set aside.

If the Player picks up the skat, he then discards any two cards. These cards are added to his tricks and count for him in the scoring.

If the Player sets aside the skat, then: at Suit or Grand, the skat goes to the Player after the play; at Reject, it goes to winner of the last trick; at Null, it is ignored.

Having declared a handplay Suit or Grand, the Player may seek to increase the value of his game by declaring "open." In this event, he places his hand face up on the table; the base value of his game then becomes 59 (whatever the suit or Grand named).

PREDICTION. The Player may, before the opening lead, seek to increase the multipliers applicable to his game, by making a prediction (which is in effect a contract): *Schneider,* that he will take at least 91 points in tricks; or *Schwarz,* that he will take all the tricks.

THE PLAY. After the Player has named the game and
disposed of the skat, play begins. The opening lead is made
invariably by forehand. A hand must follow suit to a lead
if able. (At a suit game, the lead of a jack calls for the
named suit, which may not be the same as the suit of the
jack.) If unable to follow suit, a hand may play any card.
A trick is won by the highest trump played, or, if it contains no trump, by the highest card played of the suit led.
The winner of a trick leads to the next.

OBJECT OF PLAY. This depends on the game. In *Suit* or
Grand: to win valuable cards in tricks. In *Null*: to win no
trick. In *Reject*: to take as few points in tricks as possible.

The values of cards taken in tricks at Suit or Grand are:

Each ace	11
Each ten	10
Each king	4
Each queen	3
Each jack	2

The total of points in the pack is 120.

BID MADE OR LOST. At a Suit or Grand, the Player loses
if he fails to fulfill a prediction, or fails (without prediction) to take at least 61 points in tricks. He also loses if he
has overbid—that is, if the value of his game is found finally
to be less than his bid (as can happen regardless of what he
wins in the play).

MATADORS. At a Suit or Grand, the ♣ J and all additional
trumps in unbroken sequence with it are called matadors.
A hand is said to be "with" so many matadors when it holds
the ♣ J and "without" so many matadors when it lacks the
♣ J. For example, a hand whose highest trump is the ♢ J
is "without three," while a hand holding ♣ J, ♡ J at top
is "with one" because the ♤ J is missing. The number of
matadors that the Player is "with" or "without" is one of
the multipliers affecting the value of his game; it is the most
uncertain, since he has to bid without knowledge of what is
in the skat.

MULTIPLIERS. The full list of multipliers is given below.
The point labeled Automatic is commonly called the "game
point." Since a Player is bound to be either "with" or "without" at least one matador, the minimum total of multipliers
is 2.

	MULTIPLIERS
Automatic	1
Matadors (with or without)	*Varies*
Handplay	1
Plus any one applicable item:	
Schneider made, not predicted	1
Schwarz made, not predicted	2
Schneider predicted and made	3
Schneider predicted, Schwarz made	4
Schwarz predicted and made	5

SCORING. The Player alone scores, except in Reject. If he makes his bid, he is credited with the full value of his game (which may be far more than his bid). If he fails in a Suit or Grand, he loses the amount of his bid at handplay, or twice the amount of his bid if he took the skat.

At either Null game, the Player wins or loses the fixed value according as he makes or loses in the play.

At Reject, the player who takes the fewest points in tricks scores 10, or 20 if he wins no trick. If two players tie for low, the one who did not take the last trick as between them scores the 10. If one player takes all the tricks, he loses 30, the others scoring nothing. If each player takes 40 points, forehand alone scores 10 (being deemed the winner since he named the game).

The score is usually recorded on paper. When a session ends, the average of final totals is determined. (A player can have a minus score.) Then each player pays or collects according as his total is above or below the average.

IRREGULARITIES IN SKAT

MISDEAL. There must be a new deal if a card is faced in dealing or if the dealer departs in any way from correct procedure and attention is called to the error before the first bid.

WRONG NUMBER OF CARDS. If after the bidding has begun a hand or the skat is found to have the wrong number of cards, the error must be corrected: a player not involved draws the extra cards from the long hand and gives them to the short hand. A player whose hand was incorrect may not bid. If the error is discovered after the bidding has closed, the Player loses his game if his hand is incorrect, or wins his game if his hand is correct and an Opponent's is not.

LOOKING AT THE SKAT. If a player turns and looks at either skat card when not entitled to do so, he is barred from bidding and penalized 10 points.

WRONG DISCARD. If the Player discards more or less than two cards, then plays to the first trick, he loses his game.

REVOKE AND MISPLAY. If the Player fails to follow suit when able, he loses his game, but either Opponent may instead require the error to be corrected and play to continue (to increase the Player's loss). If an Opponent leads or plays out of turn or revokes, the error must be corrected if possible and the deal played out; in tournament play the Skatmeister (director) must rule whether the Player could have made his game without the misplay. (In social play, this matter is settled by agreement, or the players adopt the rule that an Opponent's misplay gives the Player his game automatically.)

STRATEGY OF SKAT

For a trump bid the hand should usually hold at least five trumps. The normal minimum for a handplay bid is eight cards that are trumps, aces, and tens. This may be reduced to seven if the player wishes to use the skat. It is unwise to bid in the hope that the skat will furnish a trump or other specific card, but proper to expect the skat to strengthen the hand by one trick. In discarding, the normal policy is to reduce short suits, keeping long suits intact. Sometimes a ten not guarded with the ace must be discarded in order to save it.

The Player should usually lead trumps. By pulling two trumps for one, the Player protects his side cards. He should not overlook the opportunity to discard unwanted cards, instead of trumping, when an Opponent leads a suit of which he is void.

The Opponents should try to keep the Player "in the middle," that is, throw the lead to the Opponent on the right so that he can lead through the Player. They should watch for chances to *schmier* (discard) aces and tens to each other, to keep them from falling to the Player.

SCHAFKOPF

Schafkopf (German for "sheepshead") is an old Middle European game, some features of which were incorporated in Skat. Whereas Skat became codified, Schafkopf has continued to be played under a variety of rules. The variant here described is the one most prevalent in the United States.

PLAYERS. Three. Four or five may sit at the table and take turns staying out of the deal.

CARDS. A pack of 32; from a regular pack of 52 discard all ranks from two to six inclusive. There is a permanent trump suit of fourteen cards, which rank: ♣ Q (high), ♠ Q, ♡ Q, ◇ Q, ♣ J, ♠ J, ♡ J, ◇ J, ◇ A, ◇ 10, ◇ K, ◇ 9, ◇ 8, ◇ 7. In nontrump suits the rank is: A (high), 10, K, 9, 8, 7.

THE DEAL. Each player receives ten cards, dealt in batches of 3-4-3. After the first round of the deal, two cards are dealt face down on the table as the *widow*.

THE PLAYER. Beginning with the player at left of the dealer, each in turn has the chance to take the widow (if it has not been taken before his turn). Whoever takes the widow becomes the Player. He discards any two cards face down. The other two combine in temporary partnership against him.

THE PLAY. The player at left of the dealer leads first, regardless of who is the Player. A hand must follow suit to a lead if able. (Remember that all queens and jacks and diamonds are trumps, and call for other queens or jacks or diamonds.) A hand unable to follow suit may play any card. A trick is won by the highest trump played, or, if it contains no trumps, by the highest card played of the suit led. The winner of a trick leads to the next.

SCORING. The object of play is to win high cards in tricks. The point values of the cards are:

Each ace	11
Each ten	10
Each king	4
Each queen	3
Each jack	2

There are 120 points in the pack. The Player undertakes to win a majority, 61 points or more. If he succeeds, he scores a number of *game points*, as follows:

For winning 61 to 90 points in cards	**2** game points
For winning 91 or more points (*Schneider*)	**4** game points
For winning all the tricks (*Schwarz*)	**6** game points

The two cards discarded by the Player after taking the widow count for him at the end of play.

If the Player fails to take a majority, a number of game points is deducted from his score, as follows:

Player wins 31 to 60 points, loses	**2** game points
Player wins less than 31 (*Schneider*)	**4** game points
Player wins no trick (*Schwarz*)	**6** game points

The player who first scores 10 game points wins a game.

LEAST. If all three players decline to take the widow, the hand is played at the game *least,* in which the object is to win as few points as possible. The widow is set aside but is added to the last trick. The rules of play are as usual.

In Least, if one player takes all the tricks, he loses 4 game points. If one alone takes no tricks he wins 4 game points. If each takes one or more tricks, the one who gathers the least in point values wins 2 game points. If two players tie for least, the 2 points go to the one (as between them) who was not last to take a trick. Should each player gather 40 points, the 2 game points go to the player at right of the dealer. (The theory is that he "declared the game" by making the third pass.)

IRREGULARITIES. Follow the rules of Skat.

STRATEGY. As there are fourteen trumps, an average share is about five. No length of less than seven trumps, possibly six if very strong, warrants taking the widow. Nontrump aces may be counted as tricks, but lower cards, even tens, are not countable. However, a long strong side suit (with consequent shortness in the other two suits) greatly strengthens the hand. With a two-suited hand, the Player should of course try to establish both suits as quickly and cheaply as possible. If long only in trumps, the Player must try to limit his loss in side suits, by using his high cards to catch tens and kings and by discarding useless small cards on tricks not worth trumping.

SIXTY-SIX

SIXTY-SIX is usually played two-hand, though it can be played by three or even four. It will appeal to you as being much like Pinochle, though simpler. The fact is that Sixty-Six is believed to be the ancestor of Pinochle. Despite its great age, the game continues to be widely played, especially in Germany, Austria, Switzerland, and among emigrants from those lands.

THE PACK comprises 24 cards, made by discarding all cards below the nines from a regular pack. The cards in each suit rank: A (high), 10, K, Q, J, 9.

To decide the first dealer, the custom is to cut cards (not draw them from from a spread pack). Each player lifts a packet and shows the bottom card. If equal cards are cut, the pack must be reshuffled and both players cut again. Higher card marks the first dealer.

The dealer shuffles the pack, has it cut by the opponent, then deals two hands of six cards each, three cards at a time. The rest of the pack, put face down, becomes the *stock*. The top card of the stock is turned face up and placed partly underneath the stock: this is the *trump card*. It decides the trump suit for that deal.

THE OBJECT OF THE GAME is primarily to win valuable cards in tricks. The count is as in Pinochle: ace 11, ten 10, king 4, queen 3, jack 2 (nines count nothing). Additional points may be scored by *melding* and by winning the last trick.

EARLY PLAY. Non-dealer makes the opening lead. During the early play, the second player to a trick may play any card he pleases—he need not follow suit. A trick is won by the higher trump, or by the higher card of the suit led if it contains no trump. The winner of a trick leads to the next.

After each trick, both players restore their hands to six cards by drawing one card each from the top of the stock, the winner of the trick drawing first.

A player holding the nine of trumps (called *dix*) may exchange it for the trump card just before drawing from the stock. He may do this even if his opponent wins the current trick, but he himself must have previously won at least one trick. (If the last face-down card of the stock is the dix, it may not be exchanged for the trump card, since this is drawn by the opponent in the same final turn.)

FINAL PLAY. After the stock is exhausted, a new rule of play comes into force. In the last six tricks, the second hand playing to a trick must follow suit if able; if unable, the hand may play any card. The winner of the last trick scores 10 points for it.

CLOSING. At any turn to lead during the early play, a player may *close* by turning down the trump card. Such closure brings into force the rule of final play, the hands then being played out with no further drawing from the stock.

MELDING. A *marriage* is a king and queen of the same suit, counting 40 in trumps or 20 in a plain suit. A player holding a marriage may show it in any turn to lead (early or final play) and then lead one of the cards. He scores for the marriage at once if he has previously won a trick, or when he wins his first trick (in case of a marriage shown by the opening leader).

SCORING. The deal is won by the player who first reaches 66 points. Practically every deal is won by *declaring out* during the play. That is, a player who believes he has reached 66 claims the deal, and his claim stops the play at once. If the claim proves correct, the claimant scores 1 *game point;* if it is incorrect, the opponent scores 2 game points. The first to accumulate 7 game points wins a game.

If a deal is played out without a claim, the tricks are examined and the total scores determined. If one player has 66 or more, his opponent less, he wins the deal. If both have 66 or more, or if there is a tie at 65 each, neither wins the deal, but the winner of the next deal receives 1 additional game point.

The winner of a deal, with or without a claim, scores 2 game points if the loser won less than 33 points in play *(schneider)*, or 3 game points if the loser failed to win a single trick *(schwarz)*.

If a player closes and then fails to reach 66, his opponent

scores 2 game points, or 3 if said opponent had not yet won a trick at the time of closure.

PENALTIES

There must be a new deal if either hand receives too many cards, and the error is noted before both have played to the first trick; otherwise, the play continues. When for any reason a hand is found to have too many or too few cards, and it is too late for a new deal, the hand is rectified by omitting some draws or by drawing extra cards from the stock.

Non-dealer has the option of calling for rectification or a new deal, so long as he has not looked at his hand, if the dealer gives either hand too few cards or exposes a card dealt to non-dealer, or if a card is found faced in the pack.

If a player leads out of turn, his opponent may accept the lead as regular. In any other case, a player exposing a card not intended to be played may restore it to his hand without penalty.

If a player in drawing from the stock exposes or sees a card he is not entitled to see, he must show his opponent the card he properly drew.

Revoke is failure to follow suit when able, at a time when the final rule is in force. The revoking player may correct his error without penalty before the lead to the next trick; otherwise it stands established, and the opponent of the revoker is credited with all scores made by both players on the revoke trick and all later tricks.

STRATEGY

The play hinges on marriages, since even a plain marriage is such a great help toward declaring out. Kings and queens must be saved so long as there is any chance of filling a marriage. Aces and tens should be expended freely in the early play, both to score them when opportunity offers, and also to keep the opponent out of the lead as much as possible. The jack should be deemed expendable, even as a lead in the early play, while the ace and ten of trumps should be used to win or hold early leads when any marriage is still open. The policy of building up a strong hand for the final play, natural in Pinochle, is rarely feasible in Sixty-Six.

PIQUET

PIQUET is a two-hand game, though it can be varied for play by three or four. Historical record carries it back at least 500 years. Its popularity is greatest in France, England, Germany, and other European countries.

The pack used for Piquet is 32 cards—the regular pack with all cards below the sevens stripped out. The cards rank as usual, with ace high.

To commence a game, the pack is spread face down and each player draws a card. The lower card marks the first dealer. If equal cards are drawn, both must draw again. The turn to deal alternates.

The dealer shuffles his pack (usually, two packs are used alternately), and his opponent cuts it, leaving at least two cards in each packet. Then two hands of twelve cards each are dealt, two cards at a time. The remaining eight cards of the pack are spread face down in a fan, forming the *talon*.

Non-dealer (called *majeur* or *major*) looks at his cards, and must then discard at least one of them. He may discard any number up to five. He takes enough cards from the top of the talon to replace his discards, without showing them to his opponent. If he leaves any of the first five cards in the talon, he is entitled to look at them, without showing them.

Dealer (called *mineur* or *minor*) is entitled to take all the cards of the talon left by major, but he may stand pat on his original hand if he pleases. Having discarded as many cards as he wishes (limited by the number left in the talon), he draws replacements. If he leaves any cards in the talon, he may set them aside face down, or may turn them face up for both players to see.

During the play, each player is entitled to look back at his discards, but of course must take care not to mix them with the cards in his hand.

Carte Blanche is a hand without a face card (king, queen,

or jack). A player dealt such a hand may score 10 points for it by showing it before he discards. (Dealer may wait to show carte blanche until his opponent has drawn from the talon.)

DECLARING. After the draw, non-dealer *declares* any scoring combinations he happens to hold in three categories. The categories must be taken up in the order given below; e.g., if non-dealer begins with the second, he may not score in the first. In any event, only one player may score in each category—the one who has the highest combination.

Point is the longest holding in any one suit. For example, a holding of five hearts is superior to four cards in any other suit. (The suits have no relative rank.) As between suits of the same length, the one of higher total count wins, counting ace 11, each face card 10, other cards their index value. If the two hands tie for point, neither player scores.

The score for the better point is equal to the number of cards, 5 for a five-card suit, etc.

Sequence is longest or highest sequence of three or more cards in the same suit. Any sequence of four *(quart)* beats any of three *(tierce)*. As between sequences of equal length, the higher-ranking wins; thus A-K-Q *(tierce majeur)* beats K-Q-J *(tierce mineur)*. If the two hands tie for sequence, neither player scores. But the hand with superior sequence may score all additional sequences. For example, if a suit A-K-Q-9-8-7 is entitled to score for the major tierce, the other tierce may also be counted.

The score for sequences is: tierce 3, quart 4, quint or higher (five cards or more) 10 plus 1 for each card, a total of 15 or more.

Set is the highest four of a kind or three of a kind, in a rank higher than 9. Here there can be no tie. Four of a kind beats three, and in a tie as to number the higher rank is superior. The hand entitled to score for best set may count all additional sets; having four aces, a player may also count, e.g., three tens.

The score for sets is: three *(trio)* 3, four *(quatorze)* 14.

Non-dealer must in each case initiate the comparison of hands for scoring combinations, if only to say "No sequence." Dealer responds "Good" if he cannot beat an announced combination, or "Not good" if he thinks he can. Further information is exchanged, only to the extent of settling whose combination is higher. But each combination that actually scores must be shown to the opponent. (Many players omit this *proving* of scores, leaving it to the non-scorer to infer the exact cards in an adverse combination.)

Neither player is compelled to make a claim merely because he holds a combination. Non-dealer, having only a weak suit of four cards, will often say "No point," conceding that dealer's best suit is good. A player sometimes *sinks* (fails to announce) a low trio, jacks or tens, to conceal the weakness of his hand in playing values.

SCORING. Each player mentally accumulates his scores accruing from declarations and play, and announces his new total each time he earns a new item. After the declaring, non-dealer announces "I start with . . ." giving his current total, and leads a card.

PLAY. The hands are played out in twelve tricks. Non-dealer leads first, and thereafter the winner of a trick leads to the next. A hand must follow suit to the lead if able; if unable, the hand may play any card. A trick is won by the higher card of the suit led.

The player counts 1 point for every lead he makes, and 1 point for every adverse lead he wins. (Formerly, leads of 9 or lower, and tricks won by a 9 or lower, were not counted, but the distinction has been abandoned in modern play.)

One extra point is scored for winning the last trick. The player taking a majority of the tricks scores 10 points, but if the tricks are divided six and six there is no score. For winning all twelve tricks *(capot)*, a player scores 40, which includes the score for majority and last.

PIC AND REPIC. If a player reaches 30 points in declarations alone, before the opening lead, while his opponent has no score, he jumps from 30 to 90 for *repic*. For example, a hand having all eight clubs and the other three aces would score 8 for point, 18 for sequence, and 14 for aces, the opponent scoring nothing. The total of 40 would be jumped to 100.

If a player reaches 30 points in declarations and play, before his opponent scores a point, he jumps to 60 for *pic*. For example, if non-dealer alone scores for declarations and reaches 29, his opening lead makes 30, which jumps to 60.

GAME. There are several methods of scoring games. The oldest is: the player who first accumulates 100 or more points wins a game by the difference of final totals, or double the difference if the loser failed to reach 50.

In the modern game of *Rubicon Piquet*, a game comprises six deals. The player with the higher final total wins the difference of totals, plus 100. But if the loser fails to reach 100 he is *rubiconned*, and the winner (even if he also failed to reach 100) wins the sum of the final totals, plus 100. In card clubs this game is often shortened to four deals, with the first and last deals counting double.

PENALTIES

There must be a new deal if a card is exposed in dealing. If a wrong number of cards is dealt to one hand, non-dealer may require a new deal or may let the misdeal stand. In this case, or any other where play has begun and one hand is found to be incorrect, a short hand declares, plays, and scores as usual, except that it cannot win the last trick. A hand with too many cards plays on, but cannot score anything.

If a player draws more cards from the talon than he is entitled to take, he may return the excess cards if he has not looked at them. If non-dealer draws more than five cards and looks at them, he loses the game forthwith. If dealer draws any card and sees it, before non-dealer has drawn, dealer loses the game forthwith.

If non-dealer announces sequence before point, or a set before declaring both point and sequence, he may not score in the category omitted. If a player concedes an adverse declaration to be good, he may not withdraw this concession.

If a player declares and scores a combination he does not in fact hold, he may correct his error before playing a card, and scoring in that category is corrected. Should he play a card before announcing such error, the player may not score at all in the deal, while his opponent may score for all combinations (inferior or not) as well as for points in play.

When a player through an irregularity is deprived of the opportunity to score at all in a deal, his opponent is not entitled to score pic or repic unless he would have made it without the penalty.

STRATEGY

Non-dealer should usually take all the five cards he is entitled to, trying for point and sequence at the same time.

He should discard low stoppers in worthless suits freely for this purpose, as Q x x. He should of course save his aces, and usually his kings, together with his largest suit. Three queens may occasionally be saved to try for four, but saving three jacks or tens is almost never good.

Dealer, with the opening lead against him, must look to protection in all suits possible, to split the tricks or win majority, or to avoid capot when there is any danger. His chance of winning point or sequence is slight unless he already has a long suit and a one-card draw for at least a quart. Hence dealer may often try for four queens, even four jacks or tens, in the course of saving stoppers and guards to higher cards. Dealer should usually take all the cards left, leaving any only when he can find no safe discard or happens to have an extremely strong hand.

Non-dealer should usually open his longest suit and continue to try to establish it. The advantage of the opening lead is considerable. The further play must be guided by the fall of the cards, the discards, and what can be inferred from the declarations. The play is often a "double-dummy" problem, with all cards known to both players. It is often a foregone conclusion that one player or the other will win majority through his superior high cards, and the fight then revolves around maneuvering to win last trick.

LE BATELEVR

LE PENDV

LE MONDE

SOLO *is the name of several different games. Two of them are here described. The first is a very old game derived from the European game Tarok, the game played with the ancient tarots (samples of which are illustrated above), the first playing cards indigenous to Europe. The second game is an elaboration of the first, developed in the Western United States early in the present century. Both are three-hand games.*

SOLO

THE PACK used for Solo is 36 cards—the regular pack with the fives and all lower cards stripped out. The rank in each suit is: A (high), 10, K, Q, J, 9, 8, 7, 6. Each player receives eleven cards, dealt in rounds of 4-3-4. The last three cards are left face down on the table to form the widow.

There are three possible bids, which rank in this order, low to high:

Frog is a bid for hearts as trumps. The bidder takes the widow and discards any three cards face down.

Chico is a bid to play without use of the widow, the bidder naming any suit but hearts as trumps.

Grand is a bid for hearts as trump, without use of the widow.

Eldest hand (at left of the dealer) bids or passes first. If he bids, the next player may bid higher or pass, and if he bids higher, eldest hand may bid grand to win the contract. After these two players have settled with each other, the survivor settles with the dealer.

185

Eldest hand makes the opening lead. A lead may be any card in the hand; each other hand must follow suit to the lead if able. When unable to follow suit, a player may discard or trump as he pleases. A trick is won by the highest trump, or, if it contains no trump, by the highest card of the suit led. The winner of a trick leads to the next.

At the end of the play, the widow or the bidder's discards are added to his tricks and counted with them. The two opponents combine in temporary partnership to defeat the bidder, and pool their tricks for this purpose.

The object of play is to win counting cards in tricks:

ace	11
ten	10
king	4
queen	3
jack	2
no count for lower cards	

The pack contains a total of 120 points. The trump maker collects or pays according to the number of points he takes above or below 60. If he takes just 60, there is no payment for the deal. The difference from 60 is paid by the maker to each opponent separately, or collected from each separately. The settlement is in the ratio: Frog 1, Chico 2, Grand 4. Each deal is a separate game, being settled at once, usually with chips.

The rules of Skat are followed as to irregularities and penalties.

STRATEGY

As any player of Auction Pinochle or Skat knows, an offer to play one hand against two opponents requires fairly solid values—if making the contract is vital. But in Solo, the penalty for being defeated is trifling as compared with other three-hand games. It is one of the few games in which wilful overbidding may pay. The defeat of an overbid by 5 or 10 points may cost much less than letting an opponent win the contract and name his own trump suit.

A conservative rule-of-thumb for a bid of frog is: four or more hearts with not more than four cards that are not hearts, aces, or tens. The trump length is often ignored by forward players, frog often being bid with a weak hand to goad another player into a chico when he has a good grand, or to induce him to misplay the hand if he calls grand. The bid of chico or grand—like the bid of solo in Skat—requires fairly sure values, but even here some over-bidding is natural. The bid of grand on a hand weak in high cards but long in hearts may save as against letting another player play a powerful chico.

SIX-BID SOLO

This variant doubles the number of possible bids. The six bids rank as follows, low to high:

Simple solo. The bidder (if he wins the contract) names any suit but hearts as trumps, and has to win 60 or more in tricks.

Heart solo. Hearts are trumps, and the bidder has to win 60 or more.

Misère. There is no trump; the bidder must avoid winning any counting cards in tricks (though he may win a trick without losing contract).

Guarantee solo. The bidder names any suit as trumps; at hearts, he must win 74 points or more; at any other suit, 80 points or more.

Spread misère. The same as simple misère, except that the bidder exposes his whole hand face up on the table after the opening lead.

Call solo. The bidder names any suit as trumps, and must win all 120 points (not necessarily all the tricks). He may call any card not in his hand, and the holder of that card must surrender it in exchange for any card the bidder pleases. (The naming of trumps may be deferred until after the call. If the called card happens to be in the widow, the bidder cannot obtain it.)

The widow is never used in the play, nor in the scoring of either misère game. At other games, it is added to the bidder's tricks after the play and counted with them.

All rules of play are as in Solo (page 226), except that at spread misère the opening lead is made by the opponent at the bidder's left. The object of play is the same as in Solo, and the settlement for simple solo or heart solo is the same as for a frog. The other games have fixed values as follows:

Misère	30
Guarantee solo	40
Spread misère	60
Call solo, hearts not trumps	100
Call solo, hearts trumps	150

The requirements for making the contract are stated in the list of bids. The bidder collects or pays the foregoing values to each opponent separately, according as he makes or fails to make his contract. Each deal is a separate game, settled at once with chips.

CASINO

CASINO (*often misspelled* CASSINO) *descends from French gambling games of the 15th century. It is now a great favorite among children, but that does not mean it is a childish game. On the contrary, professional card players rate it one of the most difficult to play well and an excellent training school for observation, memory, and inference.*

PLAYERS. Two. Variants for three and four are described later.

CARDS. A regular pack of 52.

POINT VALUES. The cards are used primarily to represent numbers. An ace represents one; each card from two to ten represents its index value; face cards in effect have no point value, since they may only be paired.

THE DEAL. To begin a deal, the dealer gives two cards to his opponent, two face up on the table, two to himself, then repeats this round, so that each player receives four cards and four are dealt face up on the table. After these hands are played out, the same dealer gives four more cards to each player, two at a time, but none to the table. The new hands are played out, then there is another deal, and so on: six deals exhaust the pack. There is no scoring until the pack has thus been run through. Before the sixth deal, the dealer must say "Last," since the fact that the pack is now exhausted affects the strategy of play. After the last hands are played out, all cards are gathered and shuffled and the duty of dealing passes to the other player. (Some prefer to play that the previous winner deals.)

THE PLAY. Nondealer always plays first. Each in turn must play one card from his hand. He may simply lay it face up on the table; this is called *trailing*. But he seeks when possible to *take in* cards from the table, or to *build* as a preliminary to taking in. The object of play is to capture cards from the table, in order to score points as follows:

Cards, for 27 or more cards	3
Spades, for 7 or more spades	1
Big Casino, the ◇ 10	2
Little Casino, the ♠ 2	1
Aces, each counting 1, total	4
Sweeps, each counting	1

(A player makes a *sweep* when he takes all the cards on the table at that time.)

Each player puts all the cards he captures in a single pile, face down, near himself. A sweep is marked by turning one card face up in this pile.

Cards remaining on the table after the last card of the last deal is played go to the player who was last to take in anything. But winning the residue in this way does not count as a sweep.

PAIRING. The simplest way of taking in cards is by pairing. A card from the hand may be used to take another of the same rank on the table. This is the only way in which face cards may be captured: jack with jack, queen with queen, king with king. All other cards may be taken two, three, or four at a time; if there are three aces on the table, a player may take them all with the fourth ace.

COMBINING. Two or more cards on the table may be taken by a card from the hand that is equal to their total point value. For example, 6 and 3 on the table may be taken by a 9; or 5, 4, and ace may be taken by a 10. Two or more combinations may be taken with one card; thus 7, 3 and 6, 4 may all be taken by one 10. Further, the card from the hand may capture by pairing and combining simultaneously; 9, 7, and 2 may be taken by a 9.

BUILDING. To build is to lay the card from the hand upon a card or cards on the table, making a combination equal in total to another card in the hand. For example, a player may lay a 7 upon a 2, building 9, provided that he has a 9 in his hand. Having made a build, a player may not trail at his next turn. He must take it in, or duplicate it, or increase it, or leave it temporarily while he takes in other cards.

A build may be duplicated or paired. Suppose that a player holds 10, 6, 3, and that on the table are 10, 4. He may put his 6 on the 4 and add the 10 from the table, as a build of tens. Should his opponent then trail a 7, he could place his 3 on it and add both cards to the build, deferring the capture with his 10.

A player may capture an opponent's build if he has the requisite card. The builder must state the amount of his build. If a player lays a 4 on a 4, he must say "Building fours" or "Building eight," and his opponent can take the build only with a card of the named value.

INCREASING A BUILD. A player may increase the total of a build and so change the rank of card requisite for its capture. For example, having in hand 10, 9, 3, A, a player puts the 3 on a 6 to build 9; at next turn he may add the ace and change the build to 10. The increase may be made only with a card from the hand; on a build of 6 a player may add an ace from his hand and increase it to 7, but he may not add an ace from his hand plus a 3 from the table and increase it to 10. When finally he (or his opponent) takes in the build, however, he may take with it any matching card or combination on the table.

Obviously, only a build consisting of a single combination (not paired or duplicated) may be increased. If all the foregoing provisions are observed, a player may increase a build whether it was initiated by himself or his opponent, and a build may be increased twice or even more often.

SCORING. After the pack is played out, and so divided between the two opponents, each counts what he has taken in. The total of points to be won is 11, exclusive of sweeps. It is usual to play for a game of 21 points, but among the most serious players game is either 11 points in two deals or 6 points in one deal and sweeps do not count.

COUNTING OUT. At any time during the play a player may claim that his cards taken in have already brought his score up to 21 or more (or whatever is agreed upon for game). Play ends and the cards taken in are counted. If the claim is correct, the claimant wins the game forthwith; if it is incorrect, he loses the game.

IRREGULARITIES IN CASINO

MISDEAL. It is a misdeal if the shuffle or cut is omitted and an opponent of dealer calls attention to the omission before playing any card. In three-hand play, a misdeal loses the right to deal. In two- and four-hand play, either opponent may designate which side shall redeal after a misdeal.

INCORRECT HAND. If dealer gives an opponent too many cards, that player may face the excess on the table and dealer must play the next round with a short hand. If a hand has too many cards by reason of failure to play in turn, it must trail in each subsequent turn during that round. If a hand has too few cards due to playing more than one card in a turn, it plays on with a short hand. If the stock is found short in the final round of dealing, dealer must play on with a short hand.

EXPOSED CARDS. In two- and three-hand play, a player must trail with a card he exposes prematurely, or with which he tries to take in cards illegally. In partnership play, a card named or exposed except by legal play must be left on the table as though the offender had trailed it; he and his partner may never take it in. None of the foregoing applies, however, to an exposed card that matches a build previously made by the offender.

ILLEGAL PLAY. An illegal play must be corrected on demand made before an opponent plays thereafter.

IMPROPER BUILD. If a player makes a build and cannot take it in (either because he lacks the requisite card or because the build does not fit his announcement), his opponent may add 1 point to his own score or subtract 1 point from the offender's score.

EXAMINING CARDS. Before the end of play, a player may not examine or count the cards he has taken in, except to establish a claim to game. If he violates this rule, opponent may add 1 point to his own score or subtract 1 point from the offender's score.

STRATEGY OF CASINO

In Casino "all" you have to do is keep track of the cards. Face cards go by pairs, so that if you hold one in the last hand its mate must be either on the table or in your opponent's hand. You surely can keep track of the "cash points" —aces and casinos. Take a spade in preference to another card when you can, until you have the majority. Try for cards above all else so long as you have a chance. When dealt a cash card, plan how you can possibly save it. If you are dealer, build with it as soon as possible. If you are nondealer, and nothing better offers, save it for your last play, since you will have first chance at it next deal.

An example of play:

NONDEALER   ON TABLE   DEALER

Nondealer has taken in twenty cards, dealer twenty-two.

Nondealer trails the ♡ 5. Dealer trails the ♡ 4. Nondealer put ♣ 3 on ♡ 5, building eight. If dealer should take the build, he would lose the rest of the cards, and nondealer would win the 3 points for cards and the 1 for the ace. Instead, dealer trails with the ◇ 3. Nondealer takes in his build. Dealer puts the ◇ A, ◇ 3, ♡ 4 in a build of eight. Nondealer takes the jack. Dealer takes his build plus the last card, making twenty-seven in all. Thus he wins 3 for cards and 1 for the ace—a net difference of 8 points hinging on his third play. (Nondealer cannot play better than he did.)

Royal Casino

This variant is much preferred by children. At the same time, it is regarded by some authorities as superior in its opportunities for skillful play.

The face cards are here given point values: king 13, queen 12, jack 11, and ace is 1 or 14 at the option of the holder.

All these cards may enter into building, and may be taken in triples and quadruples as well as in pairs. An optional rule is to count Little Casino as 2 or 15, Big Casino as 10 or 16. All other rules remain unchanged.

Draw Casino

This is a variant for two players. The game may be either the original or Royal Casino. There is only one round of dealing; the rest of the pack is left face down on the table as a stock. After playing a card, the player draws the top of the stock, thus maintaining his hand at four cards until the stock is exhausted.

Spade Casino

All spades are cash points: the jack counts 2, Little Casino counts 2 as usual, and each other spade counts 1. Game is 61 points and a Cribbage board is often used for scoring.

Three-Hand Casino

In three-hand, each plays for himself. Hands of four cards are dealt, with four going to the table only in the first round. Thus the pack is exhausted in four deals. The player at left of the dealer always plays first, and the turn passes to the left. All other rules are as in two-hand. Game is 21 points.

Four-Hand Casino

Two play against two as partners, the partners sitting opposite each other. Hands of four cards are dealt, with four to the table only in the first round. The pack is thus exhausted in three deals. "Last" need not be announced. One partner takes in all the cards for his side. There is actually little scope for partnership co-operation in the play, the partners merely pooling their scores. Game is 21 points.

GAMES PLAYED BY CHILDREN

CHILDREN ENJOY *card-playing from almost their earliest years and card-playing can be both educational and character-building for them if they are guided to its ideals of analytical thinking and sportsmanlike conduct. The following games are time-tested in their popularity with children. They range from the simplest games for the youngest children, such as* OLD MAID, *to true tests of skill such as* I DOUBT IT. *Children also can play and enjoy adult games such as Rummy, Casino, Dominoes, and Checkers.*

Fish

Fish is a simpler form of Authors, better suited to children. It is a good game for two players or more, up to about five players.

A regular pack is used. The cards are dealt one by one, and if there are two players, each receives seven cards. With more than two, deal five cards to each hand. Put the rest of the pack face down in the center of the table, to become the *stock*.

Each player in turn calls another by name, and asks for cards of a specified rank, as "Lucy, give me your sevens." The asker must have at least one card of this rank in his hand. If the one addressed has any other cards of that rank, he must give them up. The asker's turn continues so long as he succeeds in getting cards. Having none of the named rank, the one addressed says "Fish!" The asker then draws the top card of the stock, and the turn passes to the left.

Whenever a player gets a *book*, four cards of the same rank, he must show them and put them in front of himself. The one who gets the most books wins the game.

Children often make a rule of their own, and you had better not pull the rules book on them if they are set on it. This is the rule that the turn continues so long as the caller is successful in any way—such as if the card drawn when he is told to fish is of the rank he last named, or if it completes a book.

I Doubt It

I Doubt It is particular fun for a large group, say six to twelve. In this case, use two regular packs shuffled together. With five or less, use one pack.

Deal the cards out as far as they will go, two or three at a time until the last round. It does not matter if some players have a card more than some others.

Eldest hand begins by placing one or more cards face down in the center of the table, saying "Two aces," or whatever the number of cards happens to be. He must state this number correctly, and he must say "aces," but the cards actually may be of any rank. The next player at his left must then put some cards face down in the same pile, calling "kings" and stating the number. Play continues in the same way, each in turn calling the next-lower rank. After "twos" come "aces" again, and then "kings," the rank of the cards being circular.

If a player in his turn names the wrong rank, not the one that duly falls to him in turn, he must take up all the cards on the table and add them to his hand.

After each play, any other player may say "I doubt it." The last batch of cards played is then turned face up, and if any card is not of the rank stated, the player who put them down must take up all the cards on the table. But if the cards are correct, all of the named rank, the doubter must take all the cards on the table. If several players call "I doubt it" simultaneously, the one nearest the player's left is the official doubter.

The one who first gets rid of all his cards wins the game. He always puts his last batch of cards face up, because everybody is bound to doubt him.

While a favorite for children's parties, I Doubt It is actually a game of considerable skill. The trick is to arrange the hand with the ranks in the sequence in which they must be played; plan to be "honest" in your last five or six turns, and therefore do all your cheating early. If you are lacking some ranks near the end of your hand, it often pays to do some doubting, if these ranks are called early, in order to fill your hand. The ideal hand for going out is one with every rank represented. Or you may try getting rid of some ranks that otherwise would fall to you in your last several turns, by slipping them as "cheats" into your early plays.

Pig

Pig is a favorite "ice-breaker" for large parties, whether of children or adults. Any number may play, up to thirteen, and the more, the merrier.

From a regular pack, take four cards of a rank for each player in the game. For example, with seven players, take the aces, deuces, and so on up to sevens, discarding all higher cards. It does not matter what ranks you choose.

After shuffling, deal the cards out one at a time, thus giving each player four. The entire play consists in exchanging cards. All players take a card from their hands and place it to the left, then all simultaneously pick up the cards they find at their right. Actually, it is not important to keep these exchanges synchronized. The "ice-breaking" feature is that the etiquette of the game permits the player to scream at his right-hand neighbor, "Hurry up, I'm waiting!"

When any player gets four cards of the same rank into his hand, he must stop passing cards and put a finger to his nose. Each other player, on seeing this act, must quickly stop and put a finger to his nose. The last to perceive that the game is ended is a Pig, and is usually required to pay a forfeit.

Concentration or Memory

Concentration may be played by any number from two up. Take a regular pack of cards, shuffle it, and lay the cards

out one by one on a large table, with their faces down and
so spaced that they do not overlap.

Each player in turn must turn up any two cards, one at a
time, leaving them in their original positions on the table. If
they are a pair, he takes them and similarly turns up two
more cards. If they are not a pair, he turns them face down
again (still in their original position) and the next player to
his left plays.

The point is that by careful watching you can remember
where cards of certain kinds are. After turning up your first
card, you may remember what card to turn up to find its
mate. The object is to get as many pairs as possible, and the
one who gets the most wins the game.

This is a game that interests people of all ages.

Old Maid

From a regular pack discard one queen. Deal the others
out, one at a time, until all are dealt—they do not have to
come out even. Two to eight may play. Each player discards, face up, all his pairs (never three of a kind). Then
each player in turn shuffles his hand and offers it face down
to his left-hand neighbor, who draws one card, discards a
pair if he has drawn one, and offers his shuffled hand to his
left. Eventually one player must be left with the odd queen
and is the "old maid."

War

Two play. A regular pack is divided into halves, one for
each player, face down. Each turns up a card and the higher
card wins the other, the two cards going face down under
the winner's packet. This continues until the turned cards
are a pair; then there is "war." The pair are placed in the
center, each player adds a card, and each player turns a
card, the high card winning all six. If these third cards also
are a pair, they go in the center, each adds a card, and the
whole group goes to the winner of the next turn. Since it
takes a long time for either player to win all 52 cards, it is
usually agreed that the first to win three wars is the winner
of the game.

Authors

Originally Authors was played with special cards bearing the pictures and names of famous writers, and such cards are still available, but it is now more often played with regular playing cards. It is best known as a children's game, but in its four- and five-hand forms it is favored by many fine card-players as a game of skill. A simple version for very young players is Fish (page 195).

PLAYERS. Four to six. Three may play, but the game is then too simple for any but young children.

CARDS. A regular pack of 52.

THE DEAL. The cards are dealt face down, one at a time, until all are dealt; they need not come out even.

THE PLAY. Each player in turn asks any other player for a specific card, naming the player asked, the rank, and the suit, thus, "Joe, give me the ace of spades." If the asked player has the card he must deliver it, face up on the table. The asker must have at least one card of the rank he asks for and may not ask for a card he holds. (So by asking for the ♦ A he reveals that he has an ace but not the ♦ A.) A player's turn continues as long as the player asked has the card asked for. When an asked player refuses, his turn ends. The turn to play passes to the left.

The object is to form *books*, a book being all four cards of the same rank. When a player completes a book (or is dealt one) he immediately shows it, then turns it down on the table in front of him.

SCORING. Especially in children's games, the winner is the player who completes the most books. More serious players usually keep score with poker chips. Each time a player completes a book, each other player pays him one chip. The player who completes the most books receives an extra chip per player.

IRREGULARITIES. For any breach of the rules—asking for a card one holds, asking for a card without having a card of the same rank, failing to turn over an asked card when one has it, or failing to show a book as soon as it is completed—the offender pays a penalty of one chip to each other player.

BLACKJACK or TWENTY-ONE

BLACKJACK *and* TWENTY-ONE *are the same game, and in France, where it is very ancient, the game is called* VINGT-ET-UN. *However, the American gambling-house game (almost always called Twenty-one) is governed by simpler and more rigid rules than the home or social game (almost always called Blackjack).*

PLAYERS. Two to ten or twelve.

CARDS. A regular pack of 52. It is more convenient to use two 52-card packs shuffled together. The players should have poker chips or similar counters for betting.

THE DEAL. In gambling houses a representative of the house always deals. In home games the dealer may be changed frequently, as described below. Among some players the dealer is decided by auction, as in Baccarat (page 179).

The dealer shuffles and any player cuts. The dealer may then "burn" a card—show it, then place it face up on the bottom of the pack—or he may place a joker or blank card in that position. An ace may not be burned; the pack must be shuffled and cut again.

Cards are dealt one at a time, in rotation beginning at the dealer's left, but there are different methods depending on the betting method in use, as follows:

1. Each player places a bet before the deal. Each player including the dealer receives one card face down and then each receives one card face up.

2. Same, except that each player except the dealer receives both cards face down and dealer receives one down and one up.

3. Each player including the dealer receives a card face down. After looking at his card, each player places his bet. Dealer, after looking at his card, may double all bets. If dealer doubles, any player may redouble. Each player then receives a card face up. (This is the method usually followed in home games.)

THE PLAY. The values of the cards are: Ace, 1 or 11, as the holder wishes; king, queen, jack, ten, 10 each; any other card, its number. The object is to hold two or more cards that total 21 or as nearly 21 as possible without going over 21. For example, six, four, and ace count 21; seven, four, and ace count 12, for to call the ace 11 would put the player over 21. An ace and face card or ten in the first two cards are called a *natural,* or *blackjack,* and win the bet at once except from a player who also has a natural. A natural is shown and settlement made at once.

After the initial deal, the dealer settles with each other player separately. Each player in turn, beginning at the dealer's left, may either stand (on his first two cards, or at any later time), or may be dealt an additional card by saying "Hit me." He may continue to draw additional cards, but once he says "I stand" he may draw no more cards. All additional cards are dealt face up. If an additional card puts the player's count over 21, he must show his cards and the dealer collects the bet. The player's cards are then placed face up on the bottom of the pack.

When every player except the dealer has either stood or gone over 21, the dealer turns up his face-down card. In gambling-house games, dealer must take additional cards as long as his total is 16 or less and must stand when his total reaches 17 or more. In social games, dealer may exercise his own judgment. If dealer goes over 21, he pays each player who has stood. If he stands on 21 or less, he collects from each player having a lower count, pays each player having a higher count, and has a stand-off with each player having the same count.

As each bet is settled, the player's cards are tossed to the dealer and go face up on the bottom of the pack. Dealing continues from the same pack until the dealer reaches the face-up card, when he reshuffles all the face-up cards, has them cut, burns a card (or uses the joker), and continues dealing.

SETTLEMENT. A player may bet only against the dealer. Both a minimum and a maximum are placed on the amount a player may bet. Nearly all bets are settled at even money, but a player (not the dealer) may receive bonus payments as follows:

For a natural, 1 1/2 times the amount of the bet. (In social games, usually 2 to 1.)

For 21 or less in five cards, double; in six cards, triple.

For 21 composed of three sevens, triple; composed of 8-7-6, double.

In social games only, two special rules are widely played: 1, Ties pay the dealer; for example, if dealer and another player stand with 18 each, dealer wins. 2, Dealer as well as a player collects double for a natural. Also, in social games it is customary for a player who is dealt a natural to become the dealer when all bets for the current deal have been settled. If two or more players have naturals, the deal goes to the one nearest the dealer's left. If dealer also has a natural, he keeps the deal.

PLAYERS' OPTIONS. If a player's first two cards are a pair, such as two sixes or two jacks, he may play them as two different hands. When his turn comes, he turns both face up and places the amount of his original bet on each. Dealer gives him one card down to each. Then the player may hit, or stand on, each hand under the rules given above.

A player may turn up both his cards, double his bet, and "take one down for double." In such a case he may draw only the one card. Some games permit this only when the player's count is 11 or 10.

IRREGULARITIES IN BLACKJACK

A player who is omitted on the first round of dealing must demand a card from the top of the pack before the second round begins, or must stay out for that deal.

A player dealt two cards originally may discard one of them or may play them as two separate hands, with his original bet on each. A player dealt two cards later must discard one of them, and it goes on the bottom of the pack.

If the dealer hits a player who did not ask him to, that player may either keep the card or discard it. In the latter case it goes on the bottom of the pack.

If a player receives his first card face up, he may either bet and receive his next card face down; or he may drop out.

A player who stands on a total of more than 21 must pay double the amount of his bet, even if the dealer also goes over.

STRATEGY OF BLACKJACK

In a game in which dealer must hit 16 and stand on 17, the player's strategy should usually be: Always stand on 17 or higher. Stand on any number from 13 through 16 if dealer's showing card is 6 or lower, but hit if dealer's card is 7 through 10, or an ace. Hit 12 or under. Count an ace as 1 for any number up to 17 (that is, hit four-two-ace, counting it as 7).

Double down on 11 unless dealer shows an ace, and on 10 unless dealer shows an ace or 10-point card. Do not double down on other totals.

Always split aces or eights (most gambling houses do not permit aces to be split). Never split face cards, tens, fives, or fours. Split other pairs unless dealer's showing card is 7 or higher, or an ace.

In social games, when doubling of original bets is allowed: Dealer should double all bets on any face card or ace. A player should redouble on an ace but not on a face card.

Whether dealer should hit or not, when the choice is his, depends on how many players have stood against him and what he estimates their counts to be. A player against dealer, when several players above him have stood, should stand on low counts such as 12 or 13, for dealer will have every incentive to hit a high number and may go over.

BACCARAT and CHEMIN-DE-FER

BACCARAT, *a game related in principle to Blackjack, which is so popular in the United States, is the principal gambling card game of France and several other European countries. In recent years the original game of Baccarat has been all but replaced by its speeded-up version, Baccarat Chemin-de-fer, usually called simply Chemin-de-fer (or* SHEMMY, *or* SHIMMY*).*

Chemin-de-fer

PLAYERS. In a Chemin-de-fer game there are usually ten or more players, and almost any number can play, for it is a banking game. Every player has a chance to be banker, however.

CARDS. Several regular 52-card packs are shuffled together, usually at least three packs. The players take portions of the packs and shuffle them, trading them around to mix them thoroughly. The packs finally are placed in a device called a "shoe," from which the cards can be slid out one by one.

BETTING. There is an auction to determine the first banker, who is the one willing to bid the largest sum to be his "bank." The banker then deals three or four cards from the shoe, showing them as he does so, and tossing them into a tray reserved for discards. The game is ready to begin.

Any player may make any bet, up to the amount of the bank, that the banker will lose. The player at the banker's right has the first chance to bet; any part of the bank he does not take may be bet by the player at his right; and so on in order to the right until the entire bank is covered or until everyone has bet who wishes to. Any player may take the entire bank by saying "Banco," but when two or more players wish to banco the one nearest the banker's right has the privilege.

The banker is never liable for the payment of bets in excess of his bank.

THE PLAY. Bets being placed, the banker deals two hands of two cards each, dealing one card at a time. The hand he deals first represents all the players betting against him; the other hand is the banker's. The player who made the largest bet against the banker plays the opposition hand; and again, if there is a question of precedence, it goes to the player nearest the banker's right.

The object of the game is to hold two or three cards which count 9, or as nearly 9 as possible. The values of the cards are: Face cards and tens, 0; aces, 1 each; any other card, its number. Units of 10 points are disregarded, so that 9 + 7 count as "Six," not 16.

A player whose count is 9 or 8 in his first two cards shows his hand immediately. He has a natural and his hand wins (but a natural 9 beats a natural 8). Naturals of the same number tie, and there is a new deal.

When the result is not decided by a natural, the banker must "give" (a card) to his opponent on request; or the opponent may stand. The opponent *must* stand on 6 or 7, *must* draw to 4, 3, 2, 1 or 0, but "has the option" on 5. The additional card, if given, is face up.

Now the banker decides whether to stand or take a card.

IF BANKER GIVES	BANKER STANDS ON	BANKER DRAWS TO
Face card or ten	4, 5, 6, 7	3, 2, 1, 0
Nine	4, 5, 6, 7 (or 3)	2, 1, 0 (or 3)
Eight	3, 4, 5, 6, 7	2, 1, 0
Seven or six	7	6, 5, 4, 3, 2, 1, 0
Five or four	6, 7	5, 4, 3, 2, 1, 0
Three or two	5, 6, 7	4, 3, 2, 1, 0
Ace	4, 5, 6, 7	3, 2, 1, 0
Opponent stands	6, 7	5, 4, 3, 2, 1, 0

Neither player may have more than one additional card, giving him three cards at most. When each has exercised his option, the cards are shown. If the totals are the same, the bets are off and may be withdrawn, and new bets are placed, exactly as before, for another deal. If the opponent has a higher number than the banker's, each player collects such portion of the bank as he covered, and the player to the banker's right becomes the next banker, naming any amount as his bank (there is no further auction). If the banker has the higher total, he collects all bets and remains the banker; the original bank plus the winnings remain as the new bank, and bets are placed as explained before.

No player is forced to be or remain the banker. The banker may always retire and pass the bank along, and any player in turn may take it or refuse it. But until he passes the bank, the banker may not remove from it any part of his winnings.

Baccarat

Following are the differences between the original game, Baccarat, and the game of Chemin-de-fer described above.

1. The banker does not lose the bank when he loses a *coup* (the decision or result settling a bet). He remains the banker until he loses the entire bank or withdraws voluntarily.

2. The banker deals three hands—one to his right, one to his left, one to himself. He bets against, and plays against, the other two hands separately. Punters, or players against the bank, may bet on either the right, the left, or both (called *à cheval*). Players seated at the table with the banker have precedence in betting, those seated at his right having precedence, in order, in betting on the right, and those seated at his left similarly having precedence in betting on the left. Bystanders can bet only against what part of the bank is not covered by the seated players.

3. At the start of the game, or when a banker loses his bank or withdraws, the bank is put up at auction. The casino takes 2 1/2% of the amount of the bank. It does not participate in the results of the betting but it supplies a croupier to advise the banker.

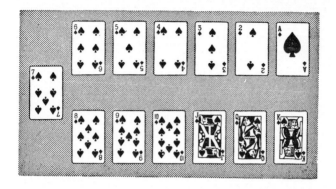

FARO *and its myriad variants were the most popular of all gambling games for centuries. By the end of the 19th century, however, it was largely supplanted by Poker, Black Jack, Craps, and other such games, and today is very little played.*

FARO

THE FARO LAYOUT, on which the patrons of a gambling house place their bets, comprises thirteen compartments, one for each rank in the pack. Suits are ignored in the game, but by tradition the layout is marked with cards of the spade suit.

Players may bet on a rank to *win* or to *lose* by placing their stakes on the appropriate compartments of the layout. A bet *to lose* is marked by *coppering* the stake, that is, placing on it a copper token furnished by the house for the purpose.

One pack of 52 cards is shuffled, then placed face up in a dealing box with an open top. The first card so exposed, called *soda,* does not enter into the betting. The bets being placed, a house dealer draws soda out of the box and puts it face up beside the dealing box to start the pile of cards that *win*. The second card is withdrawn and placed face up to start the pile of cards that *lose*. The third card, left exposed in the case, is the first card that actually *wins*.

The dealer immediately settles all bets that happen to have been placed on the first two ranks that win or lose. Bets on other ranks remain on the layout, to be settled when the first card of each such rank appears. After a due interval for the placement of additional bets, the dealer continues to the second *turn,* drawing two cards from the case, the first going on the *win* pile and the second on the *lose* pile. Bets are then settled on the identity of the *lose* card, and of the *win* card then exposed face up in the box.

Play continues in the same way until only four cards remain in the box—the last win card and three known cards in unknown order. (A house *casekeeper* keeps track of the cards that have already been drawn out of the box, for information of the bettors.) At this *last turn,* the conditions of betting change. Any bettor must place his bet on what he thinks is the order of the three cards yet unseen. If all three are alike, there is no "action." When two are of the same rank, it is a *cat-hop.*

The house pays off bets at true odds—even money on any given rank to win or lose—except in the following circumstances:

(1) When there is a *split,* two cards of the same rank showing on the same turn, the house takes half of all the bets, the other half being returned to the bettors.

(2) Payment is shortened on the last turn. The odds against *calling the turn* of three different cards are 5 to 1, but the house pays only 4 to 1. The odds against calling a cat-hop are 2 to 1, but the house pays even money.

The decline of Faro has been attributed to the fact that the house "percentage" is lower than that in any of the gambling house games that now flourish.

STUSS is a variant of Faro adapted to home play. The deal passes to each player in turn. The dealer merely holds the pack in his hand, instead of placing it in a case. The utmost care must be exercised not to expose any lower card in drawing off the top cards. Another feature that has made this variant popular with many gambling houses is that the dealer (or house) collect all the bets when there is a split.

SOLITAIRE

Solitaire *or* Patience *games, in their many differ-*
ent forms, probably have a larger following than any
other kind of card game. With rare exceptions, a soli-
taire game is a matter of laying out a "tableau," or
original layout; and then, turning up cards from the
"stock," or undealt cards, trying to build up piles of
cards which match in rank, color, suit, etc. On this basic
pattern, however, there are countless possible variants.
The ones described here are among the most popular.

Klondike

Klondike is probably the most widely known solitaire
game. It is frequently called Canfield, but actually the
game played at Canfield's in Saratoga in the gay 'nineties
was quite different. Klondike is also known under a variety
of local names, as Fascination, Demon Patience, the
Chinaman.

One regular pack is used. Deal twenty-eight cards into
seven piles. The first pile at the left has one card, the second
two, and so on up to seven in the last pile. The uppermost
card of each pile is face up; all the rest are face down. The
dealing is crosswise, one card to each pile, dealing to one less
pile each time, and turning the first card in each round face
up.

On the piles you may build in descending sequence, red on black or black on red. For example, on the ♠ K may be placed either ◇ Q or ♡ Q. All the face-up cards on a pile may be moved as a unit, and matched according to the bottom card. For example, if you have built the ♣ 7 on the ◇ 8, you can later move the two together onto the ♠ 9. When you uncover a face-down card on a pile, turn it face up. You are entitled to have seven piles, and if one is entirely removed you may put a king in the space.

Each time you free an ace, move it into a row above the piles. On the aces you may build up in suit and sequence, and to win the game you have to build each up to the king. Once played up on these foundations, a card may not be withdrawn to help elsewhere.

From the rest of the pack, the stock, turn up cards one by one. Put cards that you cannot use at once into one waste pile. You may always play off the top card of the waste pile. You may go through the stock only once.

An example beginning:

The face-up cards in your original layout are

Put the ♠ A in the foundation row and build the ♠ 2 on it. Put the ♣ 7 on the ♡ 8. Turn up the cards uncovered; suppose they are ♣ 9, ♡ K, ◇ 3. Move the pile from the left end (the ♡ 8 at bottom) onto the ♣ 9. That gives you a space, into which you can move either ♡ K or ♠ K.

Canfield

CANFIELD is named after the proprietor of a famous gambling dive at Saratoga. Here one could buy a pack of cards for $50 and play a game of Canfield under the watchful eye of the croupier, then receive $5 back for every card in the foundation piles, or $500 if he got all fifty-two cards out. Mathematicians do not attempt to calculate the odds on getting off eleven or more cards, but Mr. Canfield found them right and made a fortune.

Shuffle a regular pack and first count off thirteen cards from the top. Place them face up at your left. These cards are the *stock*. The next card of the pack is your first foundation ($5 back already!); put it above and to right of the stock. Then to the right of the stock deal four cards face up, starting your *tableau*.

Whatever the rank of the first foundation, the other three cards of the same rank are also foundations. When (and if!) they become available, put them up beside the first. Build up on the foundations in suit and sequence, ♣ J on ♣ 10, then ♣ Q, ♣ K, ♣ A, ♣ 2 and so on up to ♣ 9—the rank in the suit is circular, the ace being above the king and below the deuce. You win the game if you build each foundation up to thirteen cards.

On the tableau you may build down, red on black and black on red. For example, the ♡ J can go on either the ♣ Q or ♠ Q. One card at a time may be moved from the top of a tableau pile, or all may be moved as a unit. In the latter case, the bottom card must of course match correctly with the top card of the pile on which it is placed. For example, a pile ♣ 8, ♡ 7, ♠ 6 may be moved onto a red 9

Move the ♡ 7 up to the foundation row beside the ♣ 7. Build the ♣ K on the ♡ A. Fill the two spaces of the tableau from the stock. Then another space can be made by moving the ♡ A and ♣ K onto the ♠ 2.

You are entitled to have four tableau piles. If any pile is cleared away, making a space, fill it with the top card of the stock. After the stock is exhausted, spaces may be filled from the hand. Usually if the game reaches this stage it can be won. The great difficulty is to get all your stock cards into play.

The thirty-four cards remaining after you have dealt are the *hand*. Turn up cards from the hand in packets of three, placing them in one waste pile, face up. You may play off the top card of the waste pile onto foundations or tableau, thus releasing lower cards one by one. After you have exhausted the hand, pick up the waste pile without shuffling, turn it over, and there is your new hand. You may run through the hand by threes as many times as you wish, until play comes to a standstill.

Sometimes it would be a great help to take a card back from a foundation to make a move in the tableau. But Mr. Canfield's croupier wouldn't let you do that. It has been estimated that the average is only five or six cards played.

Accordion

Accordion is designed for the player who wants to know his fate in a hurry with no dilly-dally. The pack is dealt out, and there's an end on 't: You win or you don't, almost always the latter.

One regular pack is used. Deal cards face up, one at a time, in a row from left to right. Whenever a card is of the same suit or rank of the card at its left, or of the card third to its left, it may be moved over onto that card. For example, if your first four cards are ♠ J, ◇ 6, ♣ 3, ♠ 3, the ♠ 3 may be moved onto the ♣ 3 or the ♠ J. One move may open up others. For example, if you start ◇ 8, ♠ A, ♡ K, ♠ 8, move the ♠ 8 onto the ◇ 8 and then the ♠ A onto the ♠ 8.

Occasionally you have a choice in the order of several moves, and in this case you try to reduce the number of piles as much as possible. You win the game, ha! ha! if you get all fifty-two cards into one pile.

Golf

Golf has scope for a fair amount of skill, and it makes one of the best double solitaires where the packs are not actually amalgamated.

Use a regular pack. Deal a row of seven cards face up. Then deal four more rows on the first, making thirty-five cards in all. Overlap the cards so that you can read all indexes. This is the *tableau*.

The rest of the pack is the *hand.* Turn cards up one by one from the hand, putting them face up in one talon. You may go through the hand only once.

The object of play is to clear away the tableau, by building all the cards into the talon. One card at a time may be moved from the top of a tableau pile, if it is in sequence with the card on top of the talon. The sequence may be up or down. For example, if the cards uppermost in the layout are 6-7-8-7-6-5-4, they may be moved in that order onto the talon if it shows a 7 or 5. Suits are ignored. The ace is low and the king high. You may build 2-A-2, but when you have a king on the talon you may not put a queen on it—the sequence ends there. Occasionally you must refrain from playing off all possible queens and jacks from the tableau, saving some for kings not yet uncovered there.

The analogy with golf is that your score is the number of cards left in the tableau after you have run through the hand, and the lower, the better.

Double Golf

Two may play Golf as a double solitaire, each playing his own game with his own pack, by comparing scores at the end. Or they may play nine "holes" for lowest cumulative score. In this case, if a player clears away his entire tableau, any cards remaining in his hand are "minus strokes," and the number is deducted from his total score. Another scoring for the nine-hole game is to give one match-point to the winner of each hole separately, and five match-points to the lowest cumulative score.

Forty Thieves

Forty Thieves is also known as Napoleon at St. Helena, as it is supposed to have been the pastime with which the emperor beguiled his last exile.

Shuffle two regular packs together and deal a row of ten cards face up. Deal three more rows on the first, making 40 cards in all. Overlap the cards toward yourself so that you can read all the cards. This array is your *tableau.*

The aces are *foundations.* Each time an ace is released, move it into a row above the tableau. Build up on the aces in suit and sequence until you reach the kings. The game is won if you succeed in getting all the cards on the aces.

Illustration copyright 1939 by Whitman Publishing Company. From *100 Games of Solitaire*.

You may remove one card at a time from the top of a tableau pile, putting it on a foundation, or in a space, or on another pile if it is of the same suit and next-lower to the card on top of that pile. For example, the ♡ 5 may be placed only on the ♡ 6 on another pile. Any time you get a space in the tableau, you may use it to release cards from other piles, rearrange builds, and may fill it if and when you please by a card from the hand.

The sixty-four cards left after the deal are the *hand*. Turn cards up from the hand one by one, going through it only once. Play what cards you can on foundations or tableau. Put the ones not immediately playable in a single *talon*, overlapping so that you can read them. You have to keep track of duplicates, because it is not always advisable to make a move merely because you can. Usually you must plan from the beginning how you are going to make your first space, and this may involve not covering certain tableau cards you will need later.

The top card of the talon may be played off, releasing the next below. In the usual course of events, the talon strings out to great length before you get your first space, and then you have to plan carefully just how to dig back into the covered cards.

As in many other solitaires, kings are a nuisance. Until they can be built on foundations, kings can be moved only to spaces, which are then difficult to recover.

Spider

Spider is considered by many to be the best of solitaires, for it gives greatest opportunity to overcome the luck of the deal by skillful play.

Shuffle two regular packs together. Deal a row of ten cards face down. Deal three more rows on the first, squared up, making forty cards altogether. Then add one more card on each of the first four piles at the left. Finally, deal a row of ten cards face up on the piles.

This layout is your tableau and foundations together. The object of manipulation is to get thirteen cards of a suit on top of a pile, ace uppermost, and running in sequence from ace up to king as you go down the pile. Each time you have assembled a suit in this order, you may lift it right off and throw it out of the game. You win if you get all eight suits assembled.

On the tableau piles you may build down, regardless of suit or color. For example, the ♣ 7 may be placed on any eight. Of course when you can you try to follow suit, but it is more important to get all face-down cards into play as quickly as possible. Each time you clear all the face-up cards off a pile, turn up the next card. If you clear away a pile entirely, you have a space, and that is worth its weight in gold. You may put any available card or group of cards into a space. The only way you can get kings off, other than by assembling complete suits on top of them, is to move them into spaces. But don't be too hasty about doing so, for such spaces are the hardest to recover later. Spaces are needed to interchange cards among tableau piles so as to get suits together.

The top card of a pile is always available to be transferred elsewhere. Also, all cards in proper sequence and same suit as the top card may be moved as a unit. For example, if the top several cards are ♡ 6, ♣ 7, ♠ 8, you may move them only one at a time. But if they are ♡ 6, ♡ 7, ♡ 8 you may move one, two or three together.

Each time your manipulations come to a standstill, deal another row of ten cards face up on the tableau. Before doing so, you must fill all spaces. Then go to it again. After using up the entire pack, and making all the moves you can, that's the end of it—you either win the game or start another.

An example beginning: The face-up cards in the layout are

The first thing to do is to build the "naturals," those that follow suit. You have only one natural play, the ♡ Q on the ♡ K. The card you turn up is the ♤ 4. That gives you another natural; put the ♤ 3 on it. You turn up the ♡ A.

Next move any card that can go on either of two others, so that you may later move it again to make way for a natural, should the opportunity arise. Put the ♤ J on the ♡ Q. Should the ♡ J turn up later, you can move the ♤ J over to the ♧ Q to make way for it.

The ♧ 8 turns up. Now you have only non-natural plays left. Make a guess, and try the ♤ 7 on the ♧ 8. The ◇ K turns up— and you bemoan your bad luck in guessing! But at least that brings off the ♧ Q. Make this move at once, on the general principle of moving higher cards before lower. The ♡ 7 turns up, at present useless. The remaining play is to move the ♤ 4-3 onto the ♧ 5. The ◇ 9 turns up and now play is at a standstill. Deal another row of cards.

Cribbage Solitaire

Cribbage Solitaire depends upon Cribbage (page 78) for the scoring. Shuffle a regular pack, then deal three cards to your hand, two to your crib, and three more to your hand. Look at your hand and lay away two cards to the crib. Turn up the next card of the pack for the starter, and score your hand. Then turn up the crib and score it. Discard the eight cards used, place the starter on the bottom of the pack, and deal again. Continue in the same way until you exhaust the pack. At the end there will be four cards left; turn them up and score them as a hand, without a starter. Count for "his nobs" and "his heels" as usual, except in this last hand.

The object is to make as high a total score as possible in going through the pack. Average is about 85, so that you may consider that you win the game if you make 121.

Poker Solitaire

Poker Solitaire rewards both lucky guessing and accurate calculation of odds.

Shuffle one regular pack and deal twenty-five cards one by one, placing them in a 5 x 5 square. The skill arises in picking the best spot for each card. The object is to make as high a score as possible, counting each row and column as a Poker hand, and scoring as follows:

Straight flush	30
Four of a kind	16
Straight	12
Full house	10
Three of a kind	6
Flush	5
Two pairs	3
One pair	1

The hands are not ranked as in Poker, but in accordance with their relative difficulty in the solitaire game. A straight is hard to make, for if you play for it you risk making nothing at all or merely 1 for a pair. A full house is easier, for you can afford to play for it, scoring 6 or 3 if you fail. Flushes are very easy to make; in fact, the usual plan is to try for flushes in the columns and full houses or fours on the rows. Most of the time you will make three or four flushes without giving up any higher-scoring opportunities.

RUSSIAN BANK

RUSSIAN BANK *(called* CRAPETTE *in French) is a double solitaire in which the two play alternately. The moves are governed by strict rules of order, the penalty for violating which is to lose one's turn.*

PLAYERS. Two.

CARDS. Each player uses a regular pack of 52. The two packs should have different backs, so as to be readily sorted after a game.

RANK OF CARDS. In each suit the cards rank: K (high), Q, J, 10, 9, 8, 7, 6, 5, 4, 3, 2, A.

PRELIMINARIES. One pack is spread face down and each player draws one card. Lower card has choice of packs and seat, and has first turn. Both packs are then shuffled thoroughly.

THE LAYOUT. Each player counts off twelve cards from his own pack and places them face down at his right. This packet is his *stock*. Next he deals four cards face up in a column extending from above his stock toward his opponent. As shown by the diagram below, the two columns should be separated so as to allow for two additional columns between them. The eight face-up cards commence the *tableau*.

Each player puts the undealt remainder of his pack face down at his left; this is his *hand*.

See illustration of the layout on the next page.

THE CENTER. The space between the columns of the tableau is the *center*. Each ace, the moment it becomes available, must be placed in the center, after which cards of the same suit may be built upon it in sequence from two up to king. The first rule of order is:

I. *If an available card can be moved to the center or upon a center pile, this move must be made before any other* (except as in Rules II and III).

From the tableau depicted above, the first player must move the ◇ A to the center, then build the ◇ 2 upon it.

THE STOCK. After making all possible plays from tableau to center, in his first turn, the player must next turn the top card of his stock face up.

II. *A player must begin every turn after his first with at least one card face up on his stock.*

With regular play, there is always a card face up on a player's stock when he ends his turn. But if he commits an irregularity, it may happen that he is stopped at a time when no card is face up on his stock. In such case he must begin his next turn by exposing a stock card.

III. *On moving the last face-up card from his stock elsewhere, the player must immediately turn another card face up.*

Rules II and III are the only exceptions to Rule I.

IV. *If the stock card is playable upon a center pile, tableau pile, or tableau space, it must be so played before a card is turned from the hand.*

If a space in fact exists, the stock card must eventually be moved into it. But it is not a violation of Rule IV to refrain from making a space when possible. In fact, it is legal (and good tactics) to spread the tableau cards to fill all spaces, so as to get a look at the card from hand, before deciding about the stock card.

TABLEAU BUILDING. Cards may be built on the tableau piles in descending sequence and alternating color: red on black, and black on red; a six on a seven, queen on a king, etc. The diagram on the next page illustrates a stage of the

OPPONENT

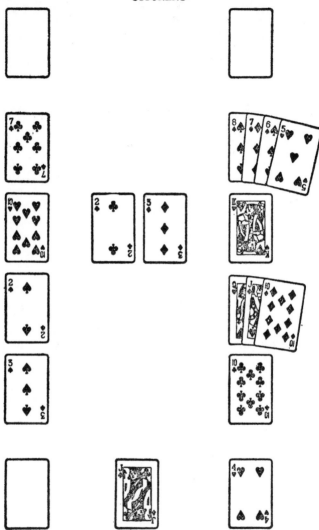

YOURSELF

tableau depicted previously, after the first player has done some building. Available for building are cards from stock, hand, and other tableau piles. One card at a time may be moved off a tableau pile (the whole pile cannot be moved as a unit).

When any of the eight tableau piles is cleared away, a *space* exists. The space may be filled by any available card (subject to rules of precedence), including the top card from any tableau pile. In the illustration, the ♡ 7 can be moved to the space so as to uncover the ♧ 8, which can then be moved upon the ♡ 9; replacement of the ♡ 7 on the ♧ 8 then leaves a second space.

The foremost object of tableau-building is to create spaces so as to get cards off one's stock. But Rule I must be borne in mind: If an uncovered card is playable to the center, it must be so played; it may not be kept in the tableau to facilitate building. Furthermore,

V. *When moves to the center are possible from both stock and tableau, the move from the stock must be made first.*

THE HAND. When the top card of his stock is unplayable (meaning among other things that all eight tableau spaces are filled), the player may turn up the top card from his hand. If this card proves unplayable, it is placed face up in a *wastepile* between hand and stock, and the player's turn ends. Should he inadvertently place it on the wastepile when it is in fact playable, his turn ends nevertheless the moment his hand quits the card.

If the card from the hand can be played, the player must then attend to any other plays thereby opened and having precedence under the rules, after which he can turn another card from his hand.

After his stock is exhausted, the player may move the card from his hand into a tableau space.

A card from the hand should be turned so that the opponent sees its face first.

The top card of the wastepile is NOT available—it can never be moved elsewhere. After the hand is exhausted, the player turns his wastepile face down (without shuffling) to form a new hand.

LOADING. At any time that tableau-building is legal, a player may get rid of available cards (from stock, hand, and tableau) by *loading* his opponent. This means building on the opponent's stock and wastepile. Such building must be in suit and sequence, but the sequence may go up or down or both ways. For example, the ♤ 8 can be placed on the ♤ 9 and then the other ♤ 9 on the ♤ 8.

STOPS. A player may call "Stop!" if he thinks his opponent has violated a rule of order. The players should then discuss and settle the fact, and if the charge is true the offender's turn ends forthwith.

In some circles, a rule is deemed violated if a player touches a card when he is bound first to move another. The usual practice in social play is to permit the stop only after the player has picked up a wrong card.

SCORING. Play continues until one player gets rid of his whole pack—stock, hand, and wastepile—into the center and tableau (and by loading). The winner scores 2 points for each card left in the opponent's stock, plus 1 for each card in the opponent's hand and wastepile, plus a bonus of 30.

IRREGULARITIES IN RUSSIAN BANK

Incorrect builds or plays may be corrected only if attention is drawn to them before the offender has completed a following play. After that the error, such as an incorrect sequence on a tableau pile, stands.

IMPROPERLY EXPOSED CARD. If a player turns and sees two or more cards at once, from stock or hand, he restores any card improperly seen and his turn ends.

STOPS. When a player violates a rule of order, his opponent calls "Stop!" The offender's turn ends and the opponent may let the incorrect play stand or require its retraction. If it was a play from the stock and is allowed to stand, the offender must at once turn up another stock card. A stop may not be called if the offender has been permitted to complete a following play.

STRATEGY OF RUSSIAN BANK

Though Russian Bank requires little more than close attention, it must be classed as a game of skill because the superior player will almost always defeat the inferior. Careful analysis is often required to make the most effective plays in the tableau, but there are no general rules.

DOMINOES

Dominoes *are thought to have been derived, in remote times, from dice—perhaps the oldest of all gaming implements. Dominoes are rectangular tiles marked with all possible combinations of numbers that can be rolled with two dice. There are twenty-one different combinations. But the number zero is always added to the set, by way of "blanks," adding seven more bones, as the pieces are called. The widely-used domino set contains twenty-eight pieces, the "heaviest" of which is 6-6. Sets are also made that run up to 12-12, containing ninety-one bones, but they are little used.*

GENERAL RULES OF DOMINOES

To begin any game, the bones are placed face down on the table and are shuffled by being moved about at random. Care must be taken not to face any domino in so doing. Each player draws a number of bones at random from this common pile, to form his hand. Dominoes are made thick and heavy enough to stand on edge on the table.

For the first play, a bone is laid face up on the table. All subsequent bones played must be matched with those already down, usually by like numbers on one end of the bone played and an *open end* of the layout. For example, if the first played is the 6-5, the next must have a 6 or a 5 at one end and be placed against the other with like ends touching. An open end of the layout is one on which it is legal to play. The number of open ends varies with the particular game and also with the circumstances. Usually these ends are self-evident, being in fact the ends of various branches, but sometimes new branches may sprout from the sides of old.

One object of a Domino game is invariably to get rid of all the bones in the hand. There may also be scoring in the course of play. The games are of two kinds according to the rule governing the play when a player has no playable bone. In the *block* game, he loses his turn. In the *draw* games, he draws bones from the common stock, called the *boneyard*, until he gets one that he can play.

The Block Game

The block game is the simplest of all Domino games. Two, three or four may play. With two, each player draws seven bones for his hand. With three or four, each takes five bones.

The player holding the highest doublet *sets* it—lays it down as the first play. The turn to play then rotates to his left. Each play is made by adding a bone to an open end of the layout, with like numbers touching. The layout always has two open ends. The two branches are built off the sides of the *set,* and all doublets are customarily placed crosswise, but this does not affect the number of open ends.

If a player cannot play in turn, he passes. The game ends when a player gets rid of his hand or when no player is able to add to the layout. The one with the *lightest* remaining hand (which may be no bones at all) wins the total of pips on all bones remaining in the other hands. The amount needed to win a game may be fixed by agreement, as 100 in three-hand play.

All that a player can do to control his destiny in this simple block game is to try to keep the largest assortment of different numbers in his hand as long as possible. For example, if a player has choice of playing the 5-4 or 5-3 on an open 5, he should choose according as he has other 4s or 3s in his hand.

Tiddly-Wink

Tiddly-Wink is the block game adapted for a large number of players, say six to nine. Each draws only three bones. The player with the highest doublet sets it. There is only one open end on the layout, three sides of the set being forever closed. Bones are played by matching as usual. If unable to play in turn, a player passes. Anyone playing a doublet, including the set, has the right to play a second time, if able. The first hand to "go out" wins, or the lightest hand if play comes to a standstill before any goes out. The winner takes a pool that is formed by equal antes from all players before the draw.

Sebastopol

Sebastopol is in effect a block game because there is no boneyard. Four play, and each draws seven bones. The 6-6 must be set, and the turn then rotates to the left of the first player. The 6-6 is open four ways, and the first four plays after the set must be upon it—no branches may be extended until all four have sprouted. In all other respects the rules are those of the Block Game.

The Draw Game

The Draw Game, at its simplest, follows the rules of the Block Game except that a player having no playable bone must draw from the boneyard until he gets one. After the boneyard is exhausted, a hand unable to play passes. The lightest hand, when play ends in a block or a player goes out, wins the total of points left in all other hands. Game may be fixed at 50 or 100 points.

Bergen

Bergen is a draw game in which the highest doublet is set and the layout always has two open ends. A player scores 2 points for *double-header* if he makes the two ends alike in number, or 3 for *triple-header* if in addition there is a doublet at one end. The winner of a deal scores 1 point. Game is 15 points.

Matador

Matador is a draw game in which adjacent ends on the layout do not match, but total 7. An open 6 calls for a 1, 5 for 2, 4 for 3, and so on. A blank is closed to the play of anything but a *matador*, one of the four bones 0-0, 6-1, 5-2, 4-3. A matador may be played at any time anywhere, without regard to the numbers, and with either end against the layout. Doublets are placed endwise, thus counting singly. For example, 1-1 is playable on a 6, not on a 5.

Sniff

Sniff is one of the best of all Domino games, especially when played by two. It may also be played by three or four. With two, each player draws seven bones for his hand. With three or four, each takes five.

First turn to play is decided by lot, and the leader may play any bone in his hand. As will be seen presently, he may score by his play. Until the first doublet is played, the layout has only two open ends. The first doublet becomes *the sniff*, and is open to play on all four sides.

The object of play is only secondarily to get rid of the hand. Foremost is to score during play. After each play the total of the numbers on the open ends is noted, and when this is a multiple of 5 the player who made it so scores the total. For example, if the leader sets the 3-2, he scores 5. If the second hand places the 2-4, and the third plays the 3-3 crosswise, the latter player scores 10.

Because sniff is open four ways, the first doublet may be placed either crosswise or endwise. For example, if the set is 3-2, scoring 5, the next hand may add the 3-3 endwise so as to score 5 also.

Although the layout is open in four directions after sniff is down, there still may be only two or three countable ends, for the sides of sniff do not count in the total until they have sprouted. A doublet other than sniff must be placed crosswise, and both its ends count in the total until it is canceled by the play of another bone on it. If the ends of sniff (as contrasted to the sides) project from the layout, they count even though they have not yet sprouted. For example, if sniff is 5-5, and branches are built off the sides until 6-6 is played on one side, 4-4 on the other, the total is 30.

If unable to play in turn, a player must draw from the boneyard until able. Some make the rule that the last two bones may not be drawn. It is well to have agreement on this point before commencing a game. A player may draw from the boneyard even if able to play without drawing— and sometimes it is worthwhile to do so.

The hand that goes out, or has the lightest count if the game ends in a block, wins the total points remaining in the other hands, taken to the nearest multiple of 5. For example, 7 counts as 5 and 8 as 10. In two-hand, the first to reach 200 wins a game. With more players, game may be 200, but usually is lowered to 100 by agreement, for there is less opportunity for scoring *muggins* points (for making the total of open ends a multiple of 5).

STRATEGY OF SNIFF

Certain bones are of intrinsic value because they give greatest probability of making a muggins score. The 5-5, 6-4, 5-0, 4-1, and 3-2 score as the set. The 5-5, 5-0 and 0-0 always make a score if played when the preceding hand has made a score. The 6-1 usually has the same effect. The 6-3, 4-2, 2-1 make a score if played after the previous hand has scored by playing the doublet of the lower number (3-3, 2-2 or 1-1). The bone that matches sniff at one end and has 5 at the other scores if played off a side of sniff after the previous hand has scored.

Especially in two-hand, there is opportunity to save such bones until they can be played to good effect. If the opponent is not too nearly out, it may be worthwhile drawing a few bones to try to avoid having to give up the 5-0 or 6-1 without scoring. Likewise occasion arises for drawing to get a particular bone that will make a score. A player with three or four more bones than his opponent is sometimes able to score in several successive turns, earning more than his investment.

CHESS

THE ORIGIN *of Chess has been the subject of innu-*
merable legends and fanciful histories. The earliest de-
scription of a game unmistakably Chess comes from the
8th century—not from an Egyptian papyrus of 4000
B.C., *as was once asserted. There is little doubt, how-*
ever, that CHESS *developed from simpler board games*
of remote times. It probably developed in India, whence
it spread to Persia and Arabia and entered Europe
through Spain and Italy. The present form of the game
as now played in most of the world was reached about
400 years ago. From India the game also spread east-
ward and in Japan developed a form markedly different
from the Western game.

PLAYERS. Chess is played by two, on a board with pieces
of special design. The pieces are made in two colors, the
darker being used by the player "Black" and the lighter
by "White."

THE BOARD. The board is a large square of 8 x 8 smaller
squares, which are colored alternately dark and light. The
board is so placed that each player finds a light square in
the corner at his right. In printed diagrams, the bottom
edge by custom represents the White side, the top edge, the
Black. (See first diagram.)

BLACK

WHITE
Starting position

The pawns indicate the squares to which the king could move (if the squares were unoccupied).

THE PIECES. Each player has 16 pieces of his own color. To begin a game, they are placed on the board as shown in the diagram. The pieces on each side are: eight pawns, two rooks, two knights, two bishops, one queen, and one king.

POWERS OF THE PIECES. There are six different kinds of pieces, and each kind has powers peculiar to itself.

The *King* (♚ and ♔) is invariably the tallest piece of the set. Its crown is usually of the shape suggested by the printed symbol.

The king moves one square at a time, in any direction, on the rank (sideward), on the file (forward or backward), or

The white queen can capture the black queen on any of the squares indicated, and a black queen on any of those squares can capture the white queen.

The white rook can capture a black rook on any of the squares indicated, and a black rook on any of those squares can capture the white rook.

on the diagonal. Of course it may not move to a square attacked by an adverse piece. The two kings can never stand on adjacent squares.

The *Queen* (♕ and ♛) is the second-tallest piece. It wears a crown with points, as in the printed symbol. It is the most powerful piece, being able to move in any direction (on a line of adjacent squares) and any distance so long as no obstructions intervene. Another way of saying it is that the queen combines the powers of the rook and bishop.

The *Rook* (♖ and ♜) is a cylindrical tower with a castellated top. It may move any distance along an unobstructed rank or file (forward, backward, sideward).

The *Bishop* (♗ and ♝) is topped by a mitre, usually marked with a cleft. It moves on diagonal lines only, any distance along an unobstructed line.

The *Knight* (♘ and ♞) has the head of a horse, and is often colloquially called a "horse." Unlike all other pieces, it moves not on a line, but from point to point. Consequently it cannot be obstructed by any intervening pieces. Its move has been described as "from one corner to the corner diagonally-opposite of a rectangle three squares by two."

The *Pawn* is invariably the shortest piece on the board. It moves only forward on the file, away from the owner's side of the board. For its first move only it has a choice of going forward one square or of jumping to the second away. After it has left its initial square, it may go only one square at a time.

CAPTURING. All pieces except the pawn capture in the same way as they move. If an adverse piece stands on a square that a king, queen, rook, bishop, or knight can move to, the move captures it. The captured piece is removed from the board, and the square it occupied is taken by its captor.

The pawn alone has a different mode of capture. It does not attack a piece standing ahead of it on the file; consequently it can be blocked without the power of fighting back. The pawn captures diagonally, on the square adjacent and forward. Thus it attacks at most two squares, and if it is at the side of the board it attacks only one.

The white bishop can capture a black bishop on any of the squares indicated, and a black bishop on any of those squares can capture the white bishop.

The white knight can capture a black knight on any of the squares indicated, and a black knight on any of those squares can capture the white knight.

The pawn has another peculiarity, the capture *en passant* (in passing). Suppose a White pawn is advanced from its initial square by a double jump, and a Black pawn stands on an adjacent file, from which it would have attacked the White pawn had it been moved one square only. The Black pawn may make the capture, moving to the square jumped over by the White pawn.

The object in allowing this *en passant* capture is to preserve the principle that an advancing pawn is bound to meet attack from the adverse pawns standing on both adjacent files. But if the *e. p.* capture is not made at once, in response to the double-jump, it may not be made at all.

THE PLAY. White always makes the first move, and thereafter the players move alternately. The object of play is capture of the adverse king. The capture is never actually made. If the king is attacked, and there is no way of escape, it is said to be *checkmated,* and the game ends. On attacking the adverse king, a player customarily warns "Check!" Contrary to popular impression, this warning is not required by the laws of Chess. However, if a player overlooks that he is checked and makes a move that does not avert the attack, he must simply retract his move and parry the attack.

The great majority of games end before a checkmate, one player resigning because convinced that he must eventually lose. A game may be drawn under circumstances detailed under "Drawn Games," on the next page.

CASTLING. Castling is a move that can be made, if at all, only once in a game. It is actually a move of two pieces at once, the king and one rook. The move is legal only if both pieces stand on their original squares and neither has moved previously; if the two or three squares between king and rook are vacant; if the king is not in check; and if the two squares the king must cross are not guarded by the enemy. Castling consists in moving the king two squares toward the rook, and then placing the rook on the square jumped over by the king.

Position in which White may castle on either side; and showing how Black could have castled on his right, or on his left.

The purpose in castling is usually twofold: (a) to remove the king to a haven of greater security (behind unmoved pawns); (b) to "connect the rooks" and bring them to central files that have been partially or wholly cleared by pawn advances.

QUEENING. If a pawn reaches the edge of the board farthest from its starting point, it is removed from the board, and the owner may substitute for it a queen, rook, bishop, or knight. The usual choice is a queen, the most powerful piece. Hence the exchange is usually called *queening*. It is legal to queen a pawn even if the owner already has a queen on the board (or any other piece that he chooses). Games with more than two queens on the board at the same time are rare, but there have been as many as five.

The importance of the queening rule is that it maintains fight in many positions that otherwise would have to be abandoned as drawn. Many times, so many pieces are "swapped off" that those remaining on the board are insufficient to force checkmate. The focus of battle then becomes the effort to force a pawn through to the eighth rank and so obtain a new queen.

DRAWN GAMES. A game may be drawn under any of the following circumstances:

Lack of Force. The pieces left on the board are too weak to force checkmate.

Perpetual Check. One player shows that he can check the adverse king without cessation.

Stalemate. The player in turn to move can make no legal move, yet his king is not in check.

Repetition. The same position (of all pieces, White and Black) recurs three times in a game, with the same player to move each time. On the third occasion, this player may claim a draw.

Fifty-Move Rule. Either player may claim a draw if during fifty moves by one player no pawn has been moved and no capture has been made, unless his opponent can demonstrate a forced win. (This is the actual effect of a rather complicated clause in the laws of Chess.)

Agreement. The players may agree to a draw. (In tournament play, not before the thirtieth turn.)

NOTATION. Several systems of notation for the chessboard are in use. The one most widely known is the "descriptive," illustrated by the diagram.

BLACK

KR1 / QR8	KKt1 / QKt8	KB1 / QB8	K1 / Q8	Q1 / K8	QB1 / KB8	QKt1 / KKt8	QR1 / KR8
KR2 / QR7	KKt2 / QKt7	KB2 / QB7	K2 / Q7	Q2 / K7	QB2 / KB7	QKt2 / KKt7	QR2 / KR7
KR3 / QR6	KKt3 / QKt6	KB3 / QB6	K3 / Q6	Q3 / K6	QB3 / KB6	QKt3 / KKt6	QR3 / KR6
KR4 / QR5	KKt4 / QKt5	KB4 / QB5	K4 / Q5	Q4 / K5	QB4 / KB5	QKt4 / KKt5	QR4 / KR5
KR5 / QR4	KKt5 / QKt4	KB5 / QB4	K5 / Q4	Q5 / K4	QB5 / KB4	QKt5 / KKt4	QR5 / KR4
KR6 / QR3	KKt6 / QKt3	KB6 / QB3	K6 / Q3	Q6 / K3	QB6 / KB3	QKt6 / KKt3	QR6 / KR3
KR7 / QR2	KKt7 / QKt2	KB7 / QB2	K7 / Q2	Q7 / K2	QB7 / KB2	QKt7 / KKt2	QR7 / KR2
KR8 / QR1	KKt8 / QKt1	KB8 / QB1	K8 / Q1	Q8 / K1	QB8 / KB1	QKt8 / KKt1	QR8 / KR1

WHITE

Each file (line of squares from the White side to the Black) is named according to the piece that stands on it originally. The ranks (lines of squares parallel to the White side) are numbered from 1 to 8, away from the player. A move is described by the name of the piece moved and the square to which it goes. The square is designated by the name of the file and the number of the rank, each player counting ranks from his side of the board.

Everything is abbreviated as much as possible. For example, if White's first move is to advance the pawn in front of his king two squares, it is recorded as P-K4. Initials are used for pieces, files, etc. K invariably means king; for knight, the symbols Kt, S, N are variously used. If White's second move is to advance his king's bishop three squares along the diagonal opened by the pawn move, it may be described fully as KB-QB4, but nowadays is abbreviated to B-B4, since there is no ambiguity.

The hyphen, by the way, is read "to." The symbol x, read "takes," indicates a capture. For example, suppose that each side moves P-K4 and White then plays P-Q4. The Black king's pawn can take the White queen's pawn; if it does so, the move is written PxP.

To illustrate the notation, here is the opening of a game:

BLACK

	WHITE	BLACK
1	P-Q4	P-Q4
2	Kt-KB3	Kt-KB3
3	P-B4	P-K3
4	Kt-B3	PxP
5	P-K3	QKt-Q2

The position reached is shown by the diagram.

WHITE

Kriegspiel

For Kriegspiel three boards and sets of chessmen are used. There is a referee, whose Chess set is in the center with the active players seated back to back, each at his own board. Each player moves his own men and the referee duplicates each move on his own board. The referee tells a player when his attempted move is impossible. Each player tries to guess what moves his opponent is making. When a player completes a legal move, the referee announces "Black (or White) has moved." When a player tries an illegal move, the referee waves his hand to prevent it but does not let the opponent know. When a move results in a capture, the referee announces, "Black (or White) captures on (the rank, file, long or short diagonal)" and removes the captured piece from the board of the player who lost it but not from the board of the player who captured. A player may ask "Any?" and be told if he has a possible capture *with a pawn*, but that is the only question he is permitted, and having asked he must try at least one pawn capture before making a different move.

CHECKERS

CHECKERS *is so called only in the United States. In England and the British dominions it is Draughts. In the Romance and Germanic languages its name is based on Dam (woman); in early times it was deprecated as "women's chess." But it has proved to be as profound, in some respects, as Chess. The nature of Checkers suggests that it had a common ancestor with Chess and Mill, but it has not been traced with certainty earlier than the 14th century. The first scientific treatise on the game was written by Peter Mallet, a French mathematician, Paris, 1668. In the 19th century the game was extensively analyzed and popularized by a great galaxy of English and Scottish players.*

PLAYERS. Checkers is played by two, on the same board that is used for Chess (see page 228), with pieces (called *checkers* or *draughts*) in the form of thick discs. All the checkers are alike in form but are provided in two colors, the darker being used by the player "Black" and the lighter by "White."

THE BOARD. As in Chess, the board is so placed that each player has a light square in the corner at his right. (In printed diagrams, the apparent colors are reversed. The

BLACK

WHITE
Starting position

BLACK

WHITE
Notation

squares printed dark represent the actual light squares; the actual dark squares are left blank so that numbers and pieces may be printed on them.) For reference purposes, the 32 dark squares are considered to be numbered as shown in the diagram.

THE PIECES. Each player has 12 pieces of his own color. To begin a game, they are placed on the board as shown in the diagram. All the pieces stand and move solely on the dark squares. At the outset, all pieces are *single men*. A single man may later become a *king,* as explained below.

THE PLAY. Black moves first, and thereafter the players move alternately. A player loses the game if he cannot move in turn; usually this is because all his pieces have been captured, but it can also come about because all his remaining pieces are immobilized. Many games are drawn by agreement, when few pieces remain and neither player has an advantage sufficient to win.

NONCAPTURING MOVE. A single man may move only forward on the dark diagonal, one square at a time (when not capturing). For example, Black can make any of the following first moves: 9-13, 9-14, 10-14, 10-15, 11-15, 11-16, 12-16. (A move is denoted by the number of the square moved from and the square moved to.)

CAPTURING MOVE. The capturing move is a jump. If a White piece stands adjacent and forward to a Black piece (e.g., B on 15, W on 18), and if the square back of the White piece on the same line (22) is vacant, the Black piece jumps over it to the vacant square (22), and then the White piece is removed from the board.

If a piece makes a capture, and then is on a square from which it can jump over another adverse piece, it continues jumping in the same turn. It may change direction during a series of jumps. For example, B on 4, W on 8, 16, 24; Black jumps 4-11-20-27.

When able to capture, a player MUST do so; he may not make a noncapturing move. (Under the traditional rule of "huff or blow," if a player violates this rule his opponent may remove from the board the piece that should have made a capture. This rule is still printed in some books, but modern tournament regulations have abolished it. When the rule is violated, the player must retract his illegal move and make the capture instead.)

It sometimes happens that a piece may capture in either of two directions, or either of two pieces may make a capture. In all such situations, the owner has free choice.

CROWNING. The row of squares farthest from the player (1 to 4 for W and 29 to 32 for B) is his *king row*. On reaching the king row, a single man is *crowned* and becomes a *king*. The opponent must immediately put on top of it another piece of the same color, and the two checkers are then moved as a unit.

The king has the same powers as a single man, plus the right to move backward as well as forward. Moves in both directions may be combined in one series of jumps. But if a single man reaches the king row by a capture, it may not continue jumping in the same turn (as a new king); it must pause one turn to be crowned.

STRATEGY OF CHECKERS

Many volumes of analysis have been published without exhausting Checkers. Here, space permits us to state only some pointers useful to beginners.

An expert once said, "Checkers is an easy game. All you have to do is to avoid losing pieces." Then he added, "Of course, the average Checker player can be depended on to fall into a two-for-one shot before he has made a dozen moves." For example, Black opens 11-15 and White answers 22-17. Black plays 12-16, thinking to go on to 20, but White plays 24-19, forcing 15-24, 28-12, and White has won a piece. Another way to do the same thing is 9-14, 22-17,

12-16, 23-18, 14-23, 26-12. The first thing a beginner has to do is to learn to avoid such simple two-for-one shots, which abound.

The loss of a single piece is normally enough to lose the game. The opponent can usually swap piece for piece and so end up with one-to-none. There are some end positions, however, where one piece can draw against two, and sometimes the sacrifice of a piece is correct because it can ultimately be regained.

A king is particularly powerful behind adverse single men, where it can attack without suffering counterattack. Therefore in the opening it is important not to let an avenue to your king row be opening up to the adverse pieces, unless you can also crown. Many a game is won by the first king. Forcing too many *cuts* (exchanges of captures) in the opening is one easy way to let the enemy through.

All these points are illustrated by the following example game. (Read down the columns.)

EXAMPLE GAME

11-15	14-17	17-21	18-15 (k)	23-27
23-19	21-14	19-15	19-16	15-19
9-14	10-17	22-25	5-9	27-31 (n)
27-23 (a)	18-14 (e)	15-8	7-2	19-24 (o)
8-11	17-22	4-11	10-14* (l)	14-18
22-18	26-17	28-24	2-7	20-16
15-22	13-22	25-29	3-10	18-23
25-9	28-24 (f)	24-19	16-11	24-28 (p)
5-14	2-6	29-25	15-8	31-27
29-25	32-28 (g)	31-26 (i)	12-3	28-32
6-9	12-16 (h)	7-10	14-18	27-24
25-22	19-12	26-22 (j)	3-7	16-11
9-13	6-10	11-15	10-14	24-19
24-20 (b)	23-18	18-11	7-11 (m)	11-7
1-5 (c)	10-17	25-18	18-23	19-15
22-18 (d)	24-19	11-7	11-15	7-2
				15-10 (q)

(a) The Defiance opening, so called because this move prevents formation of the Fife opening by 22-17, 5-9.
(b) Not good is 22-18, for after 14-17, 21-14, 10-17 Black threatens to break through and crown on 29.
(c) Other options here are 11-15 and 4-8.
(d) Now playable because Black has opened his king row.

(e) There is a safe draw by 26-22.

(f) This move and the next are dictated by the precarious position of the man on 14, which Black threatens to win by 2-6 and 6-10.

(g) Now if 6-10, then 14-9, 5-14, 23-18, 14-23, 19-16, 12-19, 24-6. White will make a king and regain his piece.

(h) Yates sprang this surprise move on Wyllie in 1876. The point of it is that the man on 14 is won and Black crowns quickly.

(i) Useless is 19-15, for then 25-22, 15-8, 22-15 and Black holds three White men with two.

(j) Of course not 19-16, 10-15, winning two for one.

(k) Thus Black gets the bind after all: The king and the man on 3 hold the three White men.

(l) 9-14 would actually lose after 2-6. But now Black threatens to make two more kings and use them to bottle up the White king. White's only chance is to sacrifice a piece in the hope of regaining it by attack on the Black single men. The star means the move is the only one that will win (or, in some cases, draw).

(m) He cannot play 7-10 because of 9-13.

(n) If 27-32, to keep White out of the double corner, then 19-23 and will threaten eventually to lock up the three Black men with two pieces.

(o) Useless is 19-23, 31-26, 23-19, 26-22.

(p) So as to meet 23-27 with 28-32.

(q) White cannot regain his piece, and the extra man wins.

RESTRICTION PLAY is the selection of opening moves by chance; this method is now used in all major tournaments. The necessity for it arises from the relative exhaustion of "go-as-you-please" Checkers; by adopting completely-known lines, expert players can infallibly avoid loss. Restriction play compels them to be familiar with the weak openings as well as with the strong.

It is well known that the strongest opening for Black is 11-15. The safest replies by White are 23-19 and 22-18. But all the seven possible first moves by Black are playable, and so are the seven White replies except 21-17 in reply to 9-14 or 10-14. Of the remaining 47 combinations, the weakest for White—and formerly *barred*—are 9-14, 23-18; 10-14, 23-18; 11-16, 23-19; and 12-16, 23-19.

In the "two-move restriction," one of the 47 combinations of Black opening and White reply is selected by chance. A match between two players comprises two games, with each player taking both the Black and White sides of the selected opening. The American championship matches now use a "three-move restriction," the opening being drawn from a list of about 150 three-move combinations that have been analyzed to be playable.

OPENINGS. Many of the opening moves and formations have acquired traditional names. After 11-15, the *Orthodox* reply is 23-19, and among alternative continuations are:

Will o' the Wisp: 9-13.
Defiance: 9-14, 27-23.
Souter: 9-14, 22-17, 6-9.
Fife: 9-14, 22-17, 5-9.
Whilter: 9-14, 22-17, 7-11.
Glasgow: 8-11, 22-17, 11-16.
Old Fourteenth: 8-11, 22-17, 4-8.
Centre: 8-11, 22-17, 15-18.
Alma: 8-11, 22-17, 3-8.
Nailor: 8-11, 26-23.
Tillicoultry: 8-11, 22-18.

Other White replies to 11-15 are:
Second Double Corner: 24-19.
Ayreshire Lassie: 24-20.

The first moves other than 11-15 are called:
Edinburgh: 9-13.
Double Corner: 9-14.
Denny: 10-14.
Kelso: 10-15.
Bristol: 11-16.
Dundee: 12-16.

CHECKERS VARIANTS

Checkers as described in the foregoing pages is so played throughout the English-speaking world. Somewhat different variants are played in the Latin and Germanic countries. Besides these national variants, there are many "minor" games played on the checkerboard.

LOSING CHECKERS is played under the usual rules, but the object of play is to get rid of one's pieces, and the first to do so wins. Though far less profound than the regular game, "giveaway" has a certain appeal in that no game can ever be drawn.

FOX AND GEESE is a juvenile pastime. The "fox" is a Black piece starting on square 2 or 3; it moves in any direction, like a king. The "geese" are four White pieces starting on 29, 30, 31, 32; they move only forward, like single men. There is no jumping nor capturing. The geese try to trap and immobilize the fox, which conversely tries to get past the advancing line. The geese can always win.

PYRAMID is another juvenile pastime, but the outcome with the best of play on both sides is still unknown, and it gives much the same opportunity for cunning as Nine-Men Morris. Each player has ten pieces, which he places in a triangle on his half of the board. The Black pieces go on squares 1, 2, 3, 4, 6, 7, 8, 10, 11, 15; the White go on 18, 22, 23, 25, 26, 27, 29, 30, 31, 32. The pieces move like single men in Checkers, only forward diagonally. Jumping is compulsory, but there is no capturing. The object of each player is to herd his ten pieces across the board into the position initially occupied by the adverse army, and the first to do so wins the game. The chief offensive tactic is to force jumps that put too many adverse pieces on one side of the board. For example, Black cannot possibly win if one of his pieces is forced to square 28 after another has occupied 32.

ELEVEN-MEN CHECKERS is one of many suggestions that have been made to revitalize this much-analyzed game. It was proposed by Newell Banks, match champion of the United States, and has received some serious attention. Each player begins with only eleven pieces; the squares to be left vacant being chosen by chance. For example, any number from 1 to 12 is drawn by lot, then this square is left vacant and also the corresponding White Square. (Thus, 32 corresponds to 1, 25 to 8, and so on.) The twelve new opening positions so created call upon the player for something more than "book" knowledge. The eleven-men variant has been played with a two-move restriction, with the desired result of reducing the percentage of drawn games.

SPANISH CHECKERS differs from the English game in these rules: (1) Having choice of captures, the player must take as many pieces as possible; (2) The king moves like a Chess bishop, any distance along an open diagonal, and captures a piece at any distance by leaping to the vacant square just beyond it.

POLISH CHECKERS is so-called because invented by a Pole: it is played chiefly in France. The board is 10 x 10, and each player has 20 pieces, posted at the outset on the first four rows of the board. As in Spanish Checkers, the player must capture the maximum of pieces when choice offers, and the king (called queen) moves like a Chess bishop. In addition, the king captures by leaping to any one of the adjacent vacant squares beyond an enemy piece: the choice must be made so as to obey the rule of maximum captures. A single man moves only forward, but may capture backward in the manner of an English king. If it reaches the king row by a jump, it must continue capturing in the same turn if possible; it does not become a king unless it comes to rest on the king row.

This game is played in Germany on a board 8 x 8, each player having twelve pieces.

NINE-MEN MORRIS *is so-called in England because of its fanciful similarity to the morris (Moorish) dances. In Germanic countries it is called the Mill, possibly in reference to the grinding process whereby the opposing army is decimated. The game is very ancient, having been traced to classic Grecian times and earlier; it has been seriously argued that Nine-Men Morris was the ancestor of Chess. But it is much less profound; in fact, it is usually looked upon as a juvenile pastime.*

NINE-MEN MORRIS

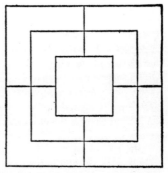

THE BOARD comprises three concentric squares, as shown in the diagram. On ancient boards, the corners were usually connected by diagonal lines, but these lines are omitted in modern play.

Two players compete. Each is provided with nine counters. First turn having been decided by lot, the players alternately place one piece on the board, on any of the twenty-four points where two lines meet. After all the pieces have been placed, the game continues by alternate moves; a piece may be moved along a line to an adjacent vacant point.

The object of play is to make a *mill*—get three of one's

own pieces in a row on the same line. A player who succeeds in so doing removes any opposing piece from the board, provided that this piece is not itself one of three-in-a-row. The game is not won by making the first three-in-a-row, but by making threes repeatedly, and removing adverse pieces, until the enemy is reduced to two men, whereupon he loses the game.

The rule is sometimes given that a player reduced to two pieces may continue play, moving his men from any point to any other regardless of lines. This rule allows two pieces to draw against three, or even four, and so increases the proportion of draws in a game that undoubtedly is a forced draw anyhow with the best of play on both sides.

It is not necessary to keep track of the identity of the individual pieces, for a player who had made three-in-a-row may move one piece off the line, then move it back, and count it as a second three-in-a-row. The art of play, in fact, largely consists in timing the "opening" of a mill judiciously, so as to avoid its destruction in case the opponent is able to close a mill of his own at this juncture. The *double mill* is a formation in which one piece shuttles between two lines, opening one mill and closing with another at each move; such a formation, once established, is a sure win.

Go-Bang

Go-BANG is a board game for two players, of the "line-up" type, with more scope than Nine-Men Morris. It is played on an ordinary checkerboard, each player being provided with twelve pieces. To commence, the players alternately place one piece on any vacant square. After all the pieces are down, play continues by alternate moves. A piece may be moved to an adjacent vacant square in any direction, horizontally, vertically, or diagonally.

The object of play is to get five of one's own pieces adjacent and on the same line in any direction. The player first to succeed in so doing wins the game.

BACKGAMMON

BACKGAMMON *(called* TRICTRAC *in some countries, and in ancient times called* TABLES*) is probably thousands of years older than Chess. Together with* PACHISI *(Parcheesi) it probably evolved from the practice of scoring the rolls of dice by moving a token along a track. About 1925 Backgammon spurted into new popularity in the United States, due probably to the introduction of the doubling rule, which gave added scope for skill as well as "pepping up" the tempo of play.*

Backgammon is played by two, on a special board with pieces resembling checkers. Each player is provided with fifteen pieces, also with two dice and a dice cup from which to cast them. The players are conventionally called Black and White, though their pieces may be of any two contrasting colors, dark and light.

THE BOARD. The Backgammon board is divided into two halves or *tables* by a center partition called *the bar.* (See diagram.) The board is conventionally placed so that the inner table is "toward the light." In each table are twelve *points*, which in the illustration are numbered for reference. (The numbers are not printed on the actual board.) The illustration shows how the pieces are set up to commence a game.

THE PLAY. The moves are governed by casting dice. Each player has two dice, and usually a dice cup. To begin a game, each players rolls one die, and the higher number plays first. If the numbers are the same, both players must roll again. The first player uses the numbers on the two dice as his first roll. (Some play that he starts with a fresh roll of his own two dice.) After that the turn alternates, and each player casts his own two dice to determine what he can do.

The object of play is to be the first to move all one's *stones* (as the pieces are called) into one's inner (or *home*)

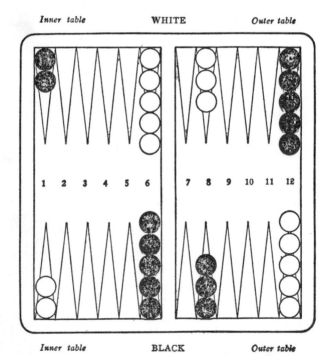

table, and thence to continue as though moving them in the same direction and off the board. The stones move from point to point, and each player heads toward his own 1-point. White moves from left to right from Black's 1-point (B1) through Black's 12-point (B12), then through W12 toward W1. Black moves in the opposite direction, W1 ... W12, B12 ... B1.

THE MOVES. Stones are advanced across a number of points corresponding to the numbers on the dice. Both numbers may be applied to move one stone, or may be applied separately to two stones. For example, if Black has first turn and his roll is 5-4, he can move one stone from W1 to W10, or one from W12 to B8 and another from the same point to B9.

Whenever a player rolls a double number, he takes that number not twice but four times. For example, on a roll of 3-3 the player makes four moves of 3 each, or a move of 3 and another of 9, etc. He moves a total of 12 points, not 6.

When two or more numbers are applied to one stone, the stone must be able to make the two moves consecutively. A stone may not land on a point occupied by two or more of his opponent's stones. For example, with 5-5 Black cannot bring a man from W1 to W11; it is true that he can put a stone on W11, but he cannot move from W1 with a 5 because the White stones on W6 prevent him from landing there.

A stone may jump over adverse stones. For example, Black with a 5-4 may move from W1 to W10 by playing first W1-W5 and then W5-W10. The five White stones on W6 are not a barricade.

A player must use both numbers of his roll (or all four of a doublet) if possible. There are times when a player could advantageously refuse to move, yet he must move in turn if he can. If he can use one number but not the other, he must use the higher number if possible. For example, if the roll is 6-5, and the player can move 6 or 5 but not both, he must move 6.

CLOSED POINTS. Any number of stones of the same color may stay on one point. If there are more than five, they are piled two or three high, to avoid encroaching on the opponent's side of the board. A point occupied by two or more men is *closed* (or *made*); a point occupied by only one man, or none, is *open*. But stones of opposite color may not stay on the same point.

BLOTS. A single stone on a point does not prevent an adverse stone from landing there. The single stone is a *blot*, and an adverse stone can land there with a *hit*. The blot is then picked up and placed on the bar. It must be *entered* before the owner may make any other move.

From the bar, a stone must enter in the adverse home table, upon an open point whose number has been cast on one of the dice. For example, if Black has a stone on the bar and rolls 5-2, he may enter on W2 or W5, whichever, if either, is open. If there is an opposing blot on the point of entry, the entering man hits it and sends it to the bar.

A compound roll will not serve for entry. For example, if the only point open in the White home table is the 5-point, Black could not enter on a roll of 4-1 or 3-2.

Until the stone enters, a player with a stone on the bar may make no other move. If his roll does not permit entry, the turn passes. If the adverse home table is entirely closed (this is called a *shutout*), he does not even roll in turn, but waits until a point of entry is opened. But, having entered, if the player has no other man on the bar he may use the rest of his roll to move any man. Thus, having a man on the bar, a player rolls 5-2; if he enters on the 2, he may now use the 5 to move any stone, including the one he just entered.

BEARING OFF. At any time when all his stones remaining on the board are in his own home table, a player may *bear off*. Bearing off consists in removing the stones from the board, never to return in that game. A stone may be borne off a point whose number shows on either die. For example, if Black rolls 4-3, he may remove a stone from B4 and another from B3. Instead of bearing off, a player may use the numbers to move inside the inner table. For example, on a roll of 5-5 Black might move four stones from B6 to B1.

When a number is rolled higher than the highest point on which the player has any stones left, he must bear off a stone from the outermost occupied point. For example, if Black rolls 6-2 and has no stone on B6, he must bear off B5, or B4 if there is none on B5, etc. But note that a player may always use the numbers in either order. For example,